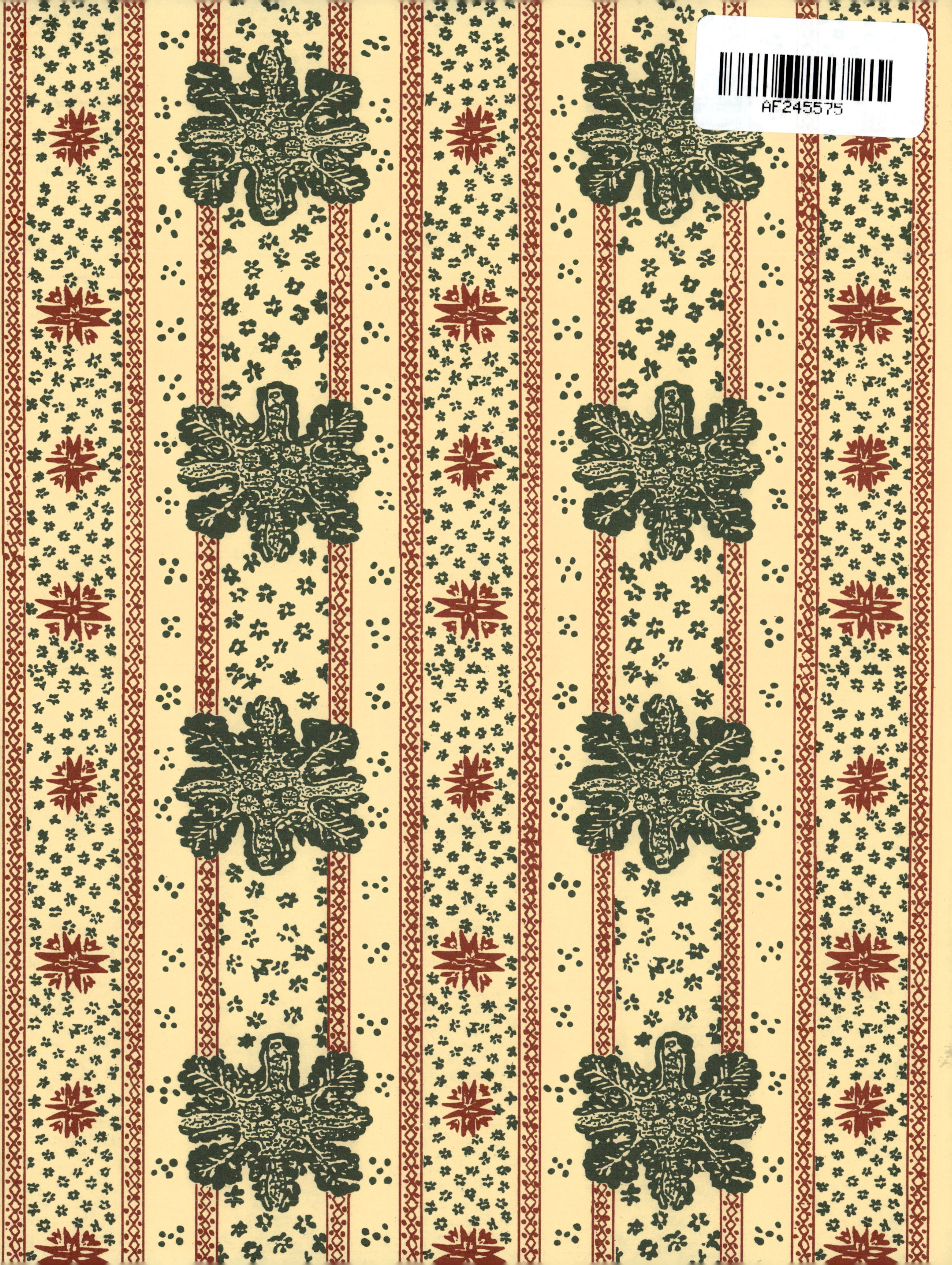

AF245575

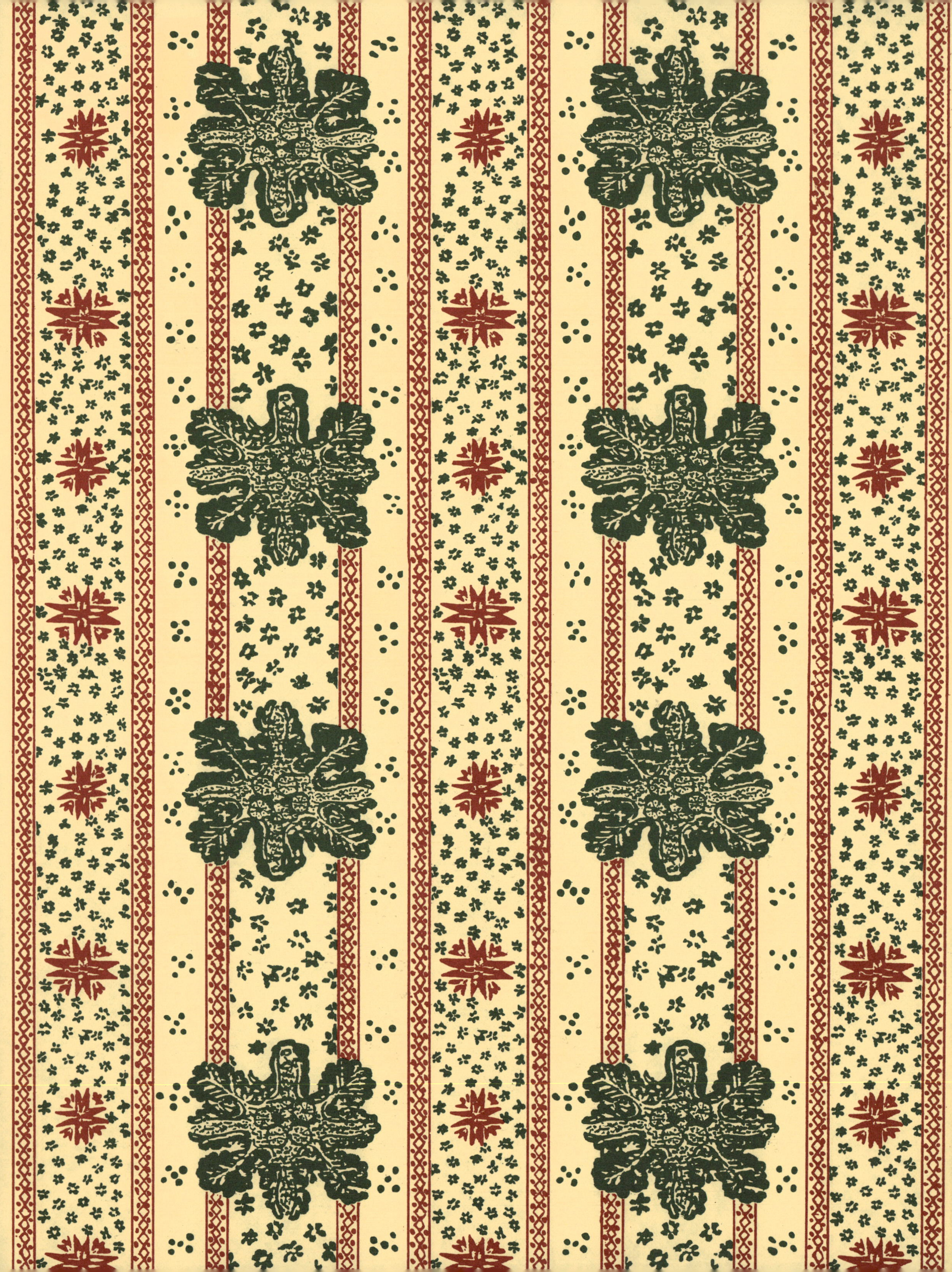

Erastus Salisbury Field: 1805 - 1900

by Mary Black

Museum of Fine Arts, Springfield, Massachusetts
February 5 - April 1, 1984

**National Museum of American Art and
National Portrait Gallery, Washington, D.C.**
June 10 - September 4, 1984

**Museum of American Folk Art and
The Metropolitan Museum of Art,
New York, New York**
November - December, 1984

**Marion Koogler McNay Art Institute,
San Antonio, Texas**
January - February, 1985

**Museum of Fine Arts
Springfield, Massachusetts**

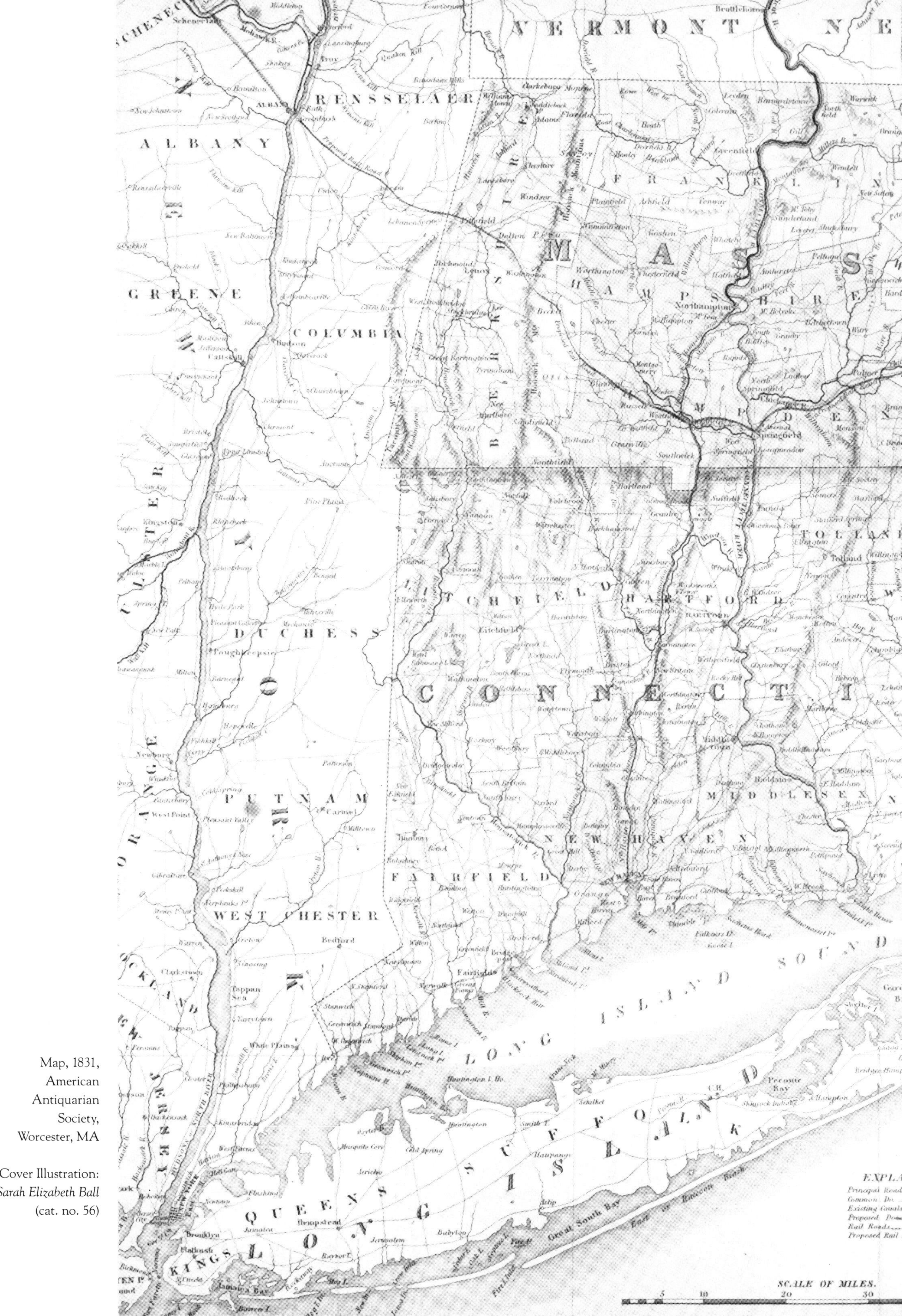

Map, 1831,
American
Antiquarian
Society,
Worcester, MA

Cover Illustration:
Sarah Elizabeth Ball
(cat. no. 56)

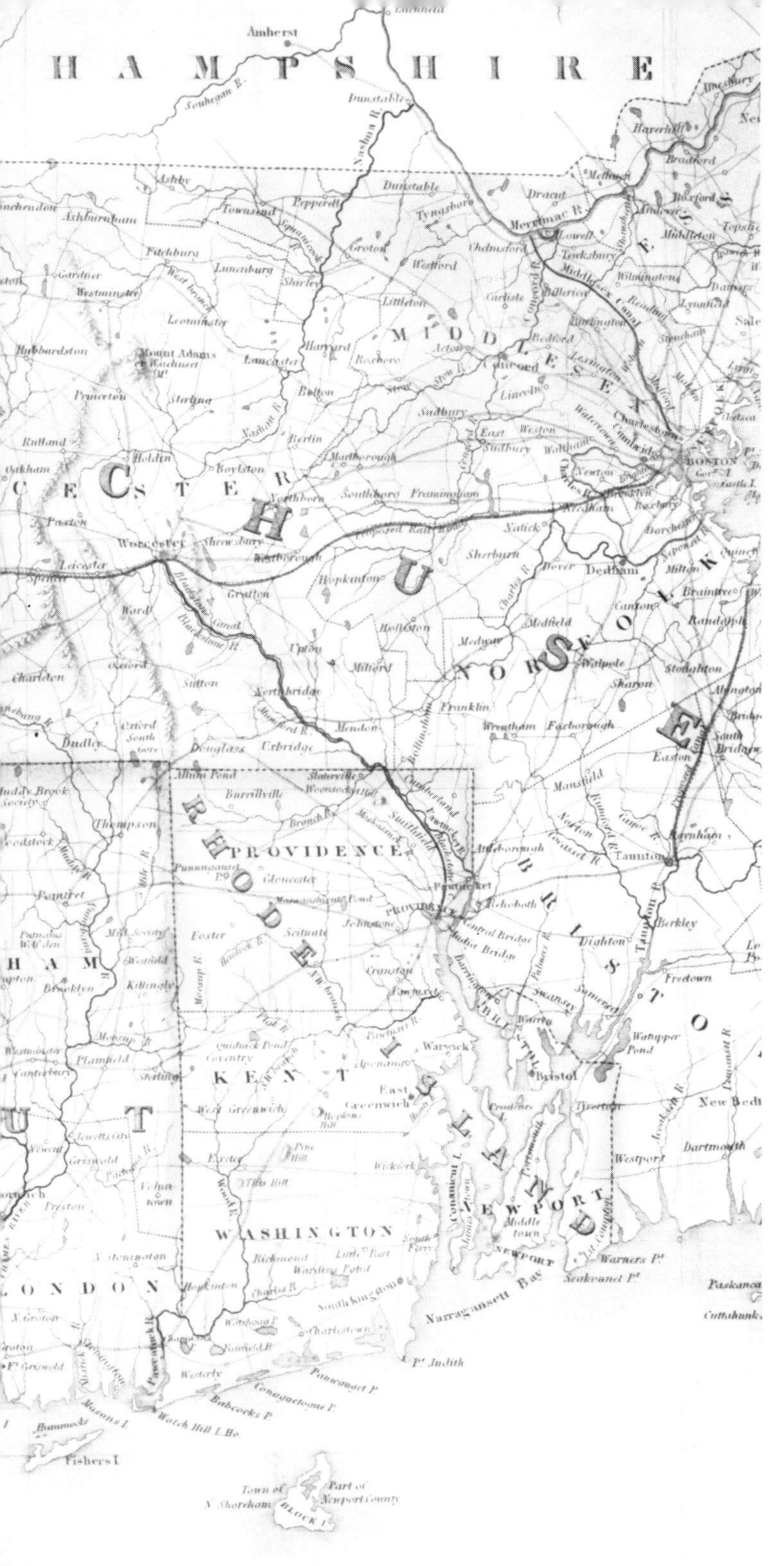

Contents

Director: Richard Mühlberger

Guest Curator: Mary Black

Curator of American Art: Martha J. Hoppin
Assistant Curator/Exhibitions: Steven Kern
Registrar: Karen Papineau
Assistant Registrar: Nancy L. Swallow
Preparator: Melvin Wachowiak
Editor: Debra Gorlin

Designer: Deborah Hewitt
Photographer: David Stansbury

Intern: Anne Marie Dowd

Printed by The William J. Mack Company,
        North Haven, Connecticut
Typesetting by The Marguerite S. Graphic Arts Service, Inc.,
        Chicopee Falls, Massachusetts

This project is supported by a grant from the National Endowment for the Arts.

The operation of the Museum of Fine Arts and all of its programs is made possible with support from the Massachusetts Council on the Arts and Humanities, a state agency.

International Standard Book Number: 0-916746-06-2
Library of Congress Card Number: 83-051142

Mary Black's earliest recollections of Erastus Salisbury Field are the four portraits of her ancestors, which hung in her grandfather's house in the Berkshires. These likenesses, or "presences," as Mary Black describes them, later became hers; and much later, as she became successively registrar, curator, and director of the Abby Aldrich Rockefeller Folk Art Center in Williamsburg, Virginia, she learned that many other paintings by this painter had been kept and treasured by his relations in the Connecticut Valley.

Field's work had been publicly exhibited as early as 1844. But it was not until 1932 when the Museum of Modern Art presented "American Folk Art, the Art of the Common Man in America" (organized by Holger Cahill) that two of Field's works, *Mr. Pearce* and *Mrs. Pearce*, of Hadley, were seen in a museum exhibition. The anonymous lender of all the entries in that exhibition was Abby Aldrich Rockefeller. In that showing the painter was as anonymous as the donor.

In 1942, when Frederick B. Robinson, then director of the Springfield Museum of Fine Arts, organized "Somebody's Ancestors" for the Springfield museum, the Pearces were shown again, alongside twenty-four similar paintings, and were for the first time identified as the work of Erastus Salisbury Field.

In 1958 three of Field's paintings achieved international fame; *Joseph B. Moore and Family,* Mr. Pearce, and *Mrs. Pearce* were sent to the Brussels World's Fair. As a result of the Brussels World's Fair exhibition and of earlier championship of Field by his great-grand-niece, Eleanor Morgan Wesson (who enlisted the support of Frederick B. Robinson), it was decided that a large number of Field's works would be brought together for the first exhibition devoted to a single artist at the Folk Art Collection in Williamsburg, which owned several portraits and religious paintings by Field. That exhibition took place in 1963.

Mrs. Wesson had inherited her interest in Field from her mother, Minnie Morgan Williams, who, as a child at Plumtrees, had watched her great-uncle at work. Another relative who had preserved Field's memory and reputation was a grand-nephew, Carey Stillman Hayward, a newspaper correspondent for *The*

Springfield Republican and *The New York Times.* After Hayward's death, his widow and children continued his interest, preserving in the family a large number of paintings, letters, books, and other memorabilia associated with the artist.

In the Connecticut Valley area Agnes Dods, an art historian who had participated in the W.P.A. index of Massachusetts portraits, kept a list of Field paintings, a current and growing record of his work. In 1963, she and Amherst professor Reginald French published a checklist of paintings which served as the catalogue of a Field exhibition at the Connecticut Historical Society. At that time the record had grown to 270 entries (including some of Field's photographs and several lost subjects). Since then, approximately one hundred additional works have been identified, among which are several groups of family portraits with four or more entries. The Bogue-Ball clan, the Merrills, and the Robbins are examples of the family series represented in this exhibition.

While the Williamsburg exhibition was on view, Arthur L. Smith, the head of Colonial Williamsburg's Audiovisual Department, proposed a series of films on folk art subjects. A biography of Field and a reenactment of the painting and Plumtrees exhibition of his eight-foot-long round-the-world panorama were the subjects of two of the films. All of the more than one hundred paintings shown in the Williamsburg exhibition were filmed on site. A two-week jaunt to the Connecticut Valley in the fall of 1963 completed the mileage for the film. Miss Dods and Mr. French were the Connecticut Valley advisers. Margaret C. and William E. Dwyer of Hadley, and Eleanor and William L.G. Hubbard of Sunderland led the filmmakers to the sites that Field had depicted, to owners of Field paintings, and, most important of all, to three Valley residents who, as children, had known Field. Mr. Dwyer's aunt, Mrs. Katherine Walsh Dwyer, was one of the participants in this film project, as were the architect Karl Putnam, and a retired schoolteacher, Miss Fanny Eastman.

To the end of her life, Eleanor Wesson maintained her interest in Field. The major collection of his work now owned by the Springfield Museum is, for the most part, her gift in memory of her son, Morgan Wesson. Her grandson, Morgan Wesson II, continued the family's interest and in 1974 made a brief pilot for a film on *The Historical Monument of the American Republic,* and prepared a light and sound exhibition for its interpretation at the museum during the year of our nation's bicentennial celebration.

The Springfield Museum of Fine Arts called upon Mary Black early in 1981 to organize this exhibition and to write this catalogue. With them, we believe that we have made an addition to folk art studies that is worthy to be numbered with the most important contributions to this field. But, from the start, I have held a personal conviction about this project. By exhibiting the full range of Field's work to a national audience, by presenting to art lovers and scholars alike the scope and depth of his subject matter, and the strengths and charm of his paintings, I have felt that we would be advancing the study and appreciation of American art in general. I hope that all who read this catalogue and who see this exhibition will agree with me that the work of Erastus Salisbury Field transcends categorization, and that his masterpieces will be numbered among those icons of art that have become a part of our national consciousness.

Our relationship with Mary Black has been a joy to all our staff, and we are proud of the results of a pleasurable and fruitful collaboration. We thank Mrs. Black for her loving kindness and patience during the long months of hard work on this publication and on the exhibition itself. Her lively belief that Mr. Field would have been pleased by what we have done has been an inspiration to all of us.

Mary Suzor, our former Curator of Collections, coordinated the organization of this exhibition from the start, and a very large portion of all the appreciation that is expressed in these acknowledgments goes to her. When she left our staff in September, 1983, to become Associate Registrar at the National Gallery of Art, Dr. Martha Hoppin, our newly appointed Curator of American Art, and Steven Kern, our newly appointed Assistant Curator/Exhibits, took over the tasks of bringing the exhibition to fruition. Our Editor, Debra Gorlin, has worked closely with Mrs. Black on the text and details of the catalogue. Nancy Swallow, Curatorial Secretary, and Karen Papineau, Registrar, efficiently processed a small mountain of paper work regarding loans, insurance, and transport.

Emil Schnorr, our Chief Conservator, and Hana Harris, his assistant, brought many of the paintings that were showing their age all too glaringly, back to a condition close to that of their youth. Mel Wachowiak assisted in this conservation effort and also designed the exhibition for its Springfield showing. Janet Gelman, Curator of Education, Lisa Maki, Assistant Curator of Education, and Kay Nichols, Education Assistant, planned the programs that will complement the exhibition in Springfield. Ms. Nichols was responsible for the writing of the helpful brochure that will accompany the exhibition throughout its tour. I thank all of the above for their good work for each of these key aspects to the success of this project, and I also thank the following staff who assisted in so many ways: Deborah Hewitt, Graphic Designer, David Stansbury, Staff Photographer, and Theodore Kapinos, Richard Dietrich, Patrick Laitres, Gerri Lockwood, Kurt Nielsen, Terry Strozzi, Steven Suse, and Elizabeth Vartanian.

Special mention should be made of Betsy Jones, Acting Director of the Smith College Museum of Art during the 1983 spring semester, who made a point of bringing the 1867 news note that changes the date of the *Monument's* creation to the attention of Nancy Swallow, who forwarded the information to Mary Black. Dr. Paul Staiti, Professor of Art at Mt. Holyoke College, kindly shared his knowledge of Samuel F.B. Morse's career.

The staffs of the National Portrait Gallery and of the National Museum of American Art have shown unusually keen interest in this exhibition from its inception, and have been important collaborators in all of our plans. I thank their directors, Dr. Allen Fern and Dr. Charles Eldredge. I am grateful to these staff members from the National Portrait Gallery: Beverly Cox, Curator of Exhibitions, Marc Pachter, Assistant Director for History and Public Programs, Robert Stewart, Chief Curator, and Kenneth Yellis, Curator of Education. At the National Museum of American Art, Charles Robertson, Assistant Director for Museum Resources, Barbara Shissler, Assistant Director of Public Programming, and William H. Truettner, Curator of 18th and 19th Century American Painting, provided invaluable assistance. I extend my appreciation to all of the other staff members at both museums who helped in so many ways.

We also received ample assistance from several staff members at various other museums: David Dangremond, Bennington Museum; Wendy Watson, Mount Holyoke College; Christopher P. Bickford, Connecticut Historical Society; Theodore E. Stebbins, Jr., Boston Museum of Fine Arts; Joan Washburn, Washburn Gallery; James D. Burke, St. Louis Art Museum; Linda Ayres and J. Carter Brown, National Gallery of Art; and John K. Howat, Metropolitan Museum of Art.

Our museum is deeply grateful to Dr. Fern and Dr. Eldridge, along with John Palmer Leeper, Director of the Marion Koogler McNay Art Institute, Philippe de Montebello, Director of The Metropolitan Museum of Art, John K. Howat, Chairman of the Departments of American Art at The Metropolitan Museum of Art, and Dr. Robert Bishop, Director of the Museum of American Folk Art, for hosting this exhibition. Thanks are also due to the National Endowment for the Arts for a generous grant in support of this exhibition, and the Massachusetts Council on the Arts and Humanities, which generously provides an annual operating grant to the museum.

Finally, but most important of all, we wish to express sincere thanks to the lenders to this exhibition who have parted with their works for over a year's time for the pleasure and benefit of a national audience.

Richard Mühlberger, Director

Museum of Fine Arts
Springfield, Massachusetts
February, 1984

Erastus Salisbury Field: 1805-1900

Leverett is a Massachusetts hill town, the first rise east of the Connecticut River. Plumtrees is a settlement directly on the river. Late in this century the two places were divided north and south by the wide U.S. highway that outlines the eastern floor of the Pioneer Valley, a new name for the region honoring its founders and first settlers. Before construction of the highway, Bull Hill Road ran directly between Plumtrees and Leverett, interrupted only by the old main road running north and south between Sunderland and Amherst.

The upland way of Bull Hill Road remains: on its south side and a few hundred yards from this winding east-west road there is a shallow depression that looks like the foundations of a small barn or shed. This is the location of the rough studio built by Erastus Field, where his grandiose plans and colorful copies of national and religious events were spun out in the last decades of the 19th century. Some of the paintings that lined the board and stone walls of the painting shed survive: nine of the series of paintings depicting the Israelites in Egypt; three or more recalling President Grant's visit to India; and at least one of the many small portraits on cardboard that the painter hawked along the roads of Leverett and Sunderland when President Garfield was assassinated in the fall of 1881.

Too large for the studio in both size and content, his nearly ten-by-fourteen foot vision of the nation's history, *The Historical Monument of the American Republic* (color insert), was brought to its final form in 1888, as Field added towers left and right to the canvas set up that summer in the Hubbard barn at Plumtrees: recorded on it already were the towers first completed in 1867.

Within his society, the small narrow one of Franklin County, he was well known: in his old age, as an eccentric and as the designer of a mythic American ziggurat. In earlier years he had been its recording artist, most of his subjects related to him by at least one branching in the small grove of Leverett and Sunderland family trees. But throughout western Massachusetts and Connecticut, into southern Vermont and New York east of the Hudson, hundreds of life-size portraits intimate at the greater renown he enjoyed as he perpetuated the faces and figures of the rural society that existed there from the mid-1820's to the mid-1850's.

Field's family had lived in the Leverett region for generations. The painter's paternal grandfather, William Field, was the great-grandson of English-born Zachariah Field, one of the earliest pioneers in central Massachusetts, "a settler at Pocumtuck before Philip's War."[1] Sometime during the 1770's, William Field relocated in Leverett, where he, like nine out of ten men at the end of the eighteenth century, made his living at farming.[2]

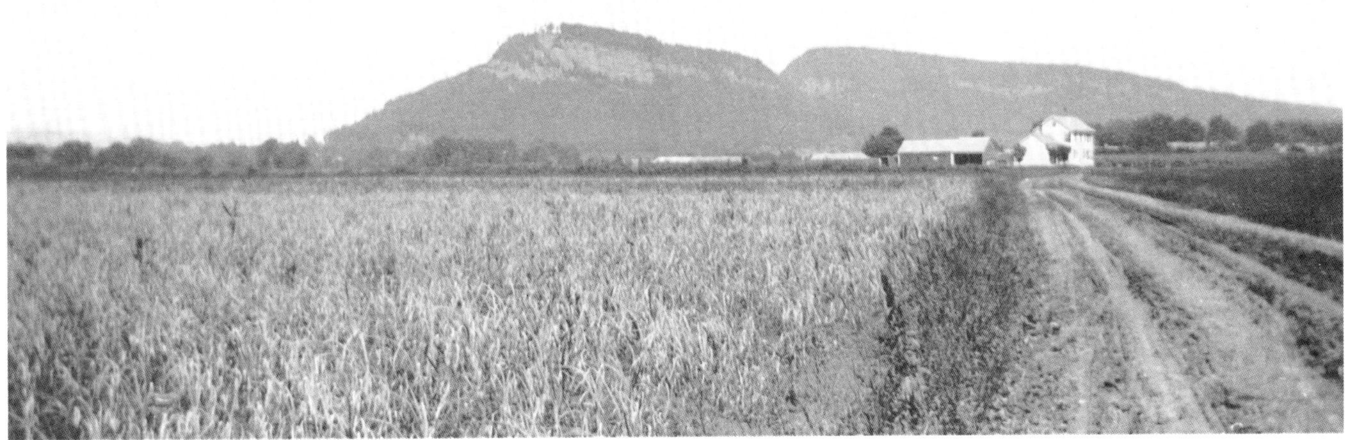

View of Mount Toby and Mount Sugarloaf, 1898

In 1747, as a boy of seven, Stephen Ashley, Erastus Field's maternal grandfather, arrived in Sunderland, he and his family migrating to the Connecticut Valley from Winchester, New Hampshire. At nineteen, on his return from an expedition to Crown Point and Canada in the last of the French and Indian Wars, Ashley moved to Long Plains, about a mile southwest of the present town of Leverett. There, he too made his living as a farmer. In 1773, he and other residents petitioned to set off the area into a new town. In March, 1774, he became one of Leverett's first selectmen.[3]

In 1762 Stephen Ashley married Elizabeth Billings, daughter of Lieutenant Ebenezer Billings of Sunderland; four years later he became a communicant there of the Congregational Church in which he had been married. In 1784 he was one of the founders of a new Congregational Church in Leverett. The seventh of the couple's eight children, Salome Ashley, was to wed Erastus, William Field's son.

Two other children, Lucretia, who married Caleb Hubbard, and Anna, who married Enos Cooley, maintained the family's connection with the Long Plains region as they spent their married lives in the tavern and the large brick house that were the principal dwellings at Plumtrees. The youngest of the Ashley children, Joseph, born in 1790, became a farmer and eventually took over the working of his father's land.

As the 19th century began, the fertile plain along the east bank of the Connecticut had only recently been cleared and cultivated, and the few families of Sunderland and Leverett who were to be the principal and common ancestors of succeeding generations were entering into the first of many complex familial relations. Near the end of the 18th century, in November, 1799, one of these marriages took place as Erastus Field wed Salome Ashley.

On a May day in Leverett in 1805, twins, the third and fourth children of the couple, were born. They were Sunday's children, and the future painter and his sister were named for their parents. Five more infants were born to the Fields between 1807 and 1816; the family eventually included three boys and six girls. Remarkably, all lived to maturity. Erastus, the longest lived, saw all but the first four years of the 19th century.

Simple, uneducated farmers populated this part of Franklin County. At the first census in 1790, eighty-six houses sheltered eighty-seven families: 524 free whites and one other freeman (who might have been an Indian or a free black). Corn, cattle, dairy products, and fruit - including the wild plums that gave the river settlement its name - were the staples of an agrarian economy. A farmer-watch-repairman, a farmer-carpenter, a farmer-teacher, and finally Erastus Salisbury Field, a farmer-painter, supplied other needs.

In 1805 New York was three days off, Boston two, and only a few of Leverett's inhabitants had ventured to either city. In his whole life Field, one of the most intrepid of Leverett's sons, never went more than two hundred miles from home. In this place, problems of the town outweighed national crises and wars.

The people of Leverett and Sunderland paid faithful attention to the precepts of the Great Awakening of the 1730's, a rededication to the Calvinist principles of colonial Congregationalism led by Jonathan Edwards from his pulpit in Northampton, twelve miles southwest of Sunderland. The record of these generations of farmers is one of frequent attendance in the church that they established, and close reading and observance of the Bible, "its own interpreter." The second awakening in the 1790's reinforced the religious beliefs of this community, as Old and New Testament continued to provide its most available source of knowledge, its instructor for achievement in this life and salvation in the next. The Bible served, as Field later recorded on the walls of his *Historical Monument,*

> as the magistrate's best rule, the parent's best guide, the servant's infallible directory, and the young man's best companion. It is the school boy's spelling book, and the learned man's masterpiece. It contains a choice grammar for the novice, and deep sayings for the sage. It is the ignorant man's schoolmaster, and the wise man's dictionary. It furnishes knowledge, witty inventions for the ingenious, and dark sayings for the grave; and it is its own interpreter.

The right to free trade with the West Indies, a concern of northern coastal merchants and shipowners from 1804 on, had little effect on the upper Connecticut Valley. The break with Great Britain over this issue in 1805 was probably of less interest to Connecticut Valley farmers than Fulton's successful trial of the *Clermont* in the summer of 1807. This event was recorded by Field as one of only three inventions memorialized in his *Historical Monument.* Field's painting of the steamboat experiment on the Hudson may, however, have been based as much on his own use of this conveyance in his travels as on its increasing usefulness for moving farm goods or importing manufactured ones. The first regularly scheduled run by steamboat on the Connecticut began from Hartford in 1824. The first American agricultural fair took place on the village common in the Berkshire County town of Pittsfield in 1807, when Elkanah Watson exhibited imported Merino sheep in an effort directed toward improvement of the poor quality of native flocks. This innovation, and the more ambitious fairs that succeeded it, might have been of even more value to the artist's relations than improved transportation. By mid-century, onions, broom corn, and shade-grown tobacco were the commercial crops that were being developed in the Pioneer Valley as agriculture continued to be the mainstay of the economy of these "cultivators," as they sometimes called themselves.

There is no record of participation in the War of 1812 on the part of area militiamen who had willingly mobilized in the Revolution to protect home, land, and belief. And few effects of President James Monroe's Era of Good Feeling were relayed to this isolated society in which only a few members broke away from their homes for higher education, marriage, or commerce.

Erastus Field's large family lived in a farmhouse with sheds and barns strung onto the main building in New England fashion. One house removed from one of the two crossroads on which village life centered, it was close to church and school and tavern, near pastures, Leverett Pond, and picturesque charcoal kilns. Field surely enjoyed all the common pleasures of a New England childhood. He helped his father and family with farming and with chores, cutting wood against snow-bound winters, and hauling and stacking it in the sheds. Ice cut from the pond was preserved under straw in high icehouses. The woods and hills were beautiful in every season, and treasures of flowers, berries, and Indian arrowheads were searched for and discovered by each child in his or her secret place.

Across the road from the Field house was a huge glacial rock, with a giant oak sprung from the earth; it dwarfed and overshadowed the frame schoolhouse that nestled close to it. School was held there each weekday in the winter months, presided over by a schoolmaster paid for and boarded by Leverett's citizens. In winter,

sleds, snowshoes, and sleighs made transportation easy for these hardy Yankees. Spring rain and mud were other matters, and the farmer's need for family help in planting time closed school early in the spring; it opened again, briefly, during the summer.

There were many country activities: skating on the pond in winter, attending church every Sunday, and sliding down the icy hills on barrel staves or in wood cartons from the box factory, one of the town's few industries. Cornhuskings, sugaring off, family parties, stolen first-of-the-year swims in the brooks and ponds, to all these pleasures, Field added a growing ease in sketching portraits of his relatives. His family encouraged him, apparently, and provided him with paints for early experiments on scraps of cardboard. He continued to draw, learning the range and the limits of his skills. Even though these were first attempts, and halting ones, they were in demand in a society that was eager for a record of its own and its ancestors' likenesses.

Hundreds of portraits that once lined the walls of American houses leave no doubt that the nation's artists, trained or untutored, were well patronized. Many examples by untutored artists survive, among them portraits of every member of the family of Captain Elisha Denison of Stonington painted by Joseph Steward late in the 18th century, and Ammi Phillips' portrayal of all the members of the family of Dr. Russell Dorr of Chatham, New York in about 1814. Erastus Field's contribution to this record includes the eleven portraits of the Caleb Hubbard family painted at Plumtrees in 1837.

Away from Boston and New York, painters like Samuel F.B. Morse, among many young academic painters, and scores of others with little or no training, served the needs of rural patrons desirous of their skills. The working dates and territories of folk painters particularly, touched, overlapped, or proceeded in unison. In the Pioneer Valley of Massachusetts, however, the ranks of artists were far from full. In Field's immediate vicinity in his youth was one noted painter, Chester Harding, born just across the river in Conway. A self-taught artist in his youth, he had early success in Pittsburgh, St. Louis, and rural Kentucky. In 1822 he located in "rooms in Northampton," where he painted "a number of heads."[4] There is no indication that he knew or cared that a young, brash, and impulsive talent was developing in Leverett. However, if it could be demonstrated that Field, at seventeen, had contact with Harding in this brief moment, it might provide a connecting link between Field and another folk artist, Joseph Whiting Stock of Springfield, the paralyzed youth who was to study with a pupil of Harding's in 1832.

Stock was ten years younger than Erastus Field, and the first notice of his career is his own record of this early instruction when he was seventeen. Despite their brief training with academic artists, Field and Stock achieved success as painters through the constant practice of their profession and the development of their own distinctive styles. The realism of the faces in Stock's portraits is generally set off against dark backgrounds. His attention to costume, decorative details, and possessions emphasizes the middle-class prosperity of his subjects, a clientele similar to Field's. While Field's attack was impetuous, with quick, broad brushwork, Stock's was meticulous to the point of fussiness.

While both painters traveled extensively, and both found subjects in New Haven, there is no other evidence of their paths joining, but only of their proceeding side by side, as Stock began and ended his career in Springfield, no more than twenty-five miles south of Leverett. Even though he was confined to a wheelchair, Stock managed a successful career as an itinerant artist and kept a careful record of his work and travels. His journal, an after-the-fact diary, was recast by the artist from account books concurrent with his painting commissions between 1832 and 1845.[5] In that thirteen-year period he painted more than eight hundred portraits and subject pieces. The pages of Stock's manuscript illustrate not only his industry, but also the patronage available to a country painter in the third and fourth decades of the 19th century.

A third contemporary of Field's in the region was Ira Chaffee Goodell, born in 1800 in Belchertown, twenty-five miles southwest of Leverett. Until his death in about 1875, his career and Field's were curiously parallel. In the 1820's Goodell worked as a portrait painter in central Massachusetts, a decade in which the Leverett youth was creating his first likenesses there. While Goodell remained in this area, Field departed. When Field was in New York City in the 1840's, Goodell was also in the city. Beyond these coincidences, there are other shared characteristics which suggest a possible acquaintance between the two

artists. During their early careers, their subjects were painted in similar poses and wore clothes of similar style. Unlike the prolific production of canvases by Field and Stock, however, Goodell's works are few, showing little development or experimentation in his style.[6]

Two half brothers, both of whom spent their adult lives as painters, Augustus and George Fuller, were in nearby Deerfield. Augustus was a deaf mute, seven years younger than Field. George, born in Deerfield in 1822, did not begin his career until 1841. While Augustus remained within the limits of rural New England society, George gravitated to urban centers, working in Boston in the early 1840's, and in New York and Philadelphia for the rest of the 1840's and all the 1850's. After six months in Europe in 1860, he returned to Deerfield where for fifteen years he devoted himself to running his family's farm. In 1875 he returned to Boston to spend the last nine years of his life as a successful landscape artist. While the late careers of both Field and George Fuller coincide in several details, there is no indication of acquaintance, either with each other or with each other's works.[7]

In 1824 Field took the momentous step of traveling to New York to study with Samuel F.B. Morse. Years later, at the end of the century, Field himself may have told a Massachusetts newspaperman the circumstances. The reporter wrote, "When a mere lad he developed a love for painting in oils which became so pronounced as he advanced in years his parents considered it wise to place their son under the instruction of some noted artist."[8] Exactly how this arrangement came about is uncertain, but in a letter to Morse dated October 13, 1824, Field's father wrote about his son's plans to study with the artist.[9] The painter and his prospective pupil might have met in May of that year when Morse visited Prospect House atop Mount Holyoke.[10] Or they may have met in Hartford. Morse (with his wife and children) spent part of the summer of 1824 in Concord, New Hampshire, and returned to New York via Portsmouth and Hartford, where he fulfilled commissions for portraits. Field's maternal grandmother, Elizabeth Billings Ashley, was born in Hartford; throughout his life there were usually family members living in this city, and the nineteen-year-old might have encountered Morse there.

One year before Field entered his studio, Morse had completed his large historical painting, *The Old*

House of Representatives (Corcoran Gallery of Art), in which portraits of members of the House enliven the magnificent interior of the chamber. Morse apparently intended to show the painting as an exhibition piece, a plan that he followed with his *Gallery of the Louvre* (Terra Museum) a decade later. Morse had received training in the London studio of the American expatriot artist, Benjamin West, between 1811 and 1815. As the result of this instruction he became a competent and sometimes inspired painter and an excellent teacher. But his acceptance by American patrons was chiefly for portraits that showed the influence of Gilbert Stuart and Washington Allston and not for the historical works of which he was most proud.

In 1824 the older painter was enjoying some success in his vocation and had established himself in New York in a studio at 96 Broadway. Exulting in a letter, he wrote, "My storms are partly over, and a clear and pleasant day is dawning upon me."[11] Just before Christmas in 1824, parted from his wife and children in New Haven, he conjured up a warmly sympathetic picture of his daily life:

> I have everything very comfortable in my rooms. My two pupils, Mr. Agate and Mr. Field, are very tractable and very useful. I have everything 'in Pimlico' as mother would say. . . I have begun, and thus far carried on, a system of neatness in my painting rooms which I could never have with Henry.[12]

The result of this new arrangement, Morse continued, was that "everything has its place, and every morning the room is swept and all things put in order. . . I have as much as I can do in painting."

Lafayette returned to America that same year, landing at Castle Garden in the Battery on Saturday morning, August 14. Over all competitors Morse won the prized commission to paint the hero's portrait for the city of New York. To a young man like Field, whose life had been the routine of Leverett's days, the coming of the general to "Professor Morse's" studio must have thrown open to him the widest view of the world that he had yet seen.

Field never forgot Lafayette's arrival and much later recorded the event in his own great exhibition piece, *The Historical Monument of the American Republic.* Indeed, from Field's frequent recollection of meeting Lafayette, that event appears to have influenced him almost more than seeing the development of his teacher's great portrait. It is uncertain whether Field was already in New York when Lafayette arrived; his later mention of the triumphal landing implies that this was the case.[13] Since, in his old age, Field recalled seeing the French general as he sat to Morse, it appears likely that his instruction in the Broadway studio began in November of this year as Morse returned to the city after spending many autumn days in Washington where he met with Lafayette and began studies for the portrait.

The painting of Lafayette, completed the following year, is one of Morse's finest works. The heroic, standing figure is dramatically posed against a red-streaked sky. The picture's grand scale may have inspired Field to paint several life-size, full-length portraits both early and late in his career. Morse's atmospheric handling of color and light and the softened contours of his figures establishing three-dimensional form, influenced Field as well. Whenever blurred or muted edges appear in later Field works, they probably derive from his training with Morse.

In February 1825, Morse's young wife died suddenly in New Haven, and the tragedy abruptly ended the master-apprentice arrangement. In all likelihood, Field had returned to Leverett by early spring, for the portrait of his grandmother, Elizabeth Ashley, dates to about that time (pl. 1). In this powerful portrait, Field underscored the craggy planes of the eighty-year old face through the use of gray shadows. The old woman's deep-sunk eyes stare intently at the viewer. She sits in a red chair, which provides a clear bright accent to an otherwise somber palette. Field frequently used the red chair to enliven many of his portraits in the next decade. His quick and sometimes sloppy method is revealed in three blotches of the same red, daubed, as though by accident, against the neutral background.

Aside from the monochromatic color, which bears some resemblance to the palette used by Morse in some of his unadorned bust portraits of men, there is little in this painting, the first to follow Field's brief study with Morse, to link it to the works of his teacher. Instead, two dimensional forms are painstakingly outlined. The folds of fabric in Mrs. Ashley's collar and cap make schematic patterns, and she is placed rigidly in the center of the canvas within unconvincing space. The planes of her face, however, in contrast to the rest of the painting, have volume and are realistically painted.

In the two years that elapsed between the Ashley portrait and the next commission of Field's that is known, it is likely that he remained near home practicing the technical skills acquired in New York. By 1826 John Quincy Adams was president; in June of that year Lafayette laid the cornerstone of the Bunker Hill Monument. On Independence Day, both John Adams and Jefferson died, coincidences that the nation marked in its memory. Half a century later, Field recalled these sonorous events on the walls of his grand *Monument.*

Late in August Field's career as an itinerant painter began. Even as his teacher established the National Academy of Design in New York (joined in this endeavor by some of his students, including Frederick Agate), Field was learning the business of portrait painting. He took to the road with his paints and canvases and by mid-September was in Charlton, just southwest of Worcester. As he continued his traveling, his brother Stillman, then living in Amherst, wrote him that their grandmother Ashley had died on the preceding Saturday, to be buried in

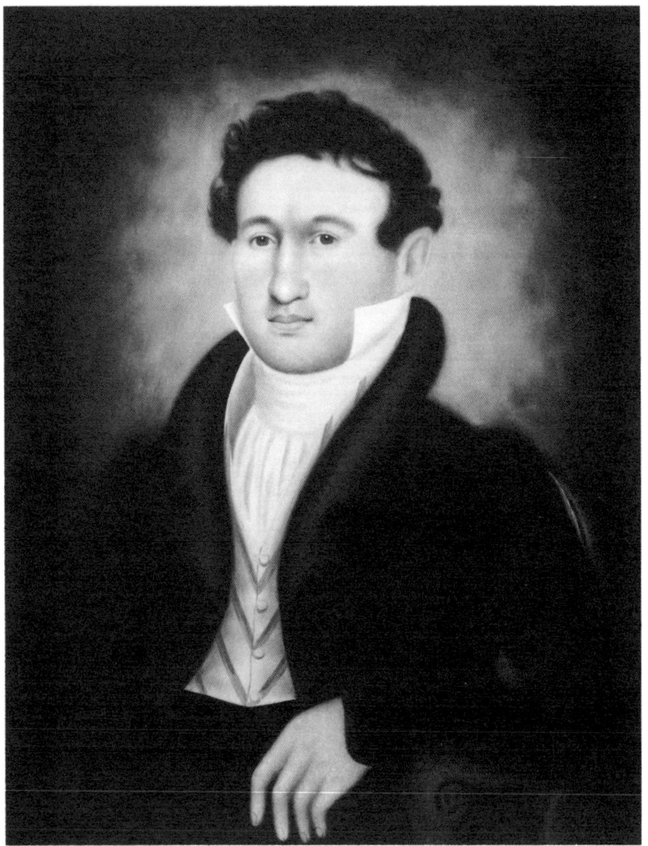

Fig. 1   *Biel Le Doyt*   (cat. no.2)

Leverett on the day of his letter, Monday, September 18. In her last illness, Stillman wrote, "I called to see her two or three times . . . she expressed great desire that all of the Grand Children would call and see her before she should be called to leave this world and its allurements."[14]

The next year, while the angel Moroni was revealing tablets of gold to Joseph Smith in a cave in Palmyra, just over the line in New York, Field, still away from home, was crossing back and forth across the central part of Massachusets, leaving behind portraits of Bay State residents. In Worcester, he painted the smooth and vapid likeness of Biel Le Doyt, a young man two years his senior, the only signed and dated portrait yet discovered from this early period (fig. 1). Except for the muted blending of tones in the shaded background, the soft edges outlining the head, and the workman-like use of a gray ground coat which he was to employ for almost fifteen years, there is little indication in this work to show that Field was influenced by Morse's example.

The Le Doyt commission was completed as the artist worked his way east from Southbridge. Late in July, 1827, addressing Field as "Dear Child," his father wrote of his own poor health, although he mentioned this as "a time of health in this town." The painter's younger sisters "Clarisy" and Eliza were home, and his twin, now married to Captain William Hubbard of Leverett, was living close by: all added notes to their father's letter. Salome was nursing a sick child, "on the bed asleep so that he cannot send his love to you." The younger girls were attending the school across the road.[15]

Nothing more is known of Field and his wanderings until June of 1828 when the only letter remaining from his youth was written to his father from Hudson, New York. His stay in Hudson gives us some idea of how an itinerant portraitist established himself in a community. Field's great-aunt, Sarah Dickinson, his grandfather Ashley's sister, lived there and helped him in "the prospect of retaining business here." His mother's brother, William Ashley, one of the town's early settlers, had come there from Amherst late in the 18th century.[16] He lived in the large brick house that he built on a hill one mile east of the landing on the river. It was the first in the neighborhood, and William claimed to himself the privilege of naming the elevation Prospect Hill.

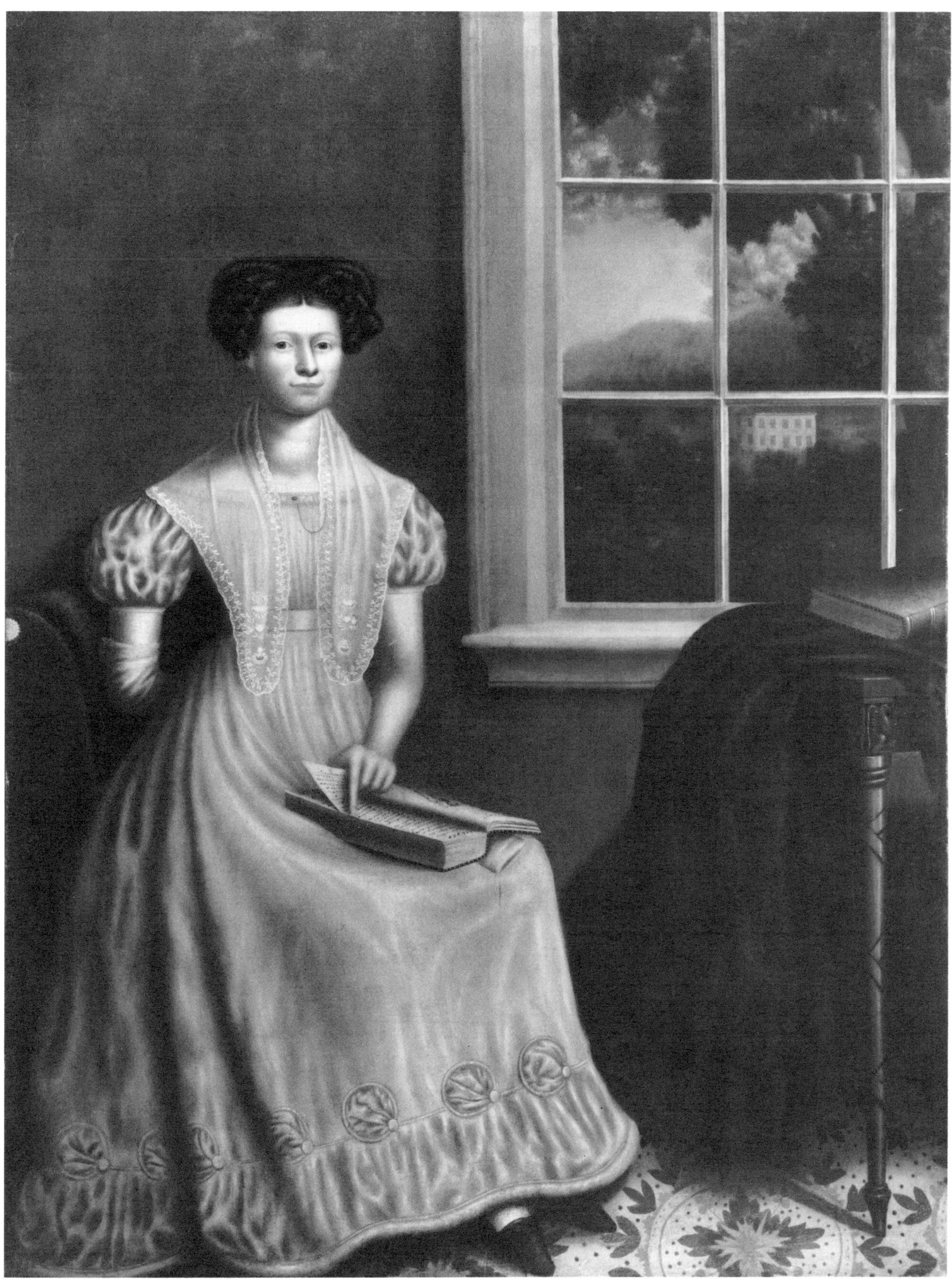

Fig. 2   *Lauriette Ashley*   (cat. no.5)

In the same letter Field wrote of using two recently finished works as samples to show prospective customers. He noted that he had already recorded "the likenesses of Mr. Fairfield, the preceptor, and Miss Frazer," both suggested as subjects by his Uncle William. Those who had seen the portraits, Erastus reported, "think they are good likenesses . . . I like it here very much so far as I have got acquainted and I think I shall tarry here as long as I can obtain business . . . Uncle William has got half a barrel of good shad put up for you . . . he will send them down the first opportunity he should have."[17]

Still at home with William and Jerusha Ashley in 1828 was the only living child of the second marriage, Lauriette, two years older than her cousin Erastus.[18] She sat to Field for his most ambitious early portrait on a large canvas about six-feet high and more than four-feet wide (fig. 2). Her collateral descendant, who presented the painting to the City Art Museum of St. Louis, was unaware of the artist's name or of his relation to his subject, although a family tradition held that the painter was a local man and one of Lauriette's admirers. Field did not marry until three years later, and the size of the portrait and the painter's attention to his cousin's face and costume suggest that this was no ordinary commission for him.

It is not only the first of Field's known portraits to show a life-sized subject full-length, but also one of the first in which a landscape view is included as part of the composition. The imposing four-square house seen through the window is almost certain to be William's dwelling on Prospect Hill. In the portrait, Morse's influence is evident in the softly blurred edges of face, arms, and hands, but the rural artist's own touch is seen in the crisp painting of architectural and decorative detail. A chair in the Grecian style, upholstered in blue, provides a setting for Lauriette, radiant in an apricot satin gown. A length of the gown's hem, corded and quilted in a design padded in trapunto, has been saved; but the marvelous yellow carpet, patterned in a geometric floral and leaf design in clear reds, blues, and yellows, has disappeared, along with the elegant table with delicately carved legs. The pose is an awkward one, especially in the positioning of the girl's right arm. The hidden arm and the single, long glove hint at a possible deformity.

Field captured a pleasant and comfortable life in his portrayal of the self-confident girl who smiled ever so slightly at her relative. It is no surprise that Lauriette's strong-mindedness is a character trait remarked upon by later generations of her family. Her grand-niece wrote of her, "not for her the lady-like pursuits of needlework and gardening."[19] She was the writer of voluminous letters, their chief subjects the Protestant Episcopal Church (in a section of the country in which most residents were members of the Dutch Reform Church), and the Abolitionist movement. Although Field and his cousin subscribed to different Protestant beliefs, his own views on abolition were consistent with hers. Their mutual support of the anti-slavery movement, and the girl's youthful attractiveness would certainly account for the painter's interest and for the grand scale of his canvas.[20]

In the year following the Lauriette Field commission of 1828, only one painting gives any indication of Field's travels, an unlocated portrait of a woman of Natick. This location, if accurate, is the most easterly of the points that he is known to have visited. In about 1829, Field was working in Wethersfield, where he painted *Gentleman of Squire Williams House* and *Lady of Squire Williams House* (figs. 3, 4). Despite the artist's difficulties with their physical proportions, similar to those he had encountered in Lauriette Ashley's portrait, they are a handsome pair. There is a rakish dash to the wings of the starched, white collar that frames the man's rugged face. Strong, broad strokes, rapidly done, represent his hair. The woman, with a big ruffled collar and bertha, is charming. The decoration on her bonnet, a spring green and Chinese-red, woven ribbon, provides a splendid burst of color. These colors, exactly complementary, are dazzling. In this portrait, as in most others, Field's shaded "cloud" background is painted in gradations from a dark margin to the warm, light grey that forms a halo outlining the head.

Just north of Wethersfield, in Hartford, Erastus Field recorded the faces of the young Gilman couple (Connecticut Historical Society). He is floridly handsome; she is delicate and timid. In East Hartford, Dr. Timothy Hall, eagle-eyed and quizzical, sat to Field, as did his wife, sweet-faced Mary Goodwin Hall (both Connecticut Historical Society). East in Coventry, in late autumn, 1830, Field painted the portraits of Samuel Wilson and his bride, Elmira Dow Wilson (private collection), who probably wore her wedding dress: a splendid, striped silk creation with a sheer, triangular, figured scarf, secured at the neckline with a ribbon fastened with an onyx and paste pin. Samuel Wilson appears prosperous in a figured waistcoat and a jacket with silver buttons.

All the portraits from the mid-1820's to about 1831 or 1832 show Field's unmistakable and characteristic difficulties in making hands and figures look real: waists are too short, shoulders too narrow, arms too long. While the bodies look awkward, his treatment of form is distinctive and oddly appealing. These early portraits demonstrate the young artist's efforts to master human anatomy and to teach himself other skills, such as modelling, color placement, and composition. Fine fabrics, jewels, and curls reflect the upper middle-class status of his clientele and add richness to the boldly scaled figures that fill the canvases. A variation on the red-upholstered chair, with wooden arms ending in curlicues like a snail's brown shell, appears frequently.

A portrait of the artist's younger brother, Phineas, is representative of Field's work in this period. Field returned to Leverett sometime during 1830, the year that Phineas came of age, and in one of his best portrayals, the artist marked the event with a fine, sure painting (pl. 3). The odd proportions are present and so is the red chair. Phineas has a broken nose; his full-lipped mouth is set in a pout; his coarse black hair is painted almost as a design in black folds. Field's use of both bright and somber colors and his sense of design result in a work that is surprisingly modern. Again, there are almost no traces left in this work to indicate that the time Field spent with Morse, the brief weeks that he prized so highly, had more than a passing effect on the development of his style and technique during the seven years in which he had worked as a country painter.

On this same visit home, Field probably painted the portraits of Franklin County's magistrate, Squire Roswell Field (Masonic Lodge, Amherst) and his wife, Sarah Graves Field (unlocated). The trial justice was the painter's distant cousin. Justice was administered in the squire's big 18th-century frame house. Justice being served, a homelier service of hard cider was dispensed in the squire's stone-walled cellar on Saturday afternoons.

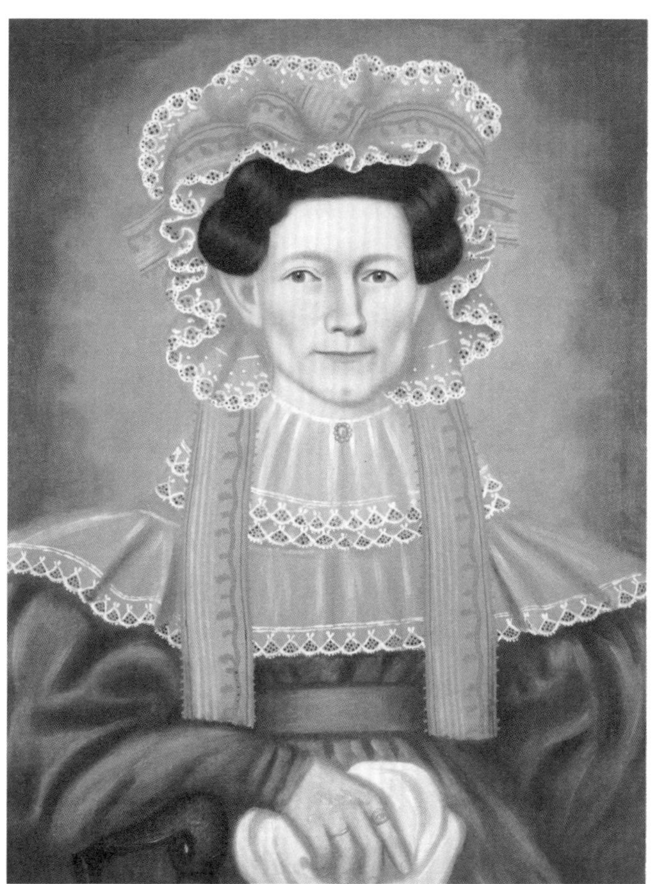

Fig. 3 *Lady of Squire Williams House* (cat. no.7)

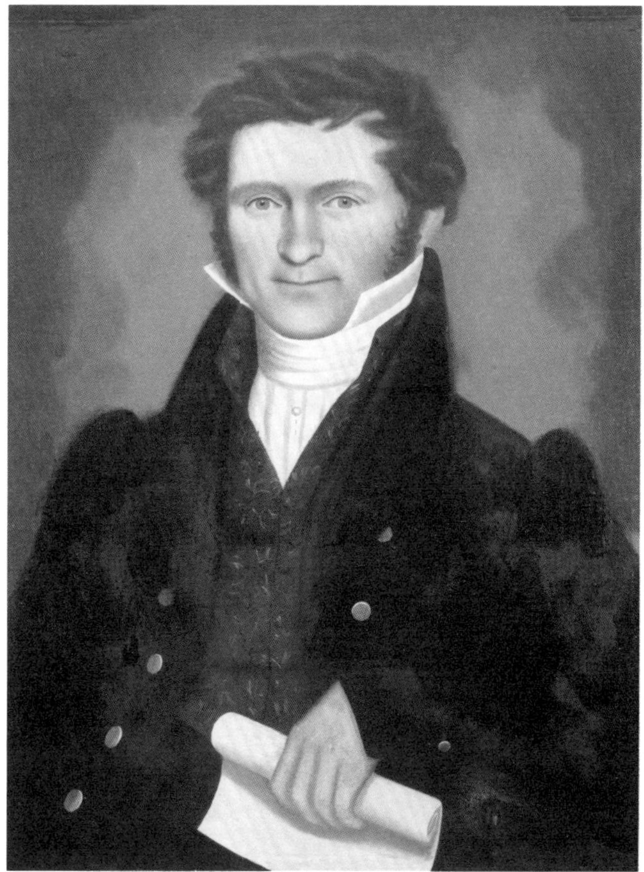

Fig. 4 *Gentleman of Squire Williams House* (cat. no.6)

As the *Liberator* began publication on the first day of 1831, Field's views on abolition were given literary expression by William Lloyd Garrison. On the Fourth of July of that year, in nearby Worcester *America* was sung for the first time. Resuming his travels in June, the artist received thirty dollars for six portraits of the family of Jedidiah Post of Glastonbury, near Hartford. Three Post children were painted together (fig. 5), representing Field's earliest group portrait as well as his earliest full-length likenesses of children.

On a Thursday afternoon, the 29th of December, 1831, Field broke from the common mold of Leverett by marrying outside the community. His bride was Phebe Gilmur (or Gilmore), the daughter of David and Mary Moore Gilmur of Ware, Massachusetts. Two unlocated Field portraits that date to this time, of the Reverend Augustus Brown Reed and his wife, Melinda Borden Brown Reed, may have been gifts to the minister who married them in the beautiful old Congregational meeting house at the west edge of Ware. While after their marriage the couple lived briefly in Hartford, where Field had prospered before, their first and only child, Henrietta, was born in Monson, twelve

miles south of Ware, on November 6, 1832. With a wife and new baby to support, Field may have felt that he had to work harder than ever as he began traveling most of the year to find portrait commissions. One imagines that he was home at holiday and harvest time, and "home" at the beginning of 1833 was Monson. But Phebe, with a baby to care for, was probably alone a great deal of the time and responsible for the house, kitchen, garden, and barnyard hens.

Field did well in these years when he worked mainly as a portrait painter even though the nation's economy was building up to the financial panic of 1837, and prices in general were low. Records of prices paid for his portraits range downward from five dollars in 1830 to four dollars for large portraits and $1.50 for smaller ones of children in 1837 and 1838. However, many of the canvases took him only a day to paint, a speed indicated by the simple, direct, three-quarter poses of the Reverend and Mrs. Frederick Marsh of Winchester Center, Connecticut, dated the 16th and 17th of April, 1833, respectively (figs. 6, 7). Furthermore, new subjects were constantly available. In 1833, in Winchester and in nearby Winsted and Torrington, he completed at least thirty portraits. This number, if

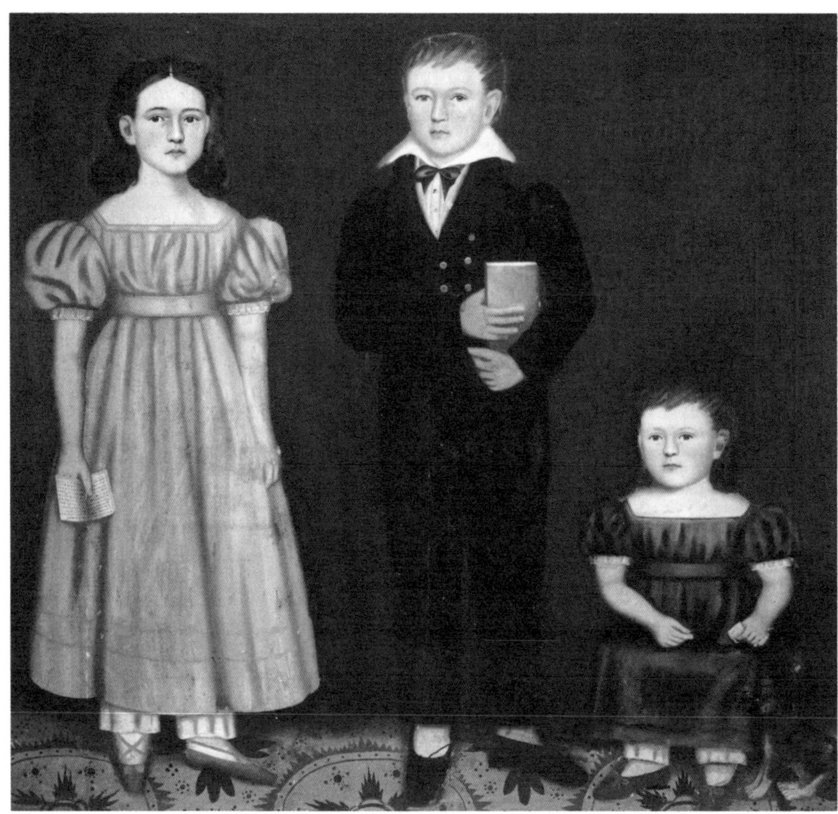

Fig. 5   *Three Post Children, Martha Elizabeth, William Warner, Laura Elizabeth*   (cat. no.16)

he worked most weekdays, would represent a little over two months labor. In addition to four portraits of members of the Marsh family, he recorded at least sixteen other residents in the immediate vicinity; the twenty portraits probably represent earnings of about one hundred dollars. When one considers prices from a central Massachusetts tavern two years later, with room and supper at twenty-five cents, Field appears to have prospered at his profession in his late twenties and early thirties.

Most of Field's commissions came through a network of family associations. Sitters were always plentiful as cousins began to marry cousins with such frequency that at the end of the century it was said of the family, "There are enough Fields in Leverett to bury all the Roots in Montague!" Relations and friends in his isolated hill town spread the word of their talented cousin and townsman. A pattern of relationships among the artist's subjects emerges as the family names of Massachusetts' subjects recur as the names of later Connecticut ones, suggesting that friends and relatives in other states also patronized him. Hubbard, Ball, Marsh, Moore, Cook, and Gallond family members, for example, as well as Fields outside the artist's

immediate family, were among the subjects that he frequently portrayed.

Field's method of working was craftsmanlike. Rapidly painted details, expressed in his distinctive shorthand, were completed with knowledgeable use of quality materials. He used a sturdy canvas, and apparently stretched his own, which he primed with a base coat of warm, light gray that occasionally shows through to the back on supports that have not been relined. Almost all the portraits of the 30's have a layer of protective varnish. Most Field paintings done in this period have at least two coats. Those completed in the Connecticut Valley could have been varnished a month or two after they were painted, but if Field were traveling, he could wait no more than a week or two before applying this glazing. Three portraits of the Chapins of Winsted, painted in 1833 (unlocated), depart from his usual method. Besides being unvarnished, these portraits, in contrast to most of Field's other commissions in this period, are on exceptionally thin canvas, the cambric or thin muslin used for transparent window shades. The lack of varnish and the fragility of the supporting fabric might indicate that these works cost less than his usual price.

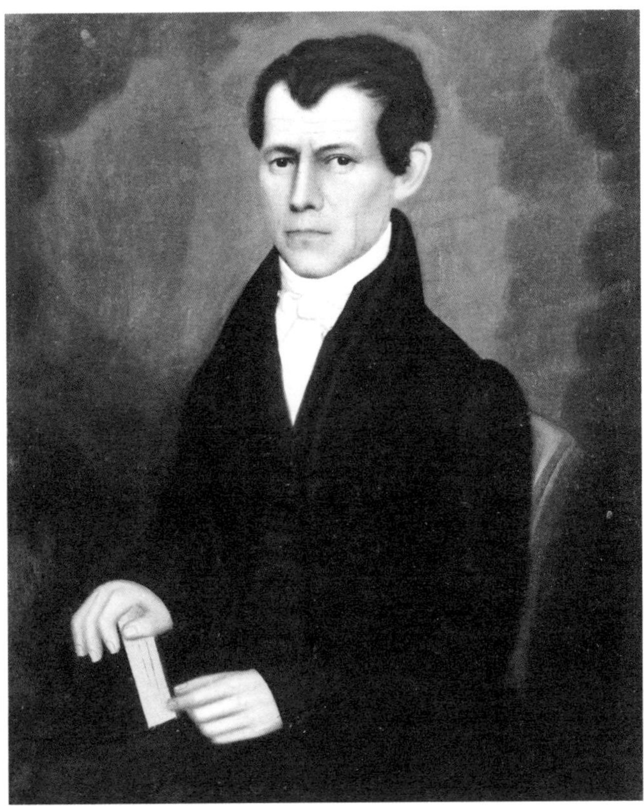

Fig. 6 *Parnell Merrill Marsh*   (cat. no.20)   Fig. 7 *Reverend Frederick Marsh*   (cat. no.19)

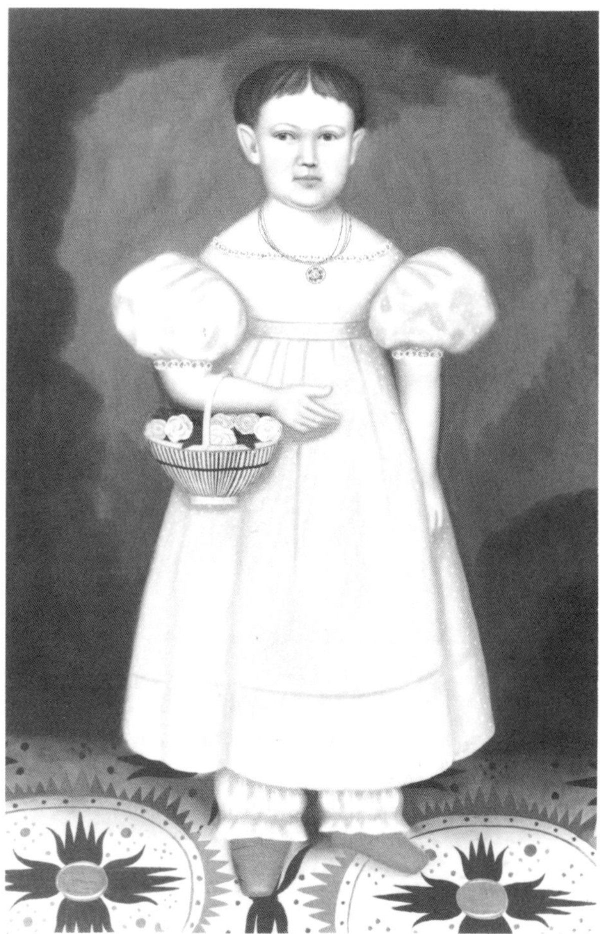

Fig. 8   *Harriet Sophia Jones*   (cat. no.27)

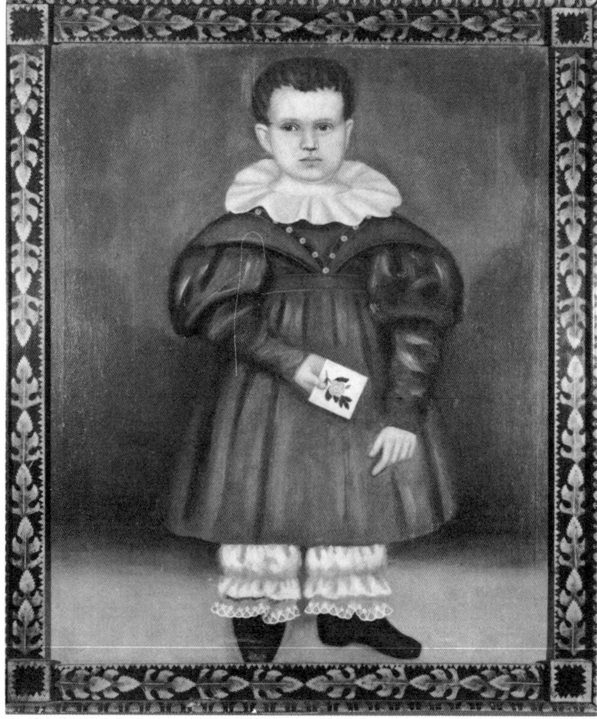

Fig. 9   *Henry Allen Pease*   (cat. no.31)

From 1825 to 1845 Field usually used either a mahogany-veneered frame with an ogee molding, or a panelled frame of the same material with block corners. Moving from Winsted in 1833 to other Connecticut locations, he began to employ black-stained frames stencilled in gold in a leaf design. These frames surround the portraits of Mr. and Mrs. Andrew Judson and their daughter, Jeannette, from Newtown (Joslyn Art Museum), and also appear on portraits of three generations of the Pease family of Suffield, Connecticut from about 1836. Only in Connecticut and only in the mid-1830's were these decorated frames used.

Field's style underwent a change in about 1833. Softer modelling and assured brushwork, quite different from the crystalline edges of the earlier portraits of about 1827 to 1832, can be seen in two of his portraits of children, *Harriet Sophia Jones,* painted in 1833 when she was only four (fig. 8), and *Henry Allen Pease,* painted in about 1836 when he was five (fig. 9). In his portrait the sulky young Henry Pease poses with a rose-painted card. These portraits of children, as well as those of Harriet Sophia's parents, Mr. and Mrs. Charles Backus Jones of Monson (figs. 10, 11), express Field's new romantic vision. The artist's pleasure is seen not only in their faces but also in the delicate details of costume and accessories over which he lingered. Field's paintings of the Jillson family suggest that he reserved this new technique for youthful sitters. Moving east of Hartford, Field painted five members of this family in 1833: Mr. and Mrs. Asa Jillson, their son and his wife (figs. 12, 13), and their young daughter, Elizabeth Camilla Jillson (pl. 6). In these paintings, while Field's portrayal of the older subjects is hard-edged, comparable to earlier figures painted in northeastern Connecticut, the younger members of the family reflect the new softness. Only a small number of portraits in this style survives.

The 1830's were a prosperous and productive time for Field. Sometime this year he was able to purchase land in Three Rivers, Massachusetts (near Palmer), another sign that portrait painting was a profitable enterprise for a skilled, rapid worker with a large prospective clientele. Field's prosperity appears to have been linked to a confident and increasingly personal style. His brief study with Morse was a more worldly experience, but now he was applying on home ground some of the basic lessons learned there. He was on his own, experimenting and finding solutions to the problems immediately before him.

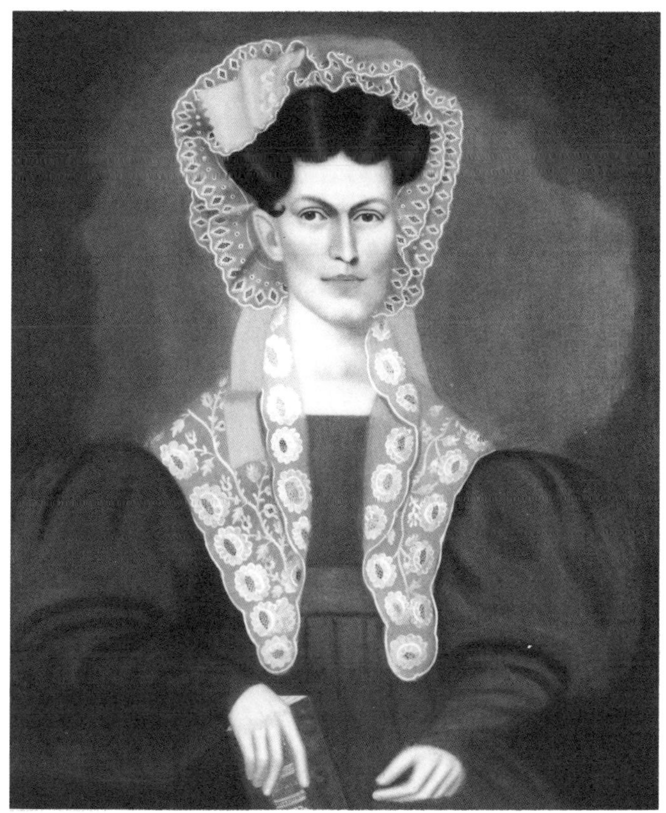

Fig. 10   *Sophia Fuller Jones*   (cat. no.26)

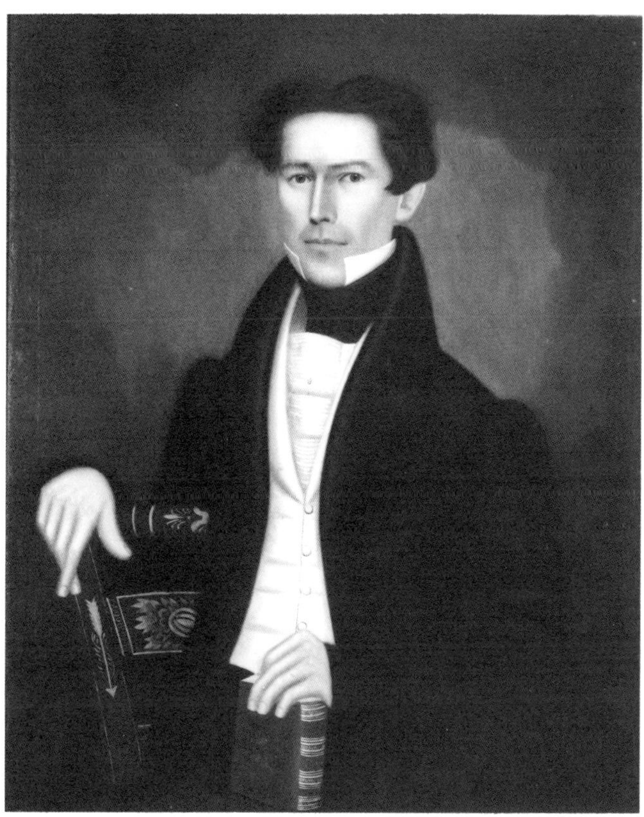

Fig. 11   *Charles Backus Jones*   (cat. no.25)

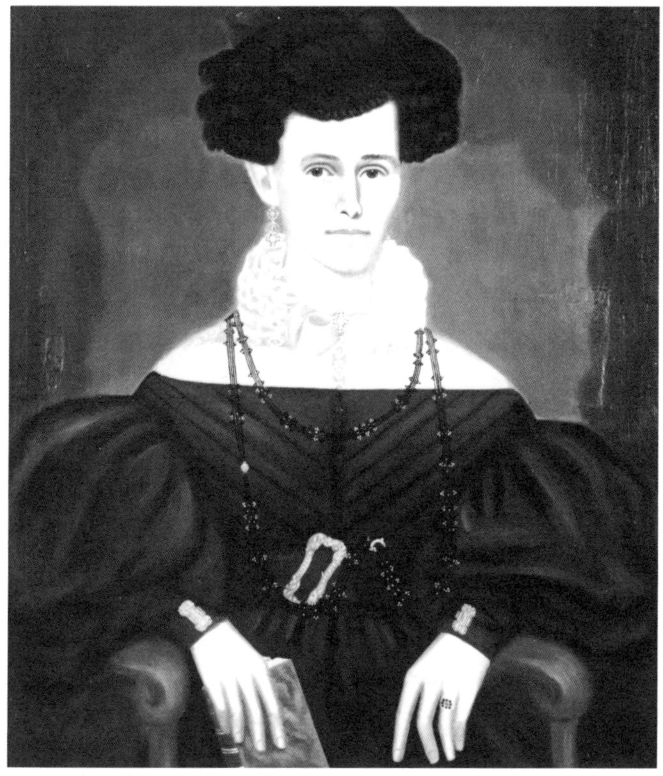

Fig. 12   *Mrs. William Lawrence (Charlotte Curtis) Jillson*
(cat. no.23)

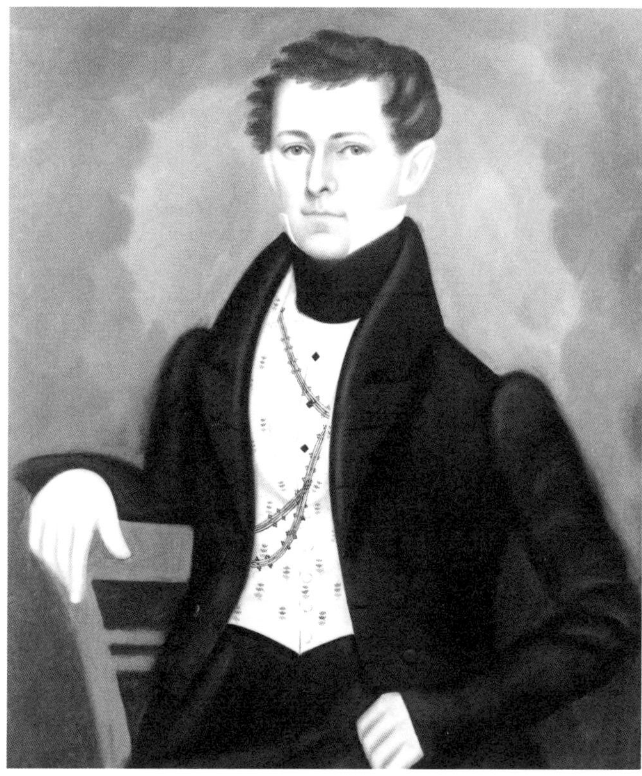

Fig. 13   *Colonel William Lawrence Jillson*   (cat. no.22)

Several striking portraits dating to about 1835 suggest this process. In each of the full-length works a child stands on a boldly patterned carpet. Backgrounds are shaded from dark tones to light warm neutral ones in billowing cloud effects. All the subjects have elfin ears and small two-knuckled fingers. The faces are shaded and highlighted in pointillist applications of gray and pink (pl. 7, 8). Patterns in lace and embroidered muslin are expressed in designs of black dots. The sweetness and charm of these children and of the adult subjects dating to the mid-1830's indicate the artist's smiling mood.

In 1834 Lafayette had died. For most Americans this event marked the end of an era. Field certainly felt a personal concern as this link with his youth was broken. A decade had passed since he had studied painting with Samuel F.B. Morse. Unlike his student, whose modest aims and provincial clientele assured his success, Morse had come close to starving as a painter. Despite talent, a few rewarding commissions, and service as founder and president of the National Academy of Design, the teacher could not make a living as an artist in New York. Most recently he had been disappointed in losing his second attempt to gain the commission for painting the remaining murals in the rotunda of the capitol in Washington. Even as his student prospered in a country situation, Morse, bitter and disillusioned, abandoned painting and began the experiments leading to the invention of the electromagnetic compass.

Repeating the marriages between cousins that were a Leverett trend, Phineas Field married Thankful, daughter of Silas Field, in November, 1834. They lived in a house on the William Montague farm, "next below the Hadley line," and close to Plumtrees where Erastus Field was to spend half of his long life. Phineas at twenty-one is remembered in his brother's painting (pl. 3). Field's 1835 portrait of his new sister-in-law shows a young woman with a beautiful, strong face (pl. 9). Her unusual coloring, tawny and golden, differs from the Anglo-Saxon pallor characteristic of most Sunderland and Leverett people. She wears a light brown dress, with a sheer white double bertha with a soft pleated edge, a style unlike the white, lace-edged, or embroidered muslin collars over black gowns worn by most of Field's young women. The simplicity of the pose is part of the painting's appeal. It is a bust portrait and there are no hands on view, thus eliminating an often difficult problem for Field. The blurred edges of the paintings of the 1820's, the stylistic traits that hint at Field's debt to Morse, are vaguely present in the

softened outlining of her head. Thankful gazes directly at the viewer, a characteristic endowing this and many other Field portraits with their special strength.

The painter probably spent most of 1835 and 1836 in and near Leverett and Plumtrees, but in the summer of 1836, he journeyed to the western part of Massachusetts. In Berkshire County hill towns he found as many enthusiastic subjects as he had in Connecticut on an earlier spring tour. In Pittsfield, Lee, and Egremont his new sitters were related to other friends and patrons in the Connecticut Valley, suggesting once more that commissions were obtained through this web of connections. The Bassetts of Lee, father, mother, brother, married son, his wife, two in-laws and a grandson, all sat to Field. The family is portrayed with a great show of realistic detail, including old Madame Bassett's noticeable mustache. Anselm Bassett, aged sixty-seven in the painting, first appeared in Lee's town records as a surveyor of lumber in 1779 (fig. 14). His son-in-law, Amos Geer Hulbert, a successful carriage manufacturer, had lived in the town since his marriage to Cynthia Bassett in 1824 (pl. 11). A member of the third generation portrayed by Field was Henry Carlton Hulbert, their son (pl. 12) not quite six.[21] The prosperity of this family is suggested by the volumes of books in the background of Amos Hulbert's portrait.

In this portrait of Amos Hulbert are characteristics that Field is almost certain to have borrowed from a fellow artist, Ammi Phillips. Such details as the lineup of books and the delineation of the subject's right hand and forearm, totally divorced from the rest of the figure and too large for accurate perspective, are found in portraits by Phillips. Phillips' 1836 portraits are of Kent, Connecticut sitters, who lived about fifty-five miles south of Lee where Field was working that same year. Field, however, might have seen Phillips' paintings in houses in western Massachusetts, as well as in those just over the Connecticut and New York state lines where Phillips had been active as early as 1811.

Again, the influence of Ammi Phillips is present in Field's *Portrait of a Miller* of about 1836, painted south of Lee in Egremont at the old tavern and grist mill at the center of town (fig. 15). The large hand, apparently separated from the subject's body, is seen once more, this time below a face that might appear at first glance to be by Phillips. Close study, however, reveals the hasty brushwork, an easy means to an end that is typical of Field. Phillips' influence on Field, never more obvious than in these two Berkshire likenesses of the mid-1830's, probably derives from Field's acquaintance with

Phillips' paintings rather than with the painter himself,
although their paths crossed frequently in the 1830's.
The most obvious difference between them lies in the
brushwork; Field's approach was quick and impetuous,
while Phillips' was meticulous and careful.

During this only known sojourn in the Berkshires,
Field painted other sitters, including a cousin of the
Sunderland Balls, Charles Ball Nye (private collection),
who was also a cousin of the Lee Bassetts. His wife,
handsomely dressed in a pale green gown and wearing
a pink tasseled stole, posed with their infant daughter,
Sylvina (fig. 16). Isaac Curtis, whose brother had married Thankful Ashley, was the subject of a portrait by
Field (unlocated) in Curtisville, now Interlaken, the
town where Ammi Phillips ended his days. In another
Berkshire portrait, Field delineated the stern Yankee
visage of Hosea Merrill of Pittsfield (fig. 17), who served
as a Green Mountain Boy in the Revolution and became an important lumber merchant and landowner
with large holdings in the Berkshires and in Onondaga,
New York. His wife, Sarah Phillips Merrill (fig. 18), two
of their sons and their wives, Phillips and Frances (figs.
19, 20), and Justus and Mary, joined the growing list of
Field's Berkshire subjects.

That summer was cold and the economy continued to founder. Crops were sparse, and fall grain
prices were high. Field, however, prospered. By this
year there were more than five hundred abolitionist
societies active in the north, and despite many other
demands in the business of country-face painting, Field
probably found time to support this cause that he,
along with most of his neighbors and family, ardently
supported. The Supreme Court of Massachusetts had
just ruled that a slave brought to the state by his
master was, by that action, made free.

Late in 1836 Field, through his own experiments,
arrived at his best and most individual portrait style,
one maintained until the early 1840's. His production
before the mid-30's included a handful of great portraits and a number of quickly drawn likenesses of
minor importance, but the portraits done from the
time he returned home to Leverett at Christmas in
1836 until the early 1840's consistently show his
mastery of oil portraiture. The draftsmanship is crisp
and the painting fresh and incisive. A regular feature
of Field's painting, his accurate delineations of
character retained their excellence. With increased
power of expression, the paintings dating from 1836 to
1840 represent his most even performance.

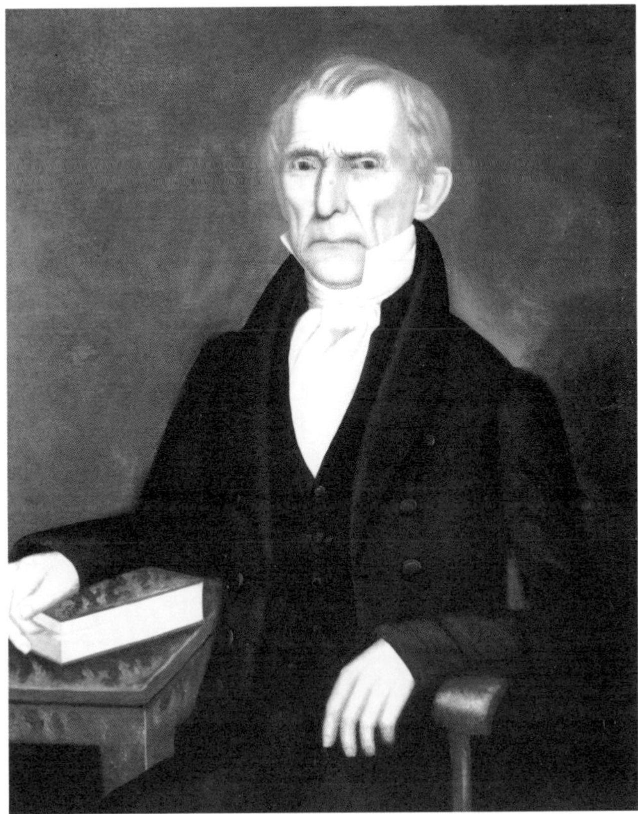

Fig. 14   *Anselm Bassett*   (cat. no.37)

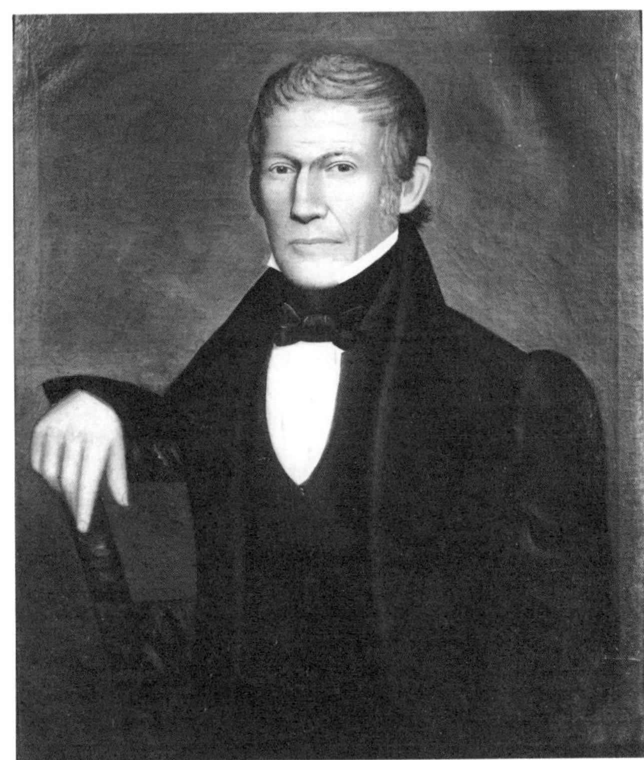

Fig. 15   *Portrait of a Miller*   (cat. no.36)

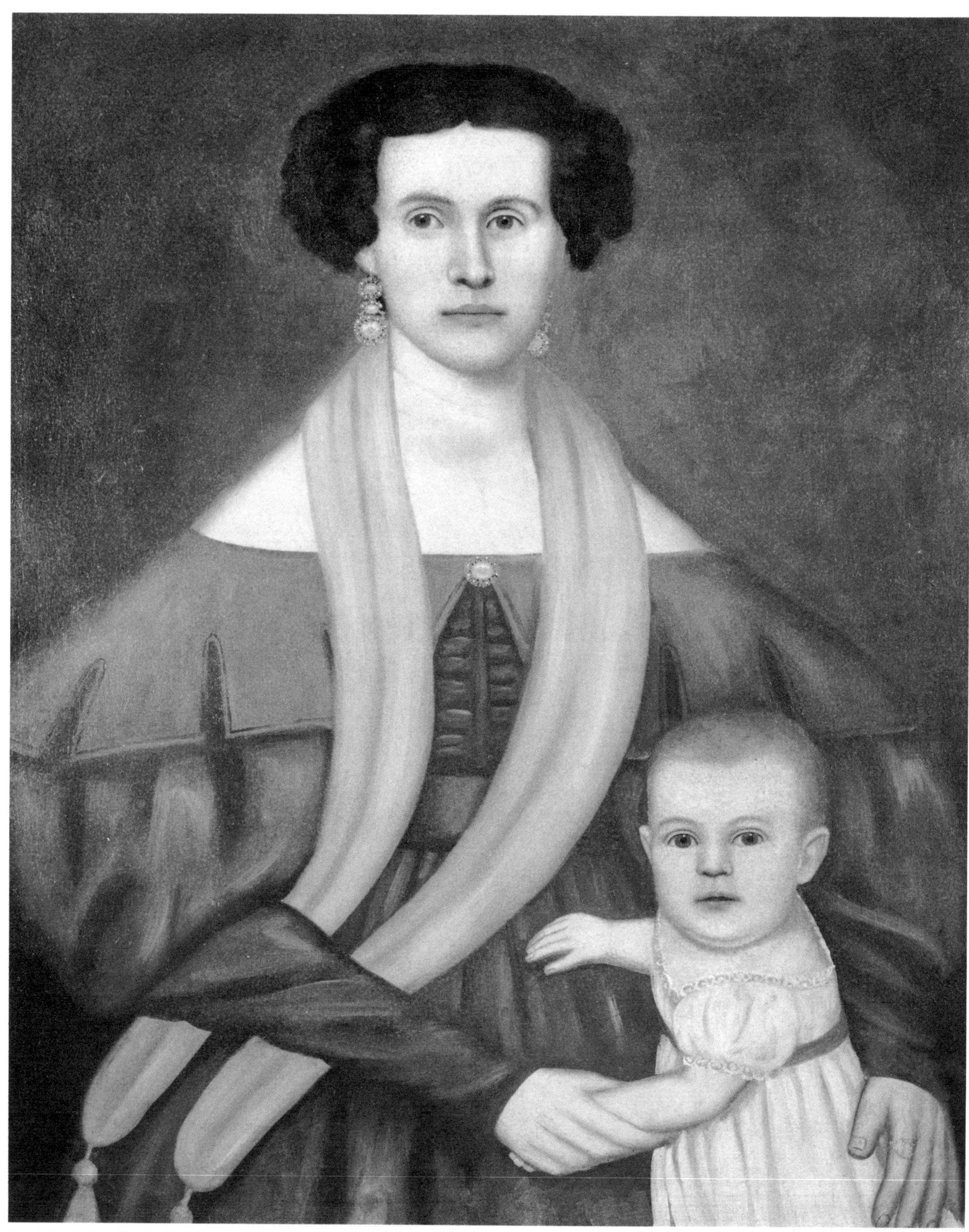

Fig. 16   *Mrs. Charles Ball Nye and Daughter Sylvina Lee*   (cat. no.40)

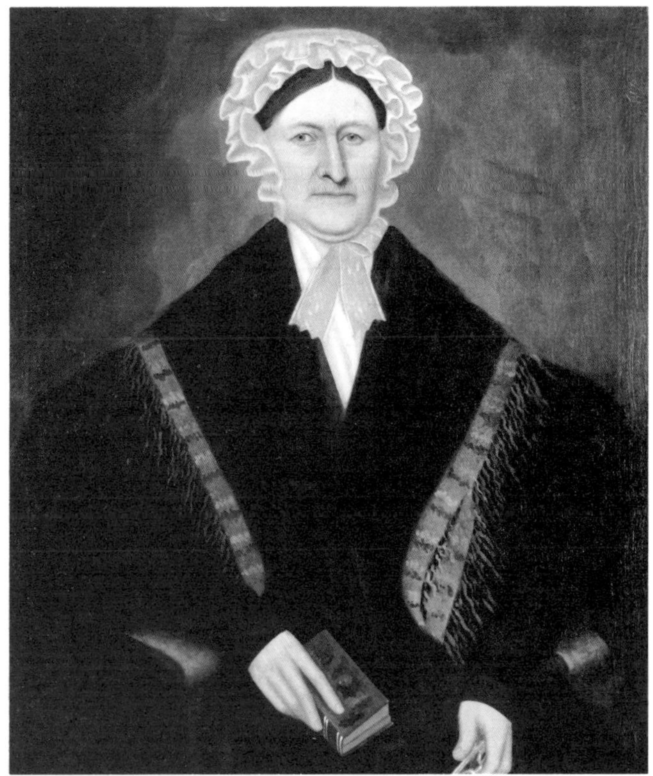

Fig. 18   *Sarah Phillips Merrill*   (cat. no.43)

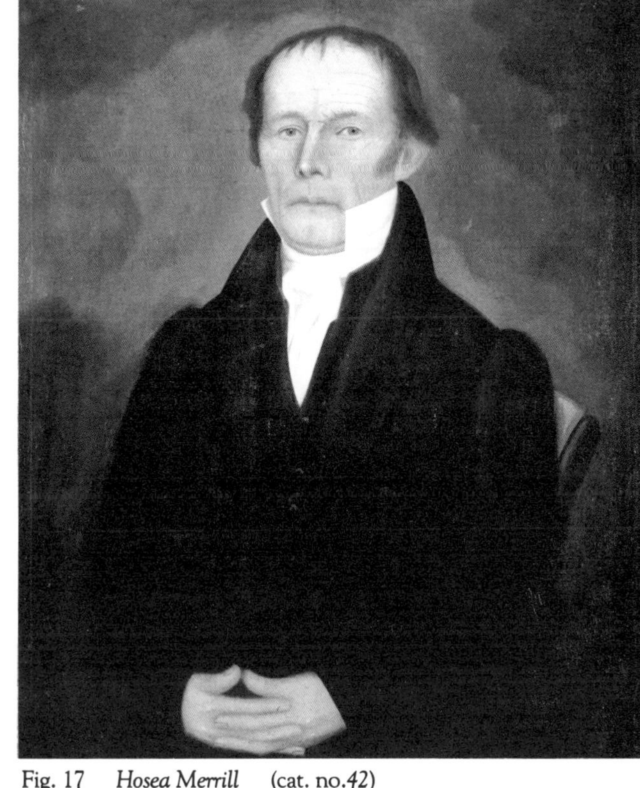

Fig. 17   *Hosea Merrill*   (cat. no.42)

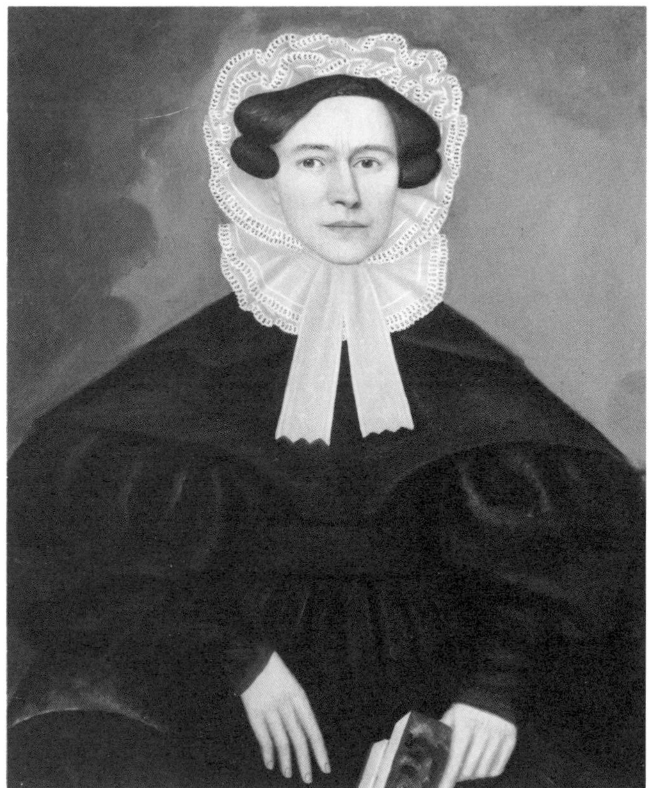

Fig. 19   *Frances Stanton Merrill*   (cat. no.45)

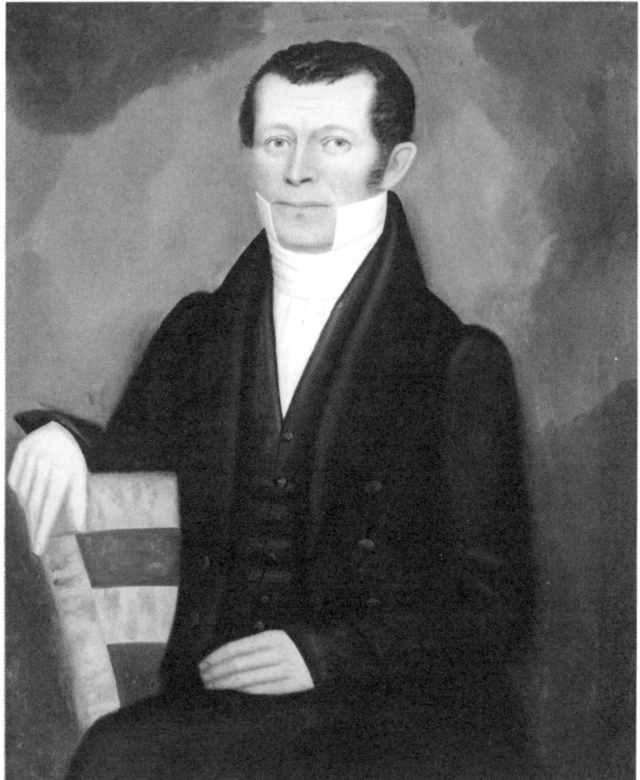

Fig. 20   *Phillips Merrill*   (cat. no.44)

Field returned from his Berkshire jaunt by December 22, 1836, when he painted a fine likeness of his brother Stillman, holding that day's *Boston Courier,* and the dark and somewhat forbidding beauty of his sister-in-law and cousin, Aurilla Field Field (figs. 21, 22). She wore her little gold and onyx pin shaped like a Maltese cross. Her face contrasts with the pale, delicate features seen in the portrait of Maryette, the artist's younger sister, but both women wear the same dress with similar collars (fig. 23). Maryette Field's husband, Austin Lysander Marsh, is shown as an attractive young man with clear, sensitive features. The long, squared-off fingers of his left hand hold a flute, and an open music book is set on the table of tiger maple and cherry next to his painted and stencilled chair (fig. 24).

Monson, Three Rivers, and Palmer are separated by short distances, and Field probably spent the first weeks of the new year in that area, painting skillful portraits of many new subjects. Among them, the self-confident Palmer physician, Dr. Marcus Shearer, and his pretty wife, Susan (Museum of Fine Arts, Springfield), sat at either end of a wine velvet Victorian sofa. Marcus' sister, Elvira Ann, and her husband, Alonzo Blanchard (both unlocated), were added to the growing roster of Field subjects as well.

By mid-February 1837 Field was again near his birthplace, painting several strong, somber portraits of the Cowls family of North Amherst. The painting is definite and sure. While the palette is almost monochromatic, there are several light touches: Eleazer Cowls' hair falls in snaky strings over his forehead like dribbles from a tipped bottle of ink (fig. 25); his wife (Worcester Art Museum), three years older than her husband, is handsome and forceful; and the two Cowls daughters (Worcester Art Museum), in their twenties, are pretty enough to show that Field enjoyed the youthful beauty of his contemporaries (fig. 26). Both girls wear sheer, starched white muslin double collars with embroidered apple designs at the edge of each layer. Old William Worthington Hunt and his able but ugly wife, preceptress of the Amherst Academy, Phoebe Caroline Dutch Hunt, were painted at about this time (both Amherst Historical Society).

From North Amherst Field moved on to Plumtrees, named by Zachariah Crocker and Caleb Hubbard, its first settlers, after the wild fruit trees in bloom when they first saw the region. Field's aunt was Caleb Hubbard's first wife and Field knew the settlement and its inhabitants from his childhood. Two big Federal houses stood there: the brick one owned by the Cooleys, and the Hubbard Tavern. Old Caleb, the tavern's proprietor, enthralled his grandchildren with stories of the bears in their dens in Sunderland Cave

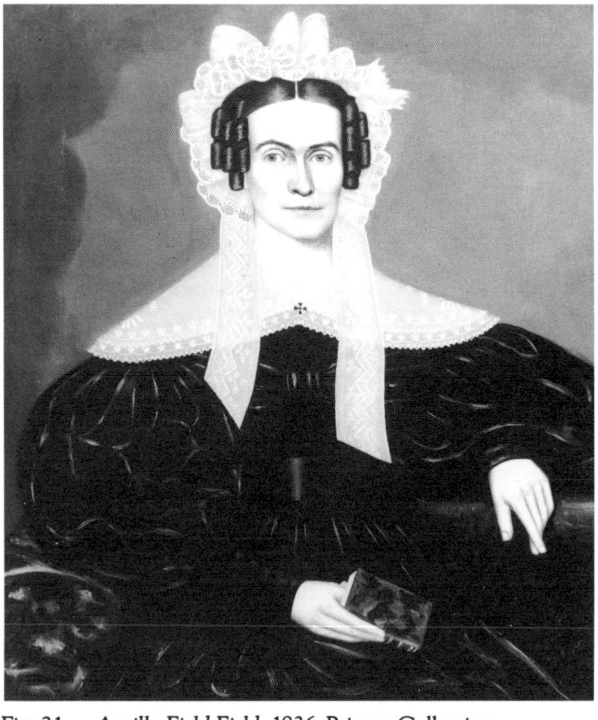

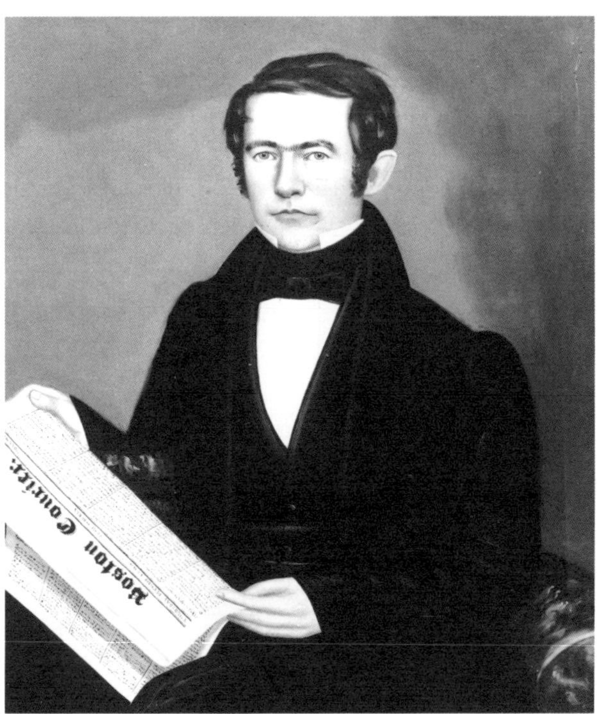

Fig. 21   *Aurilla Field Field,* 1836, Private Collection
(not in exhibition)

Fig. 22   *Stillman Field,* 1836, Private Collection
(not in exhibition)

and in the rock caverns of Mount Toby (even though the last bear near Plumtrees itself had been sighted the year of the painter's birth). He related the history of the Indian woman who lived on the northwest corner of the large Hubbard farm until 1825. Both tales bore on the last remaining traces of pioneer life in the valley. By 1837 Caleb and his wife, Caleb's son Ashley Hubbard, and the latter's second wife, Betsy Dole

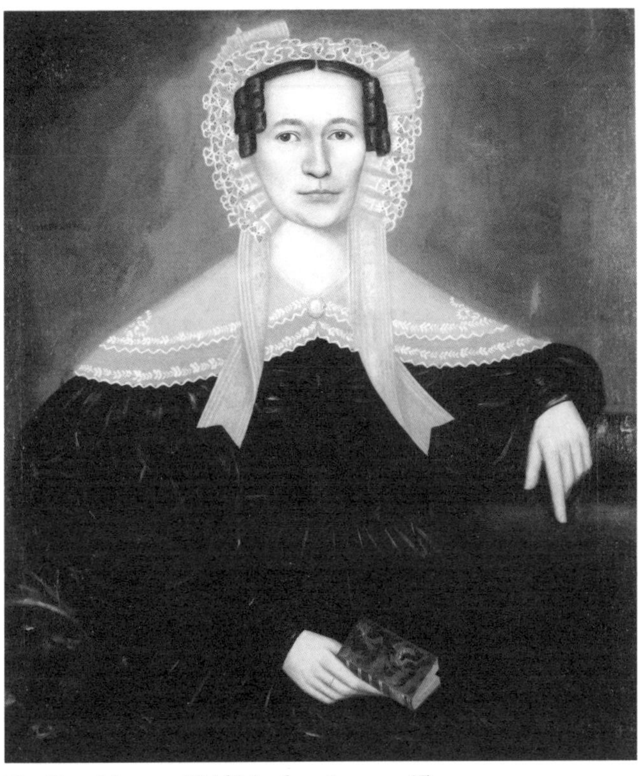

Fig. 23   *Maryette Field Marsh*   (cat. no.47)

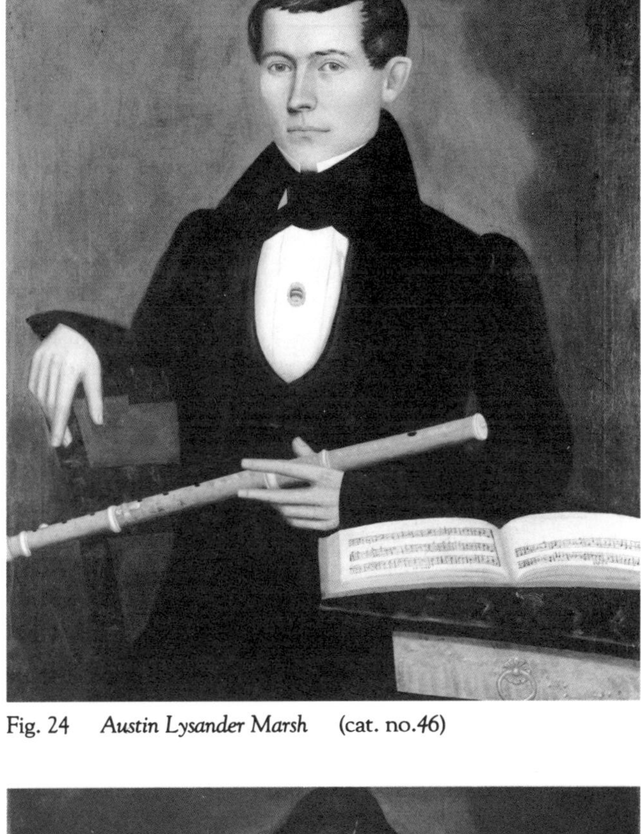

Fig. 24   *Austin Lysander Marsh*   (cat. no.46)

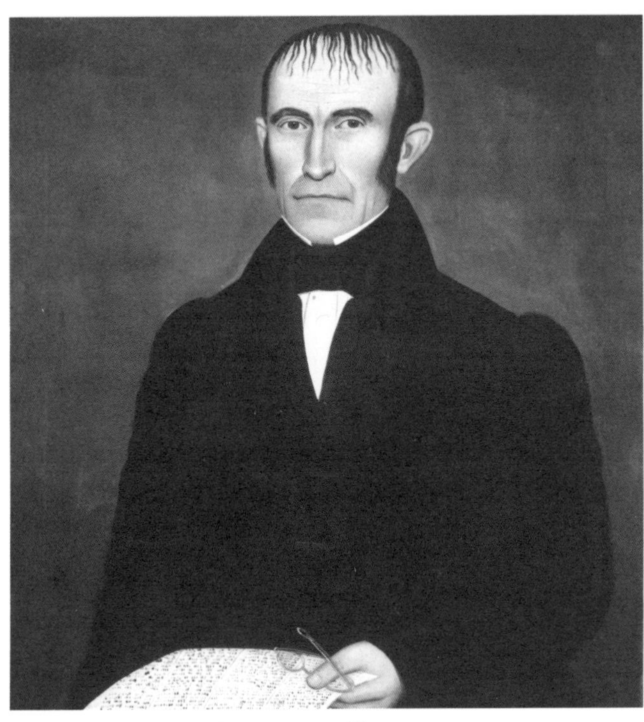

Fig. 25   *Eleazer Cowls*   (cat. no.48)

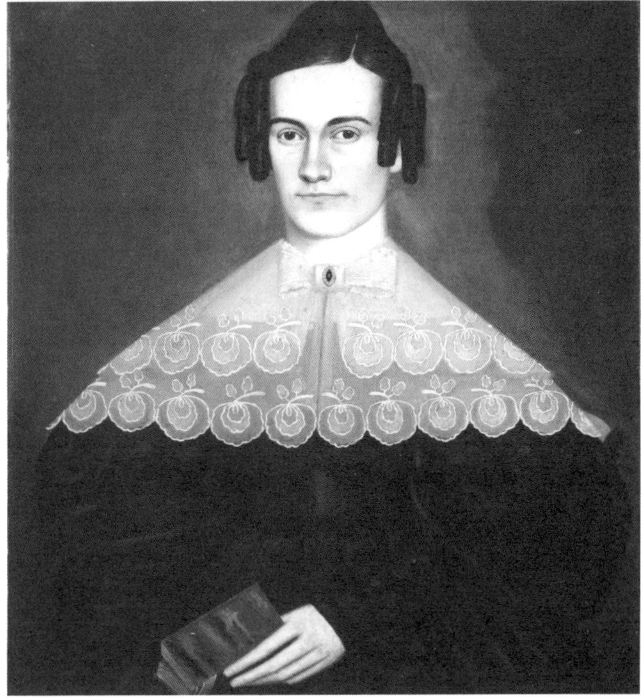

Fig. 26   *Louisa Cowls*   (cat. no.49)

Hubbard, her mother, and seven small Hubbard children, all lived in the large frame house. In 1839 it ceased to be a tavern, probably because there was no space left for paying guests.

Between March, 1837, when he painted Ashley Hubbard posed against a bright red drapery, with Sugar Loaf and Mount Toby visible beyond a white pillar, and the following February, when he was paid, Field portrayed all the members of the busy tavern household except the newest infant, another Caleb. The eleven portraits that once hung together in the north parlor of the tavern survive in the family; they form the largest known sequence of Field's likenesses of a single family. The paintings worked well together; beside the handsome and colorful portraits of the parents were their three charming sons, wearing bright yellow vests, and the two girls, dressed in grass green gowns.

During that year the Cooleys also sat to Field (private collection). Other cousins, the Wileys, lived in one of the smaller houses at Plumtrees. The painter recorded the faces of Catherine Dunn Wiley at sixty-eight (Museum of Fine Arts, Springfield) and her at-tractive daughter, Dolly Floyd Wiley (pl. 13). Holding a concertina in her long, square-tipped fingers, Dolly wears a pale green plaid taffeta dress, forever splendid in her cousin's painting. The number of books and musical instruments that appear in Field's portraits confirms the legends of lively parties and happy gatherings in Plumtrees and Leverett houses.

Yet another Field subject in this maze of family relations was Climena Everentia Ball (fig. 27), married to Zacceus Crocker, son of the founder of Plumtrees, who lived near the Wileys, Hubbards and Cooleys. She was cousin to the Wileys, Balls, and Fields. Field portrayed her as a plain, broad-shouldered, young woman in a dark dress and fancy embroidered collar. Caleb Hubbard's daughter by his first wife, Tryphena Hubbard Kellogg, posed either at Plumtrees or in Amherst for her handsome portrait by her cousin (private collection).

Despite busy times at Plumtrees, Field made side trips to Canaan, Connecticut, in 1836 and 1837 to paint more portraits, among them those of John Adams Beckley and Sarah Delia Munson Beckley (Connecticut Historical Society). John Beckley's hand-some features illustrate Field's skill; Sarah's plainness is prettified by an unusual stole. Field went on to Mon-son, where the portrait of one of the wives of the Fay family (private collection) marked this trip back to the town in which he had lived just after his marriage.

The financial panic of 1837 began on May 10, while Field was at Plumtrees. The seven lean years that followed were to have their effect on the Connecticut Valley, on Field, his relatives, and all their friends. However, when Field was finally paid in February, 1835, for the eleven Hubbard portraits, he received twenty-nine dollars. In view of the panic, this was a handsome figure, illustrating the slow spread of na-tional financial disaster from urban centers to isolated rural districts like the Pioneer Valley. The painter's cousins received full value for their money, for the paintings are examples of his best work.

In 1837 Victoria became queen, an international happening that entered the consciousness of the Pioneer Valley quicker than most events, an indication of its old families' pride in their British origins. A new career for Samuel F.B. Morse had its auspicious beginning as Field's teacher exhibited his electro-magnetic telegraph at the College of the City of New York (now New

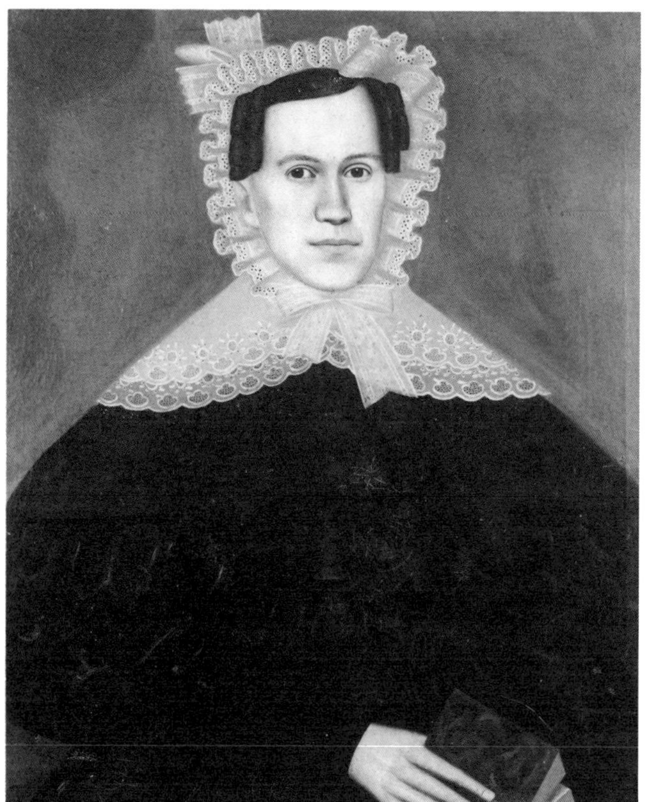

Fig. 27   *Climena Everentia Ball*   (cat. no.51)

York University's downtown campus at Washington Square), an invention that was to bring him the national honor that he had once sought in painting.

Early in 1838 Field journeyed to New Haven where he portrayed the Reverend Dyer Ball, M.D., a medical missionary, and his wife (pl. 14, 15) on their way to China (but delayed in New Haven by the panic). The evangelistic mission of the Reverend Ball is outlined in the legible message on which he was working when Field painted his portrait:

> Assist I beseech you, by sending the Bible and the means of Grace, six hundred millions of your fellow beings standing upon the verge of eternal despair, assist them *immediately* before they step from time into eternity and are beyond the limits of Grace and hope of redemption.

Despite the naturalism of both the faces and figures, mysterious red globes of light appear in the background of the paintings, recalling the seemingly haphazard flecks of red paint in Field's portrait of Elizabeth Ashley. To a romantic, provincial mind the globes might signify spiritual power.

That same year Field found new subjects and, for a change, new family names in residents of Petersham, east of the Connecticut Valley. These portraits hint at a route farther east that included a stay with the Joslin family of Westminster, where he painted the widow of Milton Joslin (Fruitlands Museums).[22] Closer to home, in North New Salem he painted portraits of an attractive carpenter and his wife (unlocated), who are identified only as residents of that town. In this painting Field described a manual skill, for on the table in front of the man an assortment of carpenter tools is displayed. The two portraits were framed together, the only time that Field's paintings were surrounded in this fashion. The double frame may be an illustration of the anonymous carpenter's skill.

Field's Petersham subjects included Jeremiah and Dorcas Gallond (Petersham Historical Society) and their daughter and son-in-law, Louisa and Nathaniel Cook, painted sometime before May, 1838. In the portrait now identified as that of Louisa Gallond Cook (fig. 28), the subject, mother of two small children, is fragile and wan; Field shows her delicacy in the last months of her life. Both she and her brisk young husband, Nathaniel (fig. 29), are pictured against a woodsy background at the confluence of two streams. A music book rests on the table beside Nathaniel.

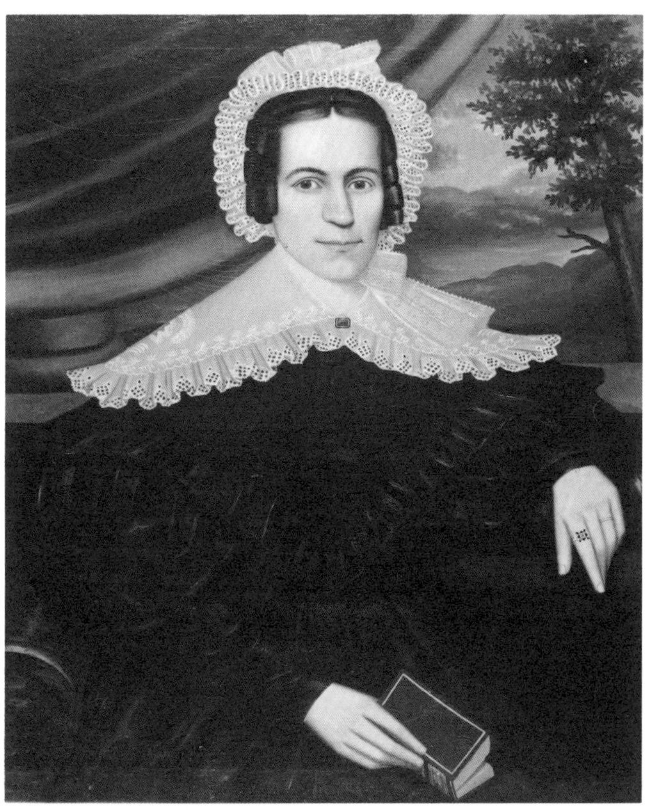

Fig. 28   *Louisa Gallond Cook?*   (cat. no.62)

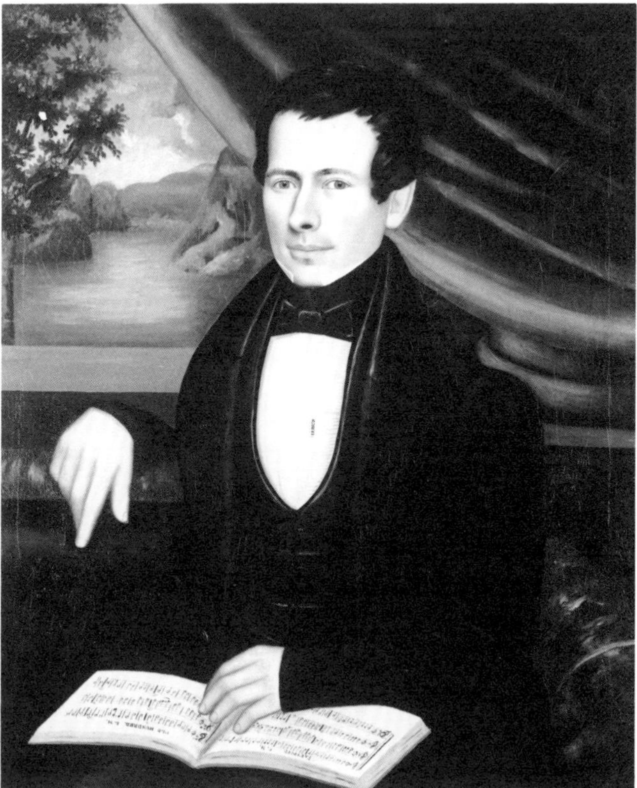

Fig. 29   *Man With a Tune Book; Mr. Cook?*   (cat. no.61)

On his return to Leverett in the spring, Field painted the winsome portrait of his niece, Stillman's daughter, Ellen Virtue Field (private collection). Her full-length likeness fills the canvas. The child stands outdoors with the Massachusetts hills in the background; she holds a basket of roses plucked from a bush growing in a stone wall beside a maple tree. The painting is a charming and sentimental performance. Her shoes, still preserved, demonstrate both Field's desire to brighten the portrait with color and his willingness to oblige his diminutive subject. Although the originals are brown leather, Ellen Field wears scarlet slippers in her portrait, a gift in paint from her uncle according to family legend. *Girl in Yellow with Red Doll* (New York State Historical Association, Cooperstown), a full-length portrait of a child standing on the now familiar double-woven carpet, was probably painted at about this time. Equal in charm to *Ellen Virtue Field,* it may represent another of the artist's small nieces.

This May, tragedy struck. Salome Ashley Field, the painter's mother, died on the 11th and was buried in Leverett, in the cemetery even then filled with ancestral Fields. Less than two weeks later, on the 23rd, his twin, Salome Field Hubbard, died and was buried near her mother's new grave. Despite his loss, Field continued to work, as shown by two fine portraits identified as Mr. and Mrs. Pearce of North Hadley (pl. 16, 17). She is a wistful, pretty, young woman with a flower decorated bonnet and a white-collared, brown dress; she has a little pin at her bosom to match the one her husband wears to hold his cravat. Mr. Pearce is red-headed. His forehead is pale from wearing a hat in the fields, but the rest of his face is red from the sun. Like the Pearces, "an American king and queen," the large figures that dominate Field's canvases are a special kind of provincial royalty.[23]

Sometime in 1839 Field painted Clarissa Gallond, wife of William Cook. (William Cook's brother, Nathaniel, was married to Clarissa's sister, Louisa; they had been painted the previous year.) Field posed Clarissa at a window overlooking a town on a river (pl. 18). While Clarissa and her husband spent most of their lives in Petersham and nearby Philipston, there is no city in Massachusetts that conforms to the one that Field illustrated. If the painter may be credited with artistic license, the river city might be interpreted as Hartford, although the three-masted vessels illustrated could never have navigated that far up the Connecticut.[24] The tree at the right of the composition is similar to the one in Ellen Virtue Field's portrait, but this time it balances a red drapery and pillar like those in Ashley Hubbard's portrait. These details were used frequently by Field at this time. Also typical of Field's portraits of women is the emphasis placed on the exaggerated slant of Clarissa Cook's shoulders: Clarissa is set against a high green hill that follows the outline of her sharply sloping shoulders, a placement which leads the viewer's eye to the subject's face.

Clarissa is a firm-featured Portia. She sits straight-backed on a horse-hair covered Victorian sofa. She wears a dark dress with a large, gold buckle at the waistline, and one of the largest and most splendid of the sheer, embroidered, and bowed muslin collars that Field loved to paint. The neckline is secured with a gold and carnelian pin; her smooth hair is held in place with a saw-toothed tortoise shell comb set high on her head. Almost certainly Field painted William Cook at the same time, but that likeness has disappeared or is now known only as one of many unidentified men. Clarissa's was nearly lost, too; in 1939, one hundred years after it was painted, it was rescued from under an old mattress at a dump near Petersham.

Field painted the masterpiece of his portrait career in 1839, when he and his family returned to the home of Phebe Field's parents on Pleasant Street in Ware, Massachusetts. Across the street from the Gilmores, in a comfortable frame house, lived Joseph Moore from Windham, Maine, a hatmaker in winter and an itinerant dentist in the summer. His wife, Almira, sister of Louisa and Clarissa Gallond, was another daughter of that Petersham family. Also living in the house on Pleasant Street were their own two children, and the two orphans of Louisa Gallond Cook. In the Moore parlor, Field painted one of the landmarks of 19th-century American painting, as the Moores and the Cook children posed in an array of elegant costumes for their nearly life-sized group portrait (pl. 19). George Francis Moore and Frederick Cook were born the same year. Since George died in 1842, and the frailer and slighter of the two smallest boys stands at the far left of the group portrait, it is believed that the figures from left to right represent George Francis Moore, Almira, Louisa Ellen Cook (two years old), Frederick Cook, Mr. Moore, and Joseph Lauriston Moore.

The portrayal of the Moore family in Ware follows an American tradition of large-scale group portraits. Earlier academic examples are John Smibert's *The Bermuda Group: Dean George Berkeley and his Entourage* (Yale University Art Gallery) and Charles Willson Peale's portrait of his own family (New York Historical Society).

Although she is gentler-faced and smaller-featured, Mrs. Moore greatly resembles her sister, Clarissa, and wears precisely the same comb, collar, gown, pin, and belt buckle that Clarissa wore for her portrait. The composition is symmetrical as it is in most Field portraits. In this large-scale canvas, almost seven-by-eight feet in size, six figures are set on an exuberantly patterned carpet with a mustard ground and a design in Indian red and dull green. Above a mahogany-veneered pedestal table is a looking glass framed in a manner reminiscent of the frames of many Field portraits. The painting, as well as some of the dress accessories and the decorative arts illustrated by Field, was in the possession of descendants of the Moore family until they were acquired by Maxim Karolik for the Museum of Fine Arts, Boston. Their use in this family portrait verifies the theory that folk portraits were painted from life, often to stock formulas, but never, or almost never, as the final touch to pre-painted and headless bodies. While no connection between the Moores of Windham, Maine, and those of Ware has been established, Joseph Moore's coming to the home town of Mary Moore Gilmore, the painter's mother-in-law, suggests a family relationship. If this were so, Field was once more following a pattern in the systematic portrayal of extended families.

The year that Field began the Moore portrait, Samuel Morse returned from Paris with Daguerre's invention. That same year he and Dr. John Draper made almost the first daguerreotypes in America, views of the growing city taken from Morse's studio rooms at the northeast corner of Washington Square in New York University's first building. It is ironic that Field's talents were soon to be outmoded in the popular demand for the reproductions of faces introduced by his teacher. Now, in New York, "Professor Morse" had returned with a new kind of image, his ultimate aim, "the application of the Daguerreotype to accumulate for my studio models for my canvas."[25]

Following his stay in Ware, Field may have made a trip to Bennington, Vermont, where he portrayed Julius Norton, the potter (pl. 20), and members of his family (fig. 30). In *Julius Norton* a piano with an open music book is shown in the background, the subject's legendary fame as a musician in Bennington County illustrated in the instrument he holds. But Field soon returned to the Connecticut Valley. Three portraits, two of them double ones, can be dated by the age of their North Amherst subjects to 1840 (private collection). William Henry Smith, his wife, and his three children were the sitters. In these works Field experimented, using a brown base and background to replace the light gray one that he had used almost exclusively since the beginning of his career. The experiment was markedly unsuccessful since it tended to muddy Field's clear palette. All the portraits of the 1840's show this change in tone, and as time passed, many became greatly disfigured as the brown base burned through the paler tints of color used in the subjects' faces.

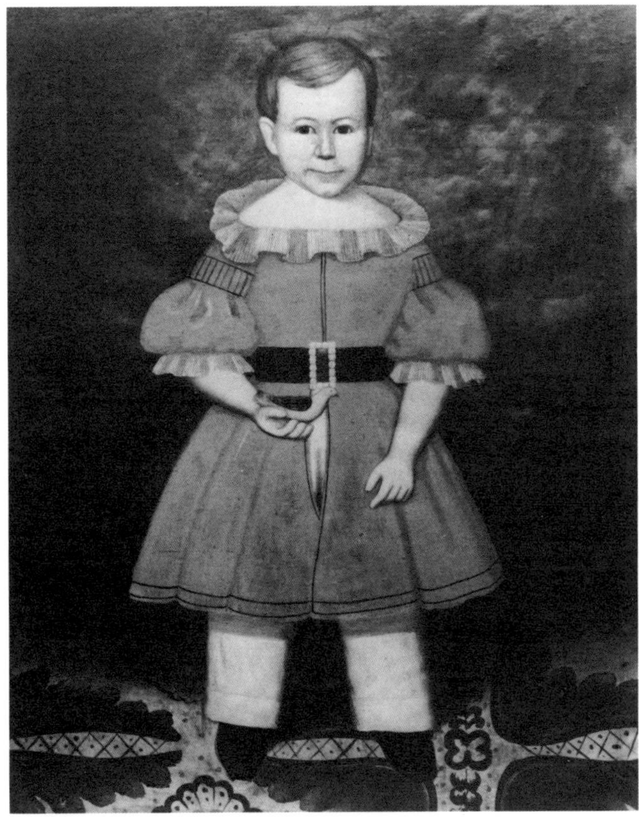

Fig. 30   *Luman Preston Norton*   (cat. no.67)

In 1841 Field left New England to spend most of the next seven years in New York City. A decline in painting commissions about 1840 suggests that he had come to the end of a once long line of patrons. It is likely that he saw the coming competition with daguerreotypists who would quickly and accurately produce small likenesses in less time than painting required, and who would charge less for their services. Perhaps Field thought that he, like Morse, could harness the new technology to his own use. At the back of his mind he might have dreamed that Morse would once more be his "Professor," instructing him in the use of the new photographic marvel. Whatever his reasons for leaving New England, Erastus Field now took the stage down the Post Road along the Connecticut River to Hartford, where he boarded the New York steamboat at 2 P.M. He arrived in the city early the next morning. The trip cost him two dollars, half the price of Caleb Hubbard's portrait.

In the *New York Directory* for 1841 and 1842, "Erastus Field, portrait painter," is listed at 58 Carmine Street in Greenwich Village, a few short blocks from the North River. Morse's studio was a turret room at New York University, five blocks east. Morse himself lived just south of City Hall on Nassau Street, about halfway between Field's address and the old studio near the Battery where the New England artist had once been his apprentice.

In 1842 the first sacred drama produced in America took place in lower Manhattan at the Park Theatre. It was entitled *The Israelites in Egypt or Passage of the Red Sea.* The entertainment was based on music illicitly borrowed from Handel and Rossini, and its English performance had been suppressed by the Bishop of London. Neither detraction is likely to have lessened Field's enthusiasm. He almost certainly saw the production and was influenced by it: it is the logical inspiration for his series of paintings on the same theme created much later.

In this decade, too, was the exhibition at the Minerva Rooms of a five-mile panorama of a voyage around the world. The trip began and ended in Boston and showed locations in the United States (including Oregon), in China, the East Indies, Egypt, Constantinople, and Europe. Forty-five years later in Plumtrees, Field painted his own eighty-foot panorama (now belonging to the Abby Aldrich Rockefeller Folk Art Center, Williamsburg, Virginia). Barely a foot high, it depicted a trip around the world beginning and ending in Boston and showing the United States (including Oregon), China, the East Indies, Egypt, Constantinople, and Europe.

One of the events of city life was a grand annual fair, the American Institute of the City of New York, which took place at Niblo's Garden most years. In this exposition were thousands of exhibits, ranging from stuffed birds to corsets, from a dozen Shaker shirts to one hundred hand-pieced quilts. Amid the myriad entries in 1842 was Morse's "Electro-Magnetic Telegraph." That same year, Erastus Field's neighbor, John Fisher, entered a model of Engine House number 14, their local firehouse. Seven blocks south of Field's first New York address lived the twins who portrayed scores of the sail and steam boats that plied the waters around Manhattan; entries 147 and 407 were watercolor ship portraits by James Bard and an oil painting of another vessel by his twin, John. (It seems entirely possible that Field, one of twins himself, knew his fellow painters.) In the 1842-43 *Directory*, Field, an "artist" rather than the preceding year's "portrait painter," was still at Carmine Street, but during the summer of 1843 he moved uptown a few blocks to 66 Bank Street.

At home in Leverett Field's sister, Maryette Marsh, died, and Elizabeth Field Cutter, another sister, took charge of the three Marsh children. A happy event took place there as the painter's sister, Julia Ann (between Maryette and Phineas), married Nathaniel Sears on Washington's birthday in 1844. Julia Ann was thirty-three and must certainly have been rated a spinster by Leverett standards. Field may have returned home for the wedding (where he might have heard of the short-lived anti-slavery community founded by Frederick Douglass in Florence, a northern suburb of Northampton). As he returned to New York that year, he brought Phebe and Henrietta back with him to share the city experience. Although Field is not listed in directories for 1844 and 1845, Phebe Field entered "one painting" at the annual fair in 1844. Her address, 151 Hammond Street, was the same one listed in the 1845-46 *Directory* for Erastus S. Field, "artist," and for the office and residence of the optician "David Gilman" (Phebe's older brother, David Gilmur or Gilmore).

Only a few works can be dated to Field's second New York period, but he probably continued to paint some portraits. Given his usual astute business practice in acquiring subjects by developing professional ties with family and friends, it is reasonable to suppose that he depended on them for patronage in the city in much the same manner as he had relied on them in the country. While Field lived in New York, it appears that his relations and neighbors entered his paintings into the fair. Since art entries in the fair indicate ownership rather than authorship and were listed by number without specific titles or the names of their creators, it is difficult to prove that this was the case.

Examples of this practice are the paintings entered by his wife and in-laws. One, indisputably by Field, survives today. It is the oil painting submitted by "M. Gillmur," an entry in the fair of 1845. "M. Gillmur" was Field's niece. (The family is also identified in New York directories as Gilmore and Gilman.) A portrait of Miss Margaret Gilmore of Ware, Massachusetts, is undoubtedly the painting exhibited in 1845 (pl. 21). In this full-length likeness, the young girl is dressed in blue, posed with a book and cat, holding a fan, and wearing red slippers. She sits in a neo-classical chair on a yellow patterned carpet. The costume, furnishings, and the warm brown base coat date the painting to Field's 1840 style.

In 1846 Abram Bogardus, a daguerreotypist, from a house east of Erastus Salisbury Field's first New York address, entered "one oil painting" as number 1073. On his return to Massachusetts Field advertised himself as a daguerreotypist in the Palmer newspaper. One might speculate that his teacher was this New York neighbor, whose mastery of the new art of photography was swapped for one or more of the New England painter's works.

In 1846-47 Field was not listed in the *Directory*, but David Gilmore was, with a residence at 641 Hudson Street. This was probably the largest New York house in which Field lived, nearly big enough for all the Fields and Gilmores who gave this as their 1846 address. At the Institute of the City of New York (held this year at Castle Garden after Niblo's Garden burned), number 712 was "one oil portrait by an artist," submitted by Mary Jane Johnston, living at 158 Hammond Street across the street from the Fields and Gilmores.

After his initial appearance in the 1841-42 *New York Directory* as "portrait painter," Field listed himself as "artist," perhaps signalling an interest in expanding his subject matter. In the mid-1840's he experimented with at least one literary theme, executing the two oil versions of the *Embarkation of Ulysses* known today, as well as a small pencil drawing of the subject (fig. 31).

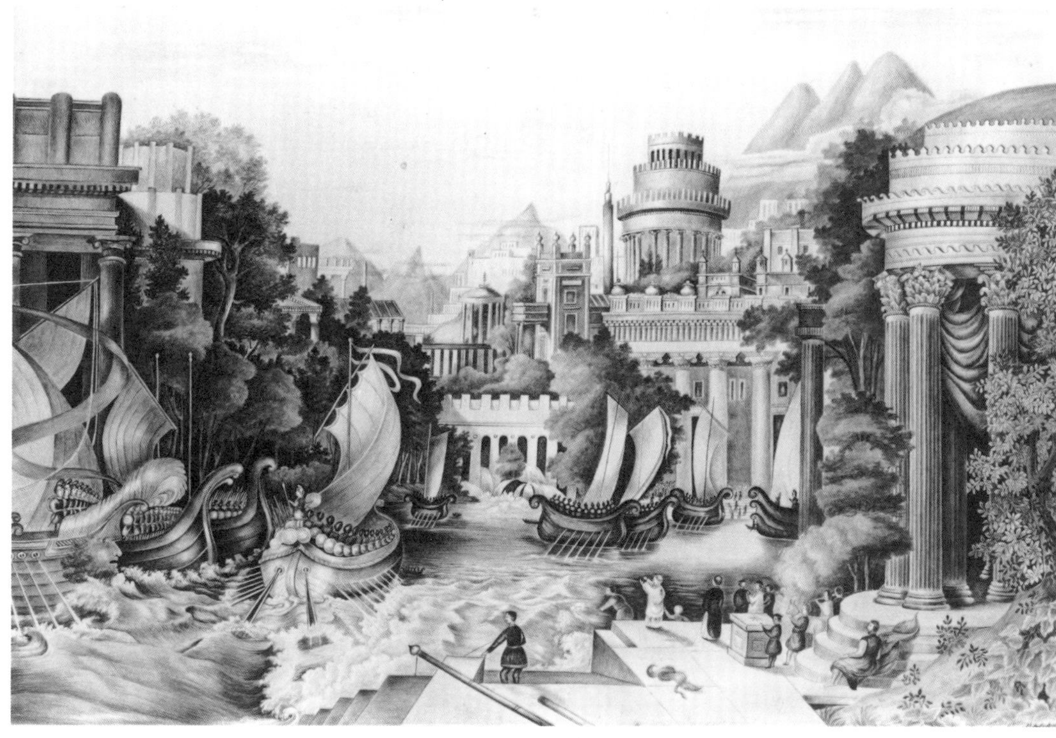

Fig. 31　*The Embarkation of Ulysses*　(cat. no.69)

One oil version belongs to the Museum of Fine Arts, Springfield (pl. 22); the second is presently unlocated. These works were copied from J.W. Appleton's engraving, *A City of Ancient Greece with the Return of the Victorious Armament*, published in London in 1840.

Other evidence for this new direction in Field's career is found in an entry in the second edition of the 1844 catalogue, printed after the fair opened, of "one watercolor drawing of the 17th Annual Fair by Benjamin J. Harrison." The original (Museum of the City of New York) is a small, almost monochromatic composition, but detailed enough to show Niblo's Garden crowded to the roof with exhibits. Among them are paintings hung floor-to-ceiling on the balcony surrounding the main floor on three sides. Although the small scale of this watercolor makes identification of specific works very difficult, one of the compositions hanging at the top of the pile, just to the right of the balcony aisle, generally conforms to the outlines of *The Embarkation of Ulysses*.

Field may also have executed a large landscape view of Castle Garden at this time. While the painting of this subject dated 1847 is unattributed, it is tempting to believe that the work was Field's (fig. 32). Its style is consistent with the *Embarkation of Ulysses*. In addition, Field's special interest in Castle Garden, the site of Lafayette's landing in America in 1824, is confirmed in his painting of this subject on the walls of his *Historical Monument*. Quite possibly, *Castle Garden* was Field's entry in the fair in 1847, identified only as "one landscape painting."

While Henrietta Field may have stayed on in New York for a time, the 1847-48 *Directory* is the last to list Field as a resident, and the entry sent by him to the annual fair in 1847 marked his final participation in that event. According to material supplied by Henrietta and other relations early in this century, Field was called home to Massachusetts in 1848 "to conduct his father's farm;" the same source states that he remained in Sunderland "some four years in the practice of his art."[26] That may have been one of his reasons for leaving the city, but undoubtedly there were others. During his time in New York he had returned to Massachusetts at least twice: the second trip was to Palmer in 1846, where he portrayed Jonathan and Sally Baggs Mooers (private collection). In Mr. Mooers painting

there is a clear reference to Field's New York sojourn, for he holds a copy of *The New York Observer*, published on Nassau Street by Samuel Morse's brother, Sidney Morse.

The photograph now became the permanent record demanded by both urban and rural society. Field was only one of the victims of the change in fashion. But with typical flexibility and good humor he seems to have adapted his ways to suit the change. He began to use his own photographic images as the source for his large and still colorful compositions. Perhaps one of his reasons for returning home was to try out this new system. Certainly Erastus Field, an artist living by his trade since he was twenty, could not "conduct his father's farm" with anything like the skill of his brothers, Stillman or Phineas, both nearby, both farmers. Farming and "the practice of his art" are not an ordinary combination of occupations, but for the next four years they appear to have been his. With the single exception of a lost portrait of four-year-old Edwin D. Marsh of Amherst, there is no painting that can be dated to this time in Sunderland. Elizabeth Field Cutter, the sister who had taken over another sister's orphans six years before, died there in 1849, and the familiar ground of Leverett cemetery was broken once more. On the 1st of March, 1851, the artist's father died.

In 1939 a Field descendant recalled that the artist lived half a century at Plumtrees.[27] While Field made a number of excursions from Plumtrees in the next fifty years, this beautiful little settlement along the Connecticut, with Sugar Loaf and Mount Toby to the west and the hills of Leverett to the east, was the permanent home to which he returned for at least part of each year. Field was later to spend the winter months away. Today Plumtrees is nearly as it was, with fields of tobacco, onions, and corn, with sugar bush, schoolhouse, tavern, and the big Federal house of the Cooleys. Four more frame farmhouses, belonging to close or distant cousins, were burned in this century and have not been rebuilt. Field's home there was a small single-story, yellow-painted cottage just south of the Cooley house. At first, he rented the place. Later, some of the Hubbards, whose portraits Field had painted when they were boys, provided it free of charge. The patriarch of that family, Caleb Hubbard, doughty old tavern keeper and Revolutionary soldier, had died the year before Field's father.

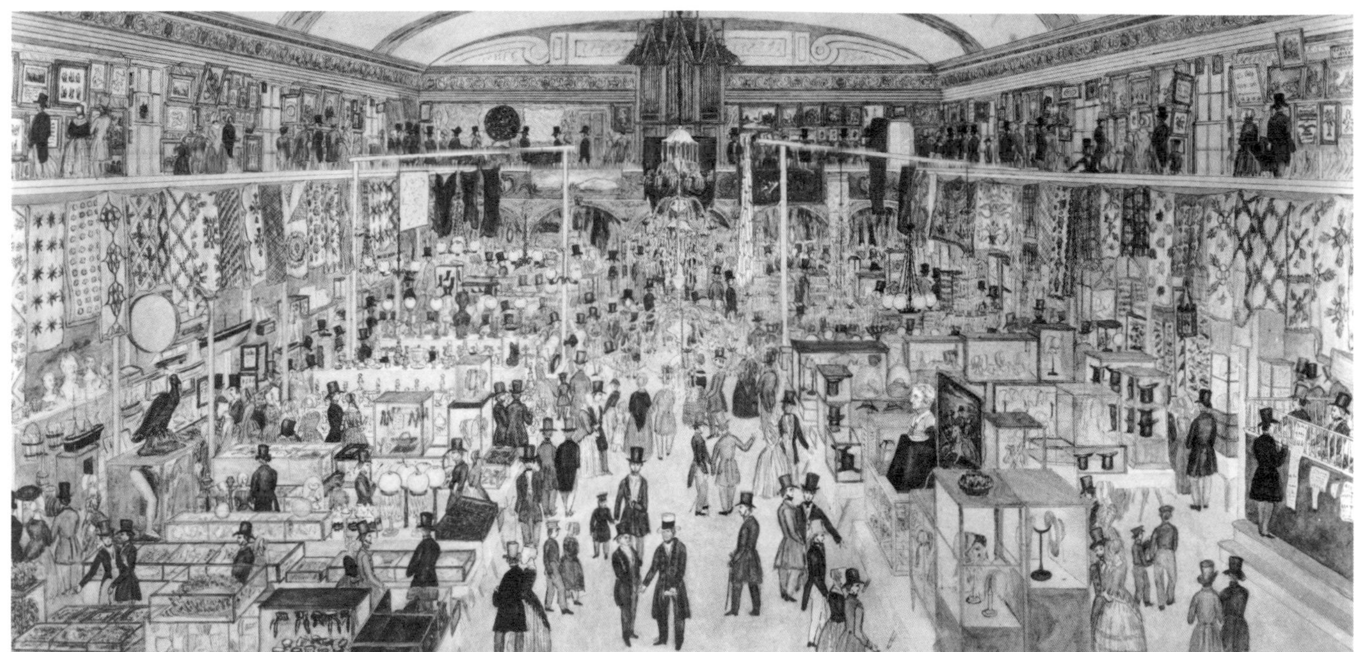

Benjamin J. Harrison. *Annual Fair of the Institute at Niblo's Garden*, detail, c. 1845. Watercolor on paper. Museum of the City of New York

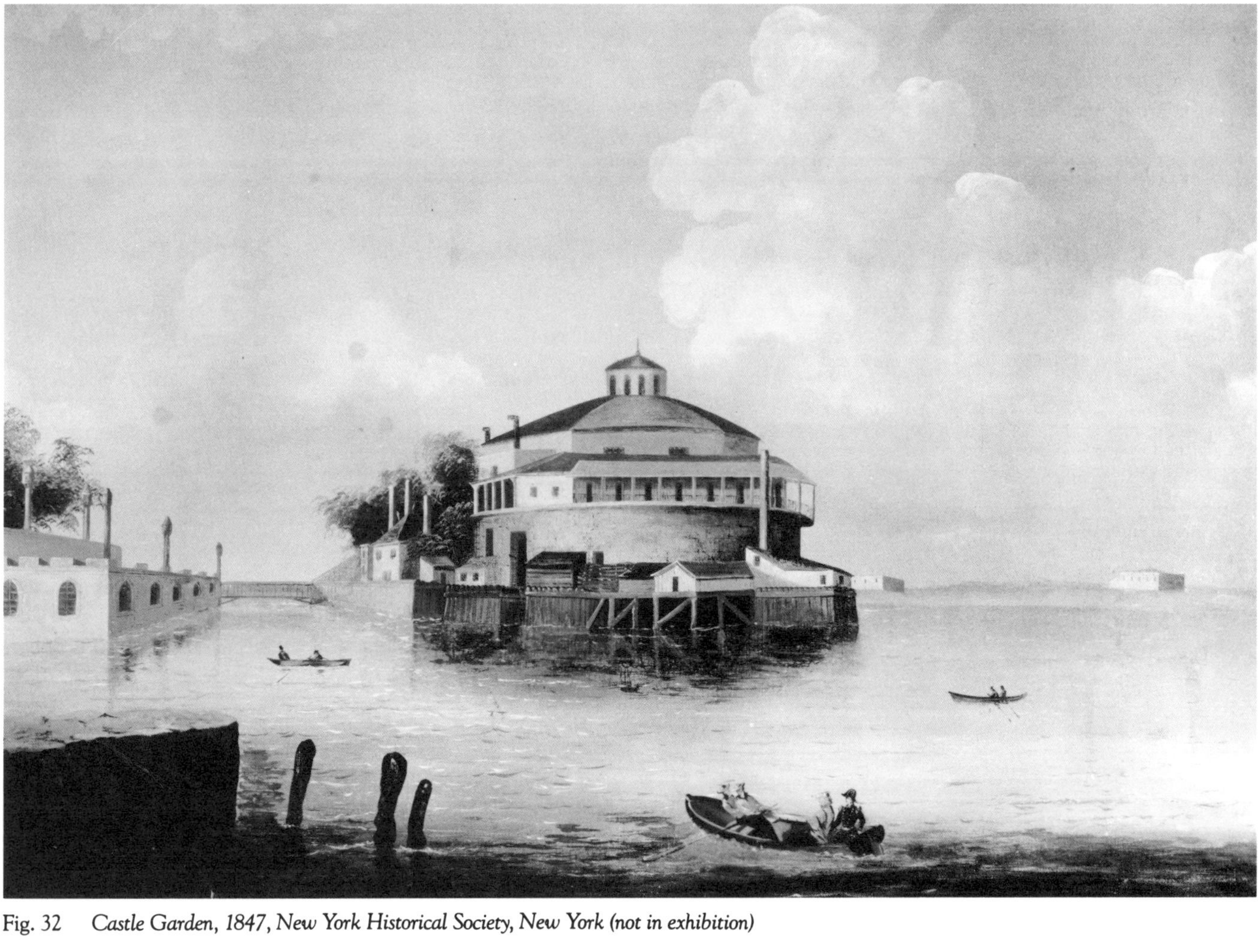

Fig. 32   *Castle Garden, 1847, New York Historical Society, New York (not in exhibition)*

The Field family returned to Palmer in 1854 as Field took a studio on the top floor of the Cross Block. Here he filled a number of painting commissions for town residents. But these figures are quite different from the looming giants who dominated his canvases before 1850. Somewhere, probably in New York, he had learned the use of the camera. From now on, Field used photographs as the basis for almost all of his portraits. He posed and photographed his subjects, then enlarged the results on canvas in color.

Figures are surrounded by empty space; faces are set squarely in the center of the compositions in individual portraits; groups are posed in flamboyant Victorian settings. In every case, the subject, formerly a rural king or queen to whom Field gave his full emphasis, is now portrayed as a small part of a larger society.

An ambrotype, which he probably colored himself, shows the artist near this turning point in his career, in about 1853 (fig. 33). He appears to be in his late forties. The photograph shows a gentle face, interesting rather than handsome. A grand-niece described him as being scarcely taller than she was at the age of nine, but in the hand-colored glass plate his frame appears sturdy and his shoulders broad. Seen beside his own impressive portraits of his brothers, Erastus of the photograph looks modest and unassuming, traits confirmed by his concentration on the personality and appearance of his subjects.

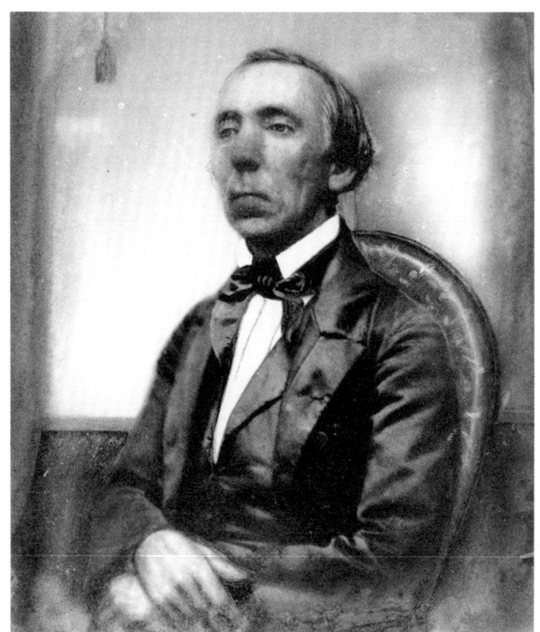

Fig. 33   *Erastus Salisbury Field*   (cat. no.106)

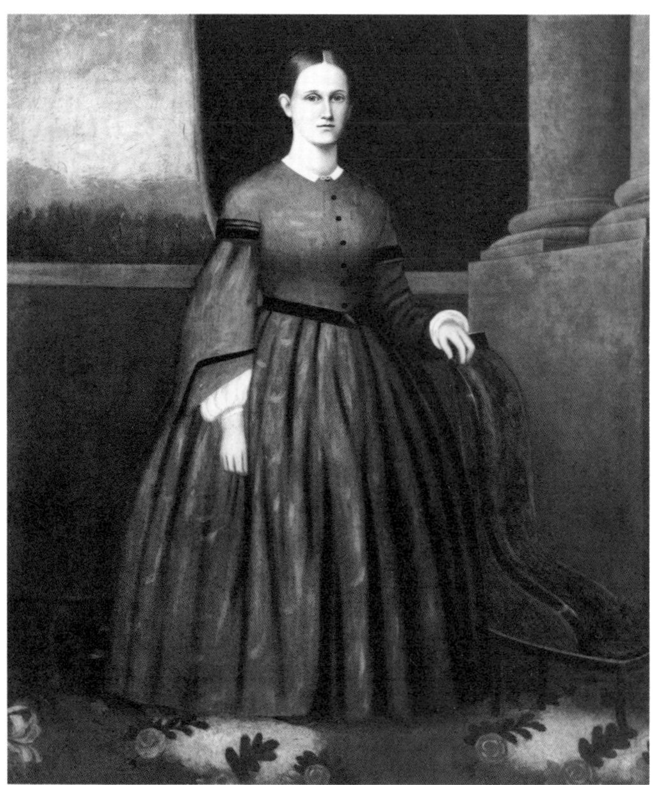

Fig. 34   *Clarissa Field?*   (cat. no.71)

A perfect illustration of Field's new experiment with photographic models is his portrait of a young woman shown full-length in an elaborate Victorian parlor (fig. 34). Even though she is identified as Clarissa Field, she could not be the painter's sister, Clarissa, who died in 1836 before the introduction of the daguerreotype into this country. The photograph from which the portrait was painted still exists, and Field copied the face exactly, even to the subject's sallow complexion. The costume is simplified a little and the background is a little more elaborate. It is a faithful copy, but an unsuccessful painting.

Moving from Palmer, Field and his family were back in Plumtrees, probably by September, 1855. Minnie Hubbard (Nancy-in-a-green-gown, subject of one of the late 1830's portraits of the Hubbard children), wrote to her sister in that month with the news that "Mr. Field's people expect to move next week," perhaps indicating that Phebe and Henrietta were already in Plumtrees and about to settle there. Nancy continued, "I have done finely in Painting - (I sent down and borrowed that little piece of Mr. F's - as it was like mine)."[28] Since Field was later to spend half the year at Plumtrees and the winter months away, it is possible

that he, too, was there that fall. The 19th-century rage
to copy the best example at hand is amusingly illustrated by Minnie's aside, demonstrating that she
and Field were both painting the same unidentified
subject. It is worth noting, however, that Field's painting provided the immediate inspiration for the one by
his young relative.

The homely facts of the 1855 harvest were recorded
in the letter. In September there was an early frost with
many of the watermelons spoiled and the broom corn
ruined. The harvest of pumpkins was "huge, loads and
loads that weigh 30 pounds and upwards." In the house,
the "lily has been in blossom and a magnificent thing -
four stalks - and 16 flowers." The Hubbard kitchen was a
busy place, and Minnie mentions making "grape jelly,
pickles - and so forth" all in a single day. From the bushels
of tomatoes saved from the frost, there were green
tomato pickles from a new recipe.

Following mention of the Field move, Minnie
noted, "I visited Sunderland Cave a week after you left -
had a very good time." Walks and hikes in the woods
to the region's many natural wonders were pleasures
enjoyed by every able person in Plumtrees. In Leverett
there was a rugged, rocky gorge called Rattlesnake
Gutter. Hiking and climbing there were only for the
energetic. It was probably during the mid-1850's that

Field set up his easel at the bottom of the gorge and
painted a colorful autumn scene (pl. 23). Six small
figures, a woman, two men, and three girls dressed in
mid-century costume, occupy the canvas. As a compositional aid, to avoid having the trees stop at mid-
trunk, Field enclosed the composition within an arched
spandrel at the top of the canvas.

In the winter of 1855 Field boarded for a few
months with the William Henry Smith family in North
Amherst, some of whose members he had portrayed
fifteen years before. While there, he painted the family
as a group, the first commission of this kind since the
Moore family of 1839. The painting of the faces is
smooth, facile, and stilted. Obviously Field's source was
not life, but a composite collection of faces from
several photographs (fig. 35). The painting's figural
groupings suggest the number of photographs: one of
Catherine Smith and her young son Seth; one of Mary
Jane; one of the next three sisters, Maria, Sarah, and
Delia; and finally, the head of the household with his
youngest daughter, Harriet. The room is the height of
middle-class elegance: pink draperies crowned with
wood valances and swagged with silk cord over lace
curtains, an upholstered Victorian sofa, and a *fauve*
carpet on the floor. Although the portraits and composition are awkward, the painting is lively and colorful.

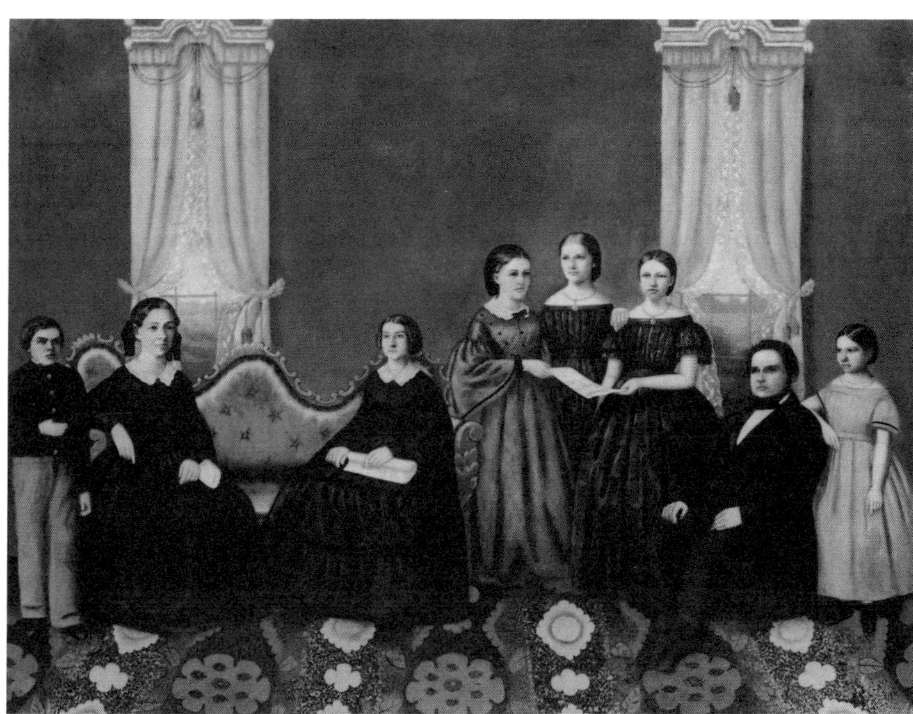

Fig. 35   *William Henry Smith and Family*
(cat. no.73)

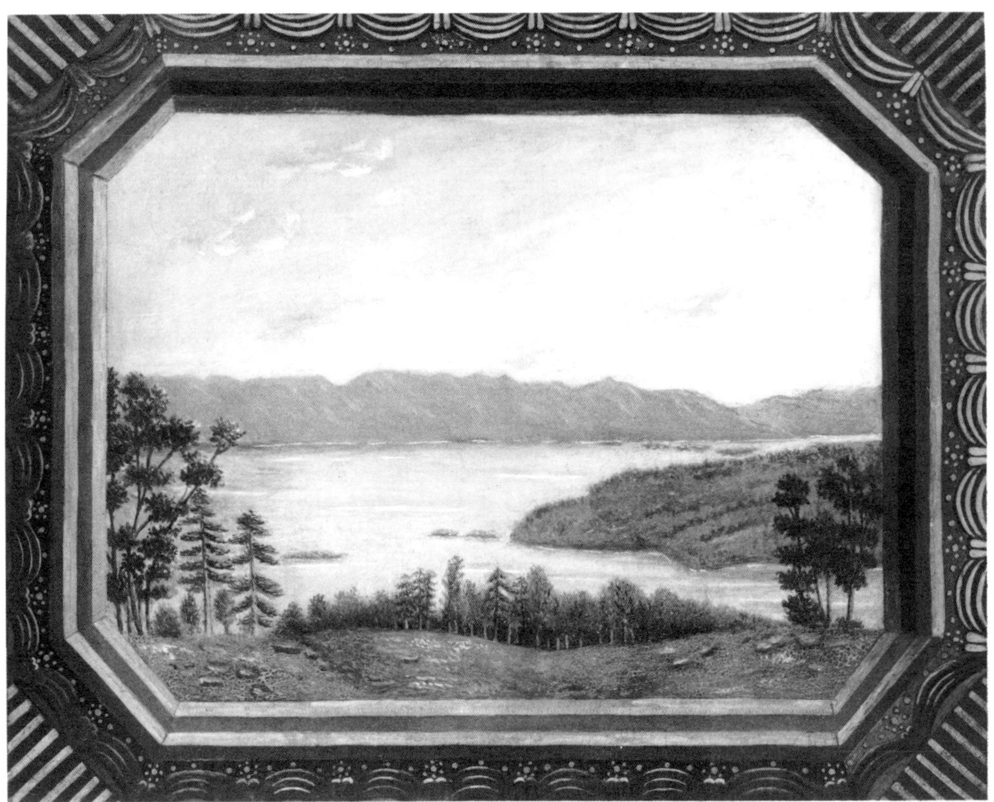

Fig. 36   Leverett Pond   (cat. no.75)

In 1857 the Fields returned to Palmer once more, their membership in the North Amherst Church transferred to Palmer's Second Congregational Church. Palmer citizens again gathered to sit for Field at his studio. Members of the Brainerd family remember posing there for photographs, and their portrait, done about 1858, is another example of Field's new photographic method (pl. 24). His ability to include an entire family in a single canvas was one advantage that he maintained over the camera's eye. Two of the children were painted posthumously. At center background hangs a small landscape somewhat reminiscent of his painting of Leverett Pond (fig. 36). He had known the pond in every season and painted it at mid-century. Field surrounded the landscape with a decorative painted border as a cheap and attractive replacement for a frame.

On the 14th of August, 1859 (the thirty-fifth anniversary of the day of Lafayette's return), Phebe died of "paralysis of the brain." She was nearing fifty-three. She was buried in the North Amherst Congregational Cemetery, and father and daughter returned to Plumtrees to live. Working still to maintain himself and Henrietta through painting, Field that year did another group portrait in North Amherst, that of the Puffer family (private collection). Despite its flaws, its photographic origins, and the gaudy Victorian interior, the painting exactly suits the taste of the time, a taste to which the artist willingly conformed.

Field at Plumtrees was hardworking and industrious, not only at the farm work necessary for board and bed, but also at his painting. In delineating four of his relatives he once more used photographs as a guide. He portrayed his daughter Henrietta as a homely little person posed at her piano (fig. 37). From the late 1850's it was she who kept house for her father until his death, contributing to the economy of the household by giving piano lessons to the local children or by dressmaking for their families (fig. 38). Occasionally they must have exasperated each other, for Henrietta had a sharp tongue, and her gentle father needed prodding into a no-nonsense Yankee mold.

In about 1865, at Stillman Field's charming Victorian house at one of the four corners near the Field family homestead in Leverett, Field did new portraits of Stillman and Aurilla in vigorous middle age (figs. 39, 40),

—36—

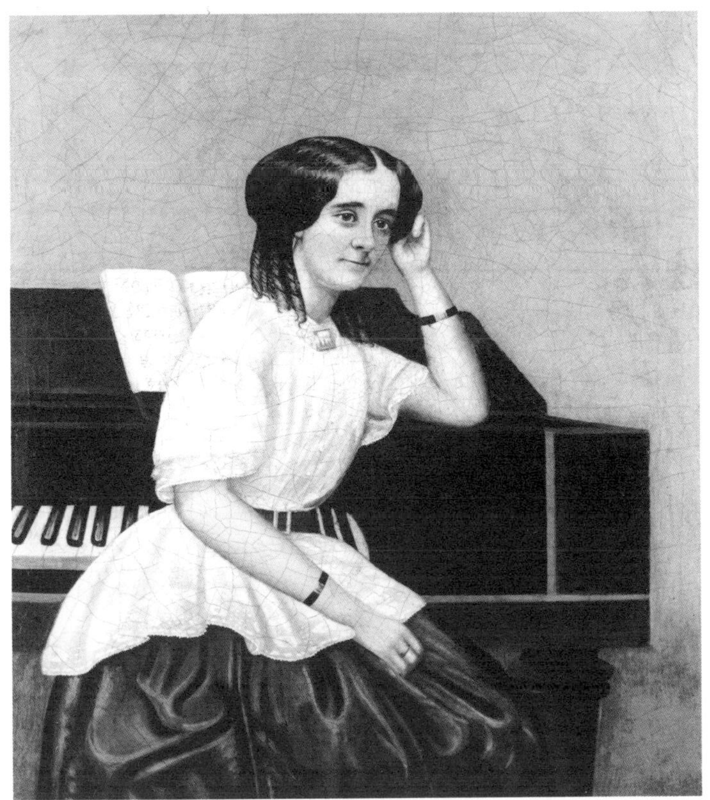

Fig. 37   *Henrietta Field*   (cat. no.78)

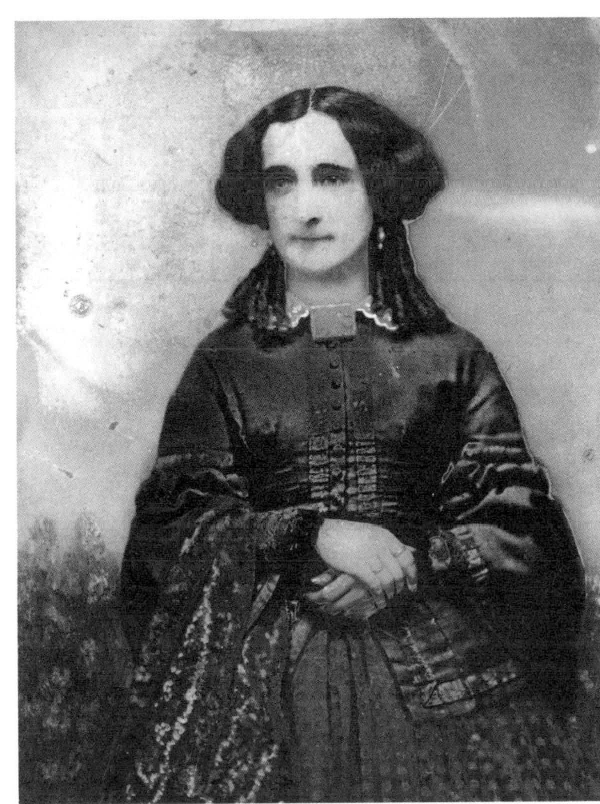

Fig. 38   *Henrietta Field*   (cat. no.107)

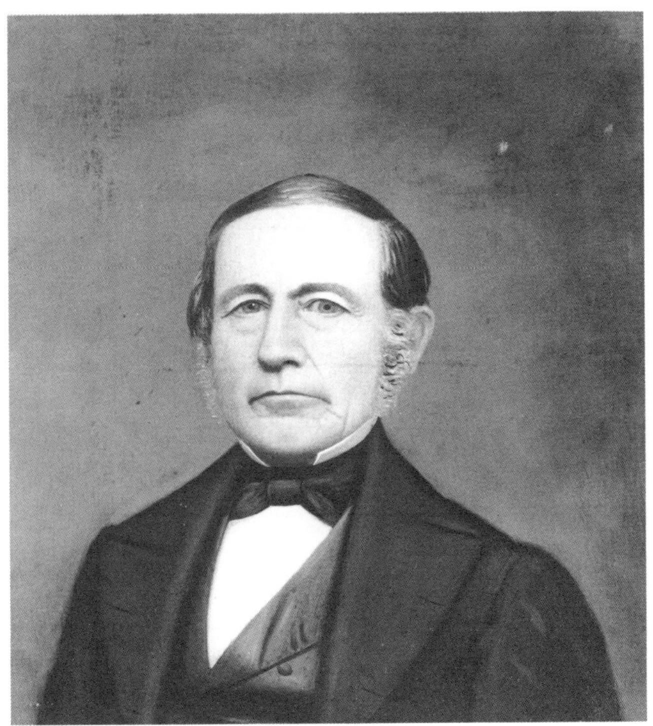

Fig. 39   *Stillman Field*   (cat. no.79)

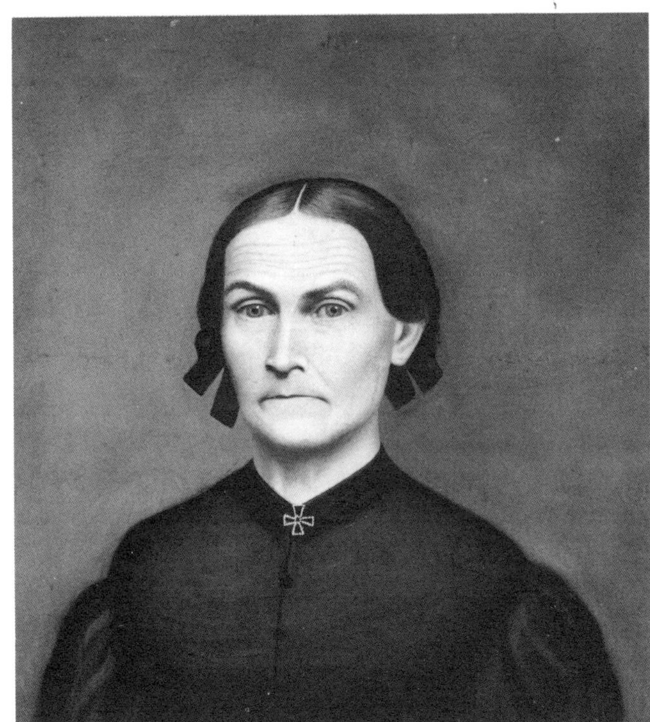

Fig. 40   *Aurilla Field Field*   (cat. no.80)

and one of their soldier son, Lucius, who had died
in 1863, during the Civil War (fig. 41). While the late
portraits of Stillman and Aurilla are in contrast to
the ones Field painted of them in 1836, they alone of
all his faces after 1850 boldly transcend the use of
photographic models. On the other hand, the portraits
of Lucius and Henrietta are the dull, static images
popular with his contemporaries.

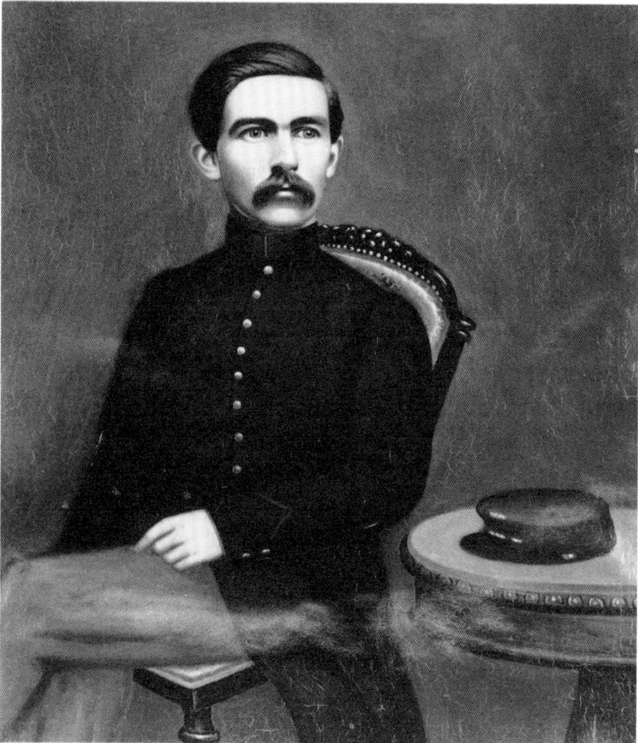

Fig. 41   *Lucius Field*   (cat. no.81)

Although they lived in a house on Hubbard land,
Field purchased an acre or two of his own across the
street from the tavern, on the east side of the north-
south road between Sunderland and Amherst. On
this land part way up Bull Hill, Field, early in his stay
at Plumtrees, dug a hole into the hillside and con-
structed a two-room studio. The building was scarcely
more than a shack. The back of the structure was set
into the hill and lined with pieces of scrap lumber. A
few small windows without frames were set directly into three walls of mismatched board on the sides and
front. Here, overlooking the tavern, Field painted. The
back room, its one earthen wall covered with boards,

held a stove and some of the wood that he cut each
spring. When the weather was warm, however, he
painted in the red barn, part of the L-shaped complex
of house, barn, and sheds that comprised the
Hubbard tavern.

While the studio was a jerry-built structure, those
who saw it recall it as a magical place. The dreamer in
Field transported him and his young audience up and
away from the rural circumstances of Plumtrees. Beginning in the 1860's, he compensated for his lack of
worldly riches by painting big, exotic pictures of great
buildings in foreign lands. Eventually, the walls of the
shack came to be lined with paintings from floor to
ceiling, all of them landscapes or subject pieces on
religious or historical themes.

Giving free reign to imagery and to dreams, he
could escape the plain facts of everyday. In the world
as it was, he planted young trees. In his vision, these
would line an avenue leading to the mansion he would
someday build behind the shack. Late in life he
started work on the mansion, excavating a large hole
for the cellar. He lined the hole with cobblestones, set
in a neat pattern, to be sure, but uneven footing for a
large farmhouse. He spent many days in building up
the crown of Bull Hill Road to even out the wagon
ruts. There is a naiveté, and a sense of propriety, in
these attempts.

After 1860 Field concentrated on the historical
and religious narratives which replaced portraits as his
chief subject matter. Frequently he based his religious
works on prints. Although it is difficult to arrange the
Biblical paintings in chronological order, *The Garden of
Eden* of about 1860 appears to be the earliest of these
subjects. He depicted the theme in two versions which
were probably painted within a few months of each
other (pl. 25; fig. 42). In them Field combined elements
from a number of published prints, creating compositions that outshine their technical limitations. John
Martin of London inspired a number of painters far
more sophisticated than Field, including Thomas
Cole. Martin's paintings were reproduced in a number
of American and English Bibles, and it may have been
one of these that Field used, for Martin's illustration of
the Temptation was certainly known to him in some
form. The landscape, and especially the trees and
mountains, were taken directly from Martin's

vocabulary. An engraving of Cole's lost *Garden of Eden*, also based on Martin's themes, was the direct source for the small waterfall and the large exotic plants at left and right foreground of Field's Gardens.[29]

The smaller of the two versions has a brilliant blue and gold *trompe l'oeil* frame painted onto the canvas itself. Until restoration in this century, Eve and the serpent had been painted out of the larger painting.

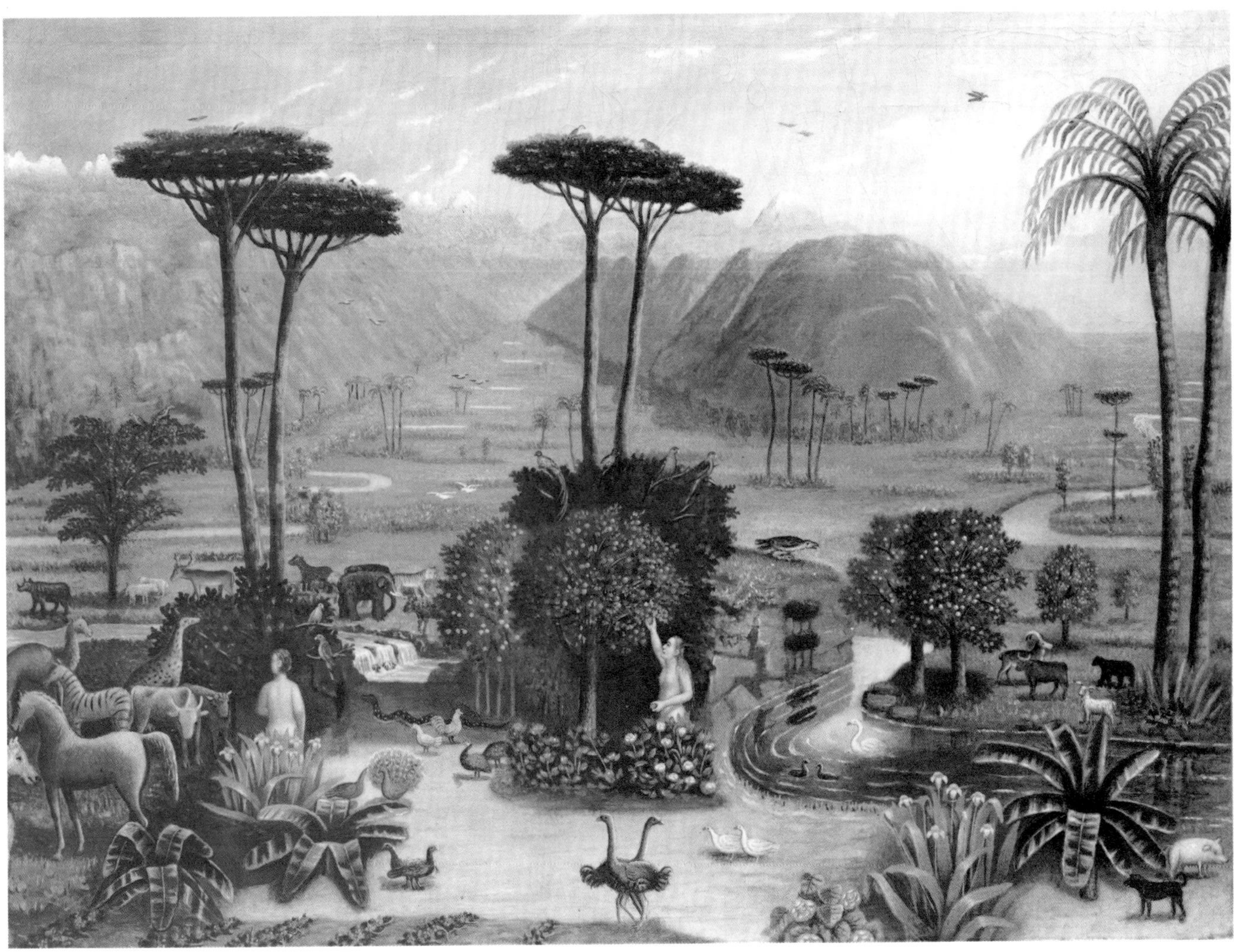

Fig. 42   *The Garden of Eden*   (cat. no.76)

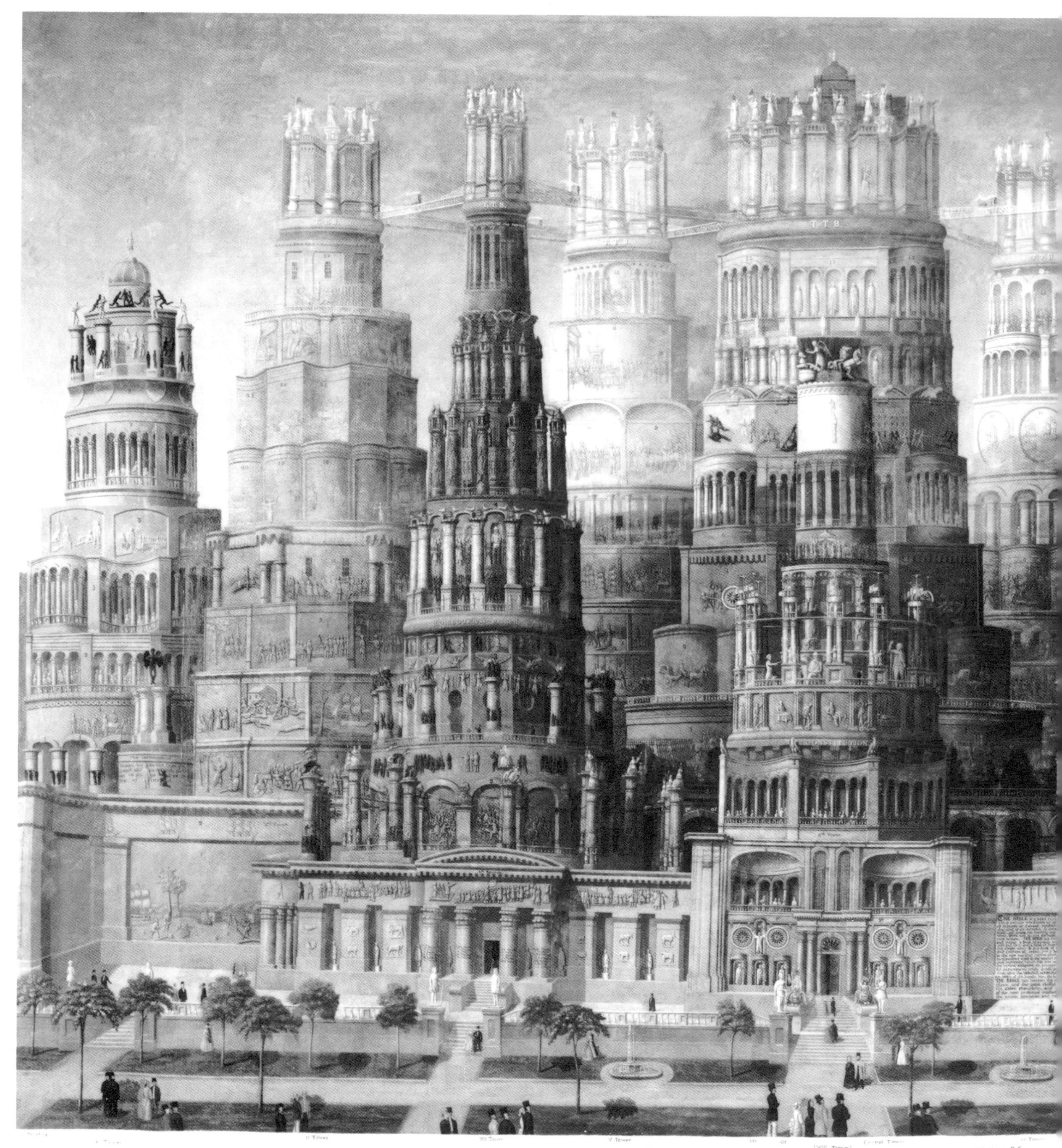

Fig. 43　*The Historical Monument of the American Republic*　(cat. no.82)

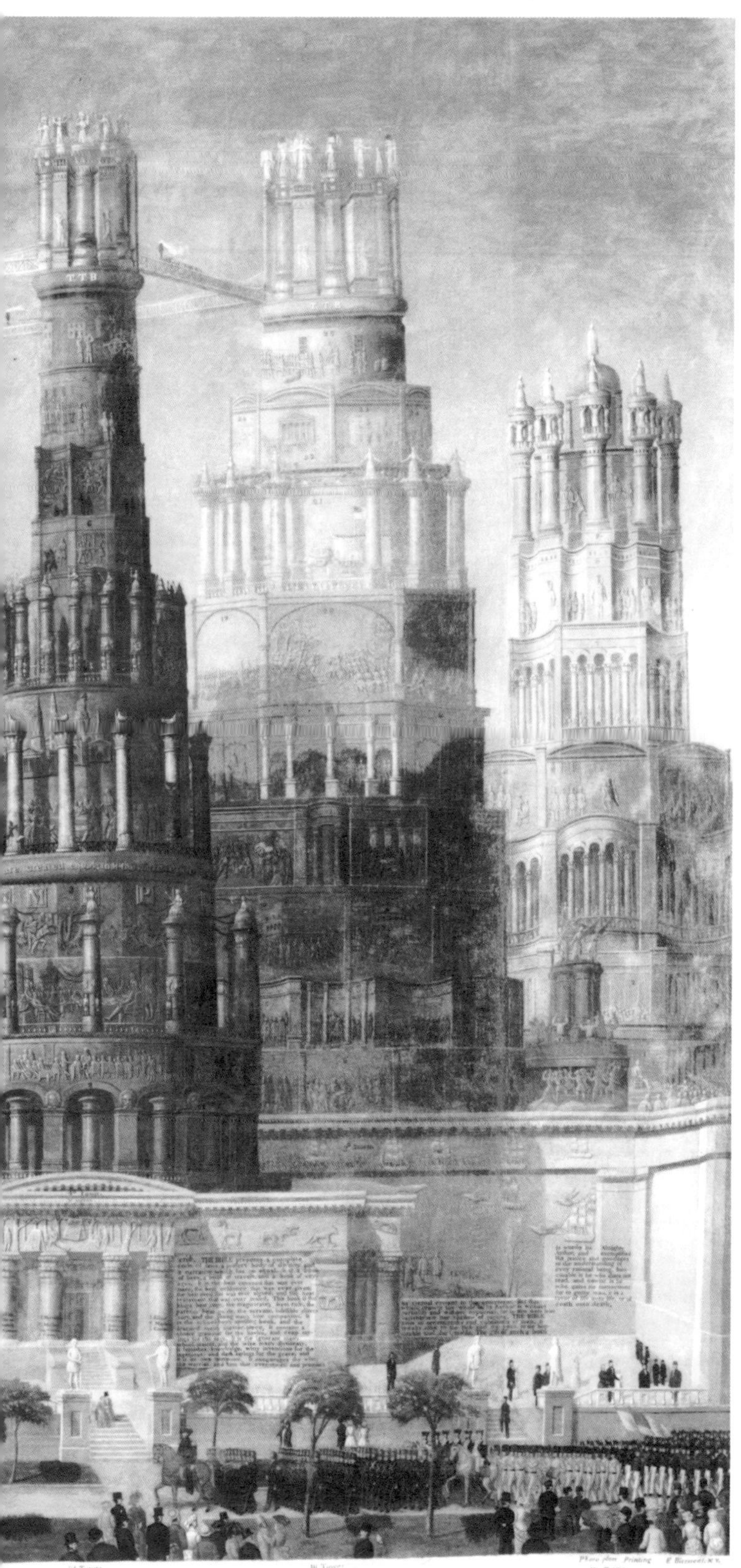

Midway through the 1860's, near the end of the Civil War, Field began work on the *Historical Monument of the American Republic,* a painting that he saw as the culmination and chief work of his long career (color insert, fig. 43). By the spring of 1867 it was brought to one stage of completion, as indicated by this notice published in the *Hampshire Gazette and Northampton Courier* on May 28, 1867:

> A new artist, E.S. Field of Sunderland, has painted a grand historical and allegorical picture twelve feet long and nine feet wide, representing the country's history from the landing of the Pilgrims to the death of Lincoln and intends to exhibit it through the States with an explanatory lecture.[30]

Eight great towers in differing architectural styles sprang high in the air from a long base that almost filled the width of the canvas. About 1876 he added the Philadelphia Centennial Exhibition Hall to the top of the central tower. Finally, in 1888 he painted the two end towers, left and right, and updated his history with illustrations of recent events.

Every level of every tower in Field's *Monument* is keyed to an incident in American history; events from the Civil War are represented allegorically. A passage from his description of the work, published in 1876, reflects this symbolism:

> On the base or main part, supporting the Third Tower, are the landing of the Pilgrims. The meaning of eagles before the vessels, you will find in Rev. 12:14. On the right of the Tower, is a war dance of the Indians. The cluster of columns above the Indians, denotes the rising States in the North, and the angels symbolize truth and righteousness. The cluster of columns to the left of the second Tower, denotes the rising States in the South, on which Satan stands, who symbolizes oppression, fraud, violence and every evil incidental to slavery.[31]

Until recently it was believed that Field completed the first stage of the *Monument* by 1875 or 1876 to commemorate the nation's centennial, but recent documentation of its actual date as no later than 1867, makes clear Field's original purpose. In Field's mind, many of the towers of his fantasy structure were dedicated to the survival of the American Republic through the crisis of civil war.

The idea of an historical painting on a grand theme had been with Field since the beginning of his career. The evolution of his plan followed a long progress likely to have been conceived as early as November 1824 when he entered Samuel Morse's studio as an apprentice student. The concept of a national art celebrating events in American history on canvas was then new, first outlined by John Trumbull in 1816.[32]

This American painter and Revolutionary War officer returned to America from England, with plans for finishing the capitol in Washington with paintings in the eighteen-by-twelve foot spaces designed for this purpose within the rotunda. Congress appropriated $32,000, an astronomical sum in that period, for Trumbull's commission for four of the eight available spaces. This "magnificent national encouragement of the fine arts" was qualified by the requirement that Congress approve both Trumbull's subjects and the appointment of the artists who were to supply the paintings for the remaining spaces. Two of Trumbull's subjects were rejected by Congress, and the final selection was for paintings of the Declaration of Independence, the surrenders of Cornwallis and Burgoyne, and Washington's resignation of his commission. A little more than forty years after Trumbull's paintings were installed in the rotunda in 1824, Field incorporated into the design for the *Historical Monument* all the images save Burgoyne's surrender.

Field's intention for the *Monument*, "to exhibit it through the States with an explanatory lecture," was an idea that might also have come from Trumbull, who completed and then exhibited all four of his paintings prior to their installation. His plans for continuing their tour were realized as he made smaller copies of the originals. The New York climate that prevailed in the 20's was one of great national pride, and the idea of showing historic paintings with accompanying lectures was one carried out by a number of painters, including John Vanderlyn and Samuel F.B. Morse. Then, for a brief moment, and later, in a longer sojourn in the city in the 1840's, Erastus Field could hardly have avoided, would indeed have sought out, the dramatic visual presentations that epitomized the spirit of the new republic.

Two large-scale paintings by Samuel Morse of notable interior architecture, *The Old House of Representatives* of 1822 to 1823, showing the architecture of the House chamber and portraits of its members, and his *Gallery of the Louvre* of a decade later, with its skillful recreation of an imaginary museum installation and gallery activity, were both shown in exhibition. Field, who was in New York the year after completion of Morse's painting of the House, might have seen the original, or, at the very least, Morse's earlier drawing. The painting of a gallery of the Louvre, which included forty-one paintings and Morse's portrait of himself instructing an art student, was shown with little success in New York and New Haven late in 1833.[33] Even if Field did not see the originals, his interest in all that Morse did would have made him aware of the designs and uses made of these elevated genre scenes. They were almost certainly part of the accumulating inspiration for his own historic and monumental observance.

Another acknowledgement of Field's indebtedness to Morse was the New England painter's undertaking of a project offered to his teacher many years before. Morse was twice disappointed in his expectations of doing one or more of the panels in the Capitol rotunda. The loss of the second commission led him to abandon painting entirely. Following assignment of the first commission to another artist, Morse's friends banded together and raised two thousand dollars for a painting on an historical subject of the painter's choice. Morse never did the work and the money was eventually returned to his patrons, but a decade later the idea was still in his mind and in those of his supporters. A letter written to him in 1847 mentions the last panel for the rotunda, once more commissioned, but not to Morse:

> I hope you may yet resume the pencil, and furnish the public the most striking commentary on their utter disregard of justice by placing somewhere 'The Germ of the Republic' in such colors that shall make them blush and hang their heads to think themselves such men.[34]

The "Germ of the Republic," transferred from Morse to Field, became *The Historical Monument of the American Republic.*

Field was as violently opposed to slavery as Morse was for it. While both men opposed secession, their divergent views made the interpretation of the *Monument* as it came from Field a far different painting than anything Morse might have created. Although it was a different composition than the one Morse might have executed, disappointment over lack of public acceptance of his work was to be as bitter for Field as it had been for his teacher.

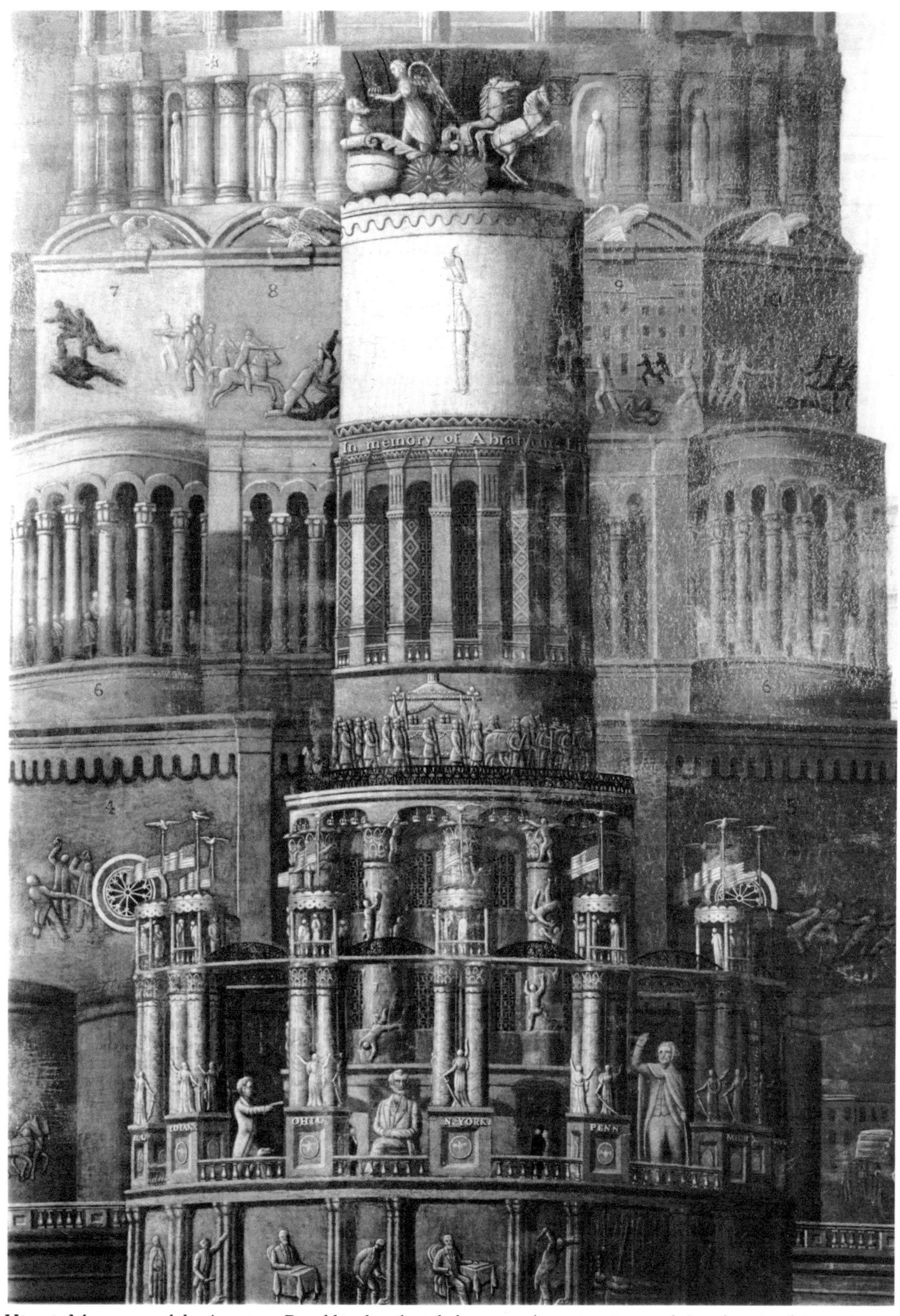

Historic Monument of the American Republic, detail, eighth tower, Assassination and Apotheosis of Lincoln.

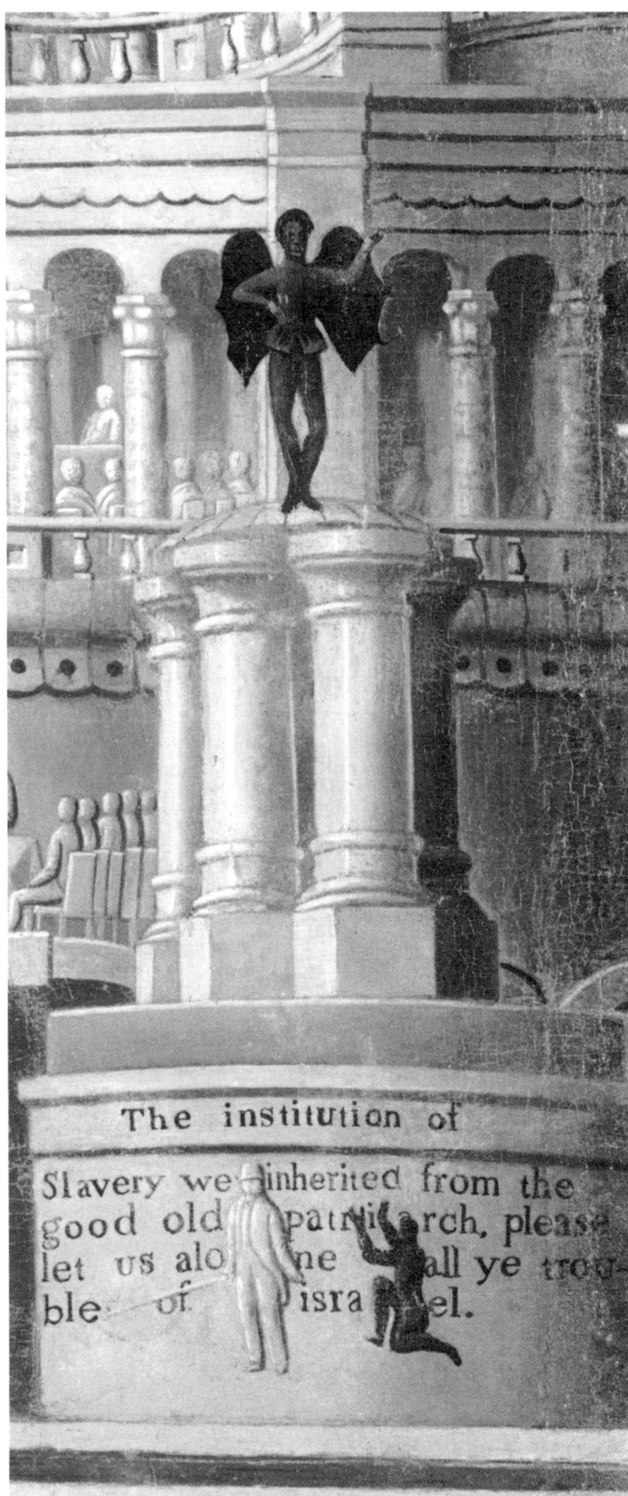

Historic Monument of the American Republic, detail, figure of Satan

Field's extraordinary contribution in the movement to provide the nation with publicly accessible images of its history was his astonishing plan for illustrating all its major events in bas-relief and bronze and stone "statues" on the towered walls of a grand national monument. His dream was no less than the actual construction of such an American ziggurat, complete to the shrine on top, the housing for a "centennial exhibition":

> A professed architect, on looking at this picture, might have the impression that a structure built in this form would not stand. The idea is this, to build after this model, (supposing such a thing took place), it would be necessary to fill up with stones or concrete in one solid mass, all but the center and entrance through each Tower, on account of the succeeding section receding. The center in each Tower could be sufficiently large for circular stairs to reach the top. The entrance from each side to the center, and also from the center to each of the platforms in each section, might be arched over to many of the sections for various purposes, and still the structure would be sufficiently solid. I am not a professed architect, and some things about it may be faulty. Be that as it may, my aid has been to get up a brief history of our country or epitome, in a monumental form.[35]

Under the top stories, the initials, "T.T.B.," The True Base of the Constitution, were to be incised. Field's crowning imagery was the aerial railway with balloon stack engines connecting exhibition rooms in seven of the eight original towers.

Field's New England ancestors had taken part in many of the early events that he planned as vignettes in his history. Other events, ones that took place in his own lifetime, suggested additional scenes. He himself had seen Lafayette in New York and established the family legend that he had been present when the French hero posed to Morse. Morse's telegraph and Fulton's steamboat were inventions of his time in which he felt some involvement and a great deal of pride. The agony of the War Between the States was the fatal outcome of conflict between two philosophies, his own belief solidly on the side of one that held that all men were by nature free and that Christian morality did not permit any of them to be held as chattels.

For some scenes Field drew on his familiarity with historic incident as it had been interpreted by artists who were his predecessors and recent contemporaries. In this way copies after Trumbull's *Battle of Bunker's Hill*; John Vanderlyn's *Landing of Columbus*; and Benjamin West's *Penn's Treaty with the Indians* were reproduced on the walls of the Monument as bas-reliefs painted in monochromatic tones.

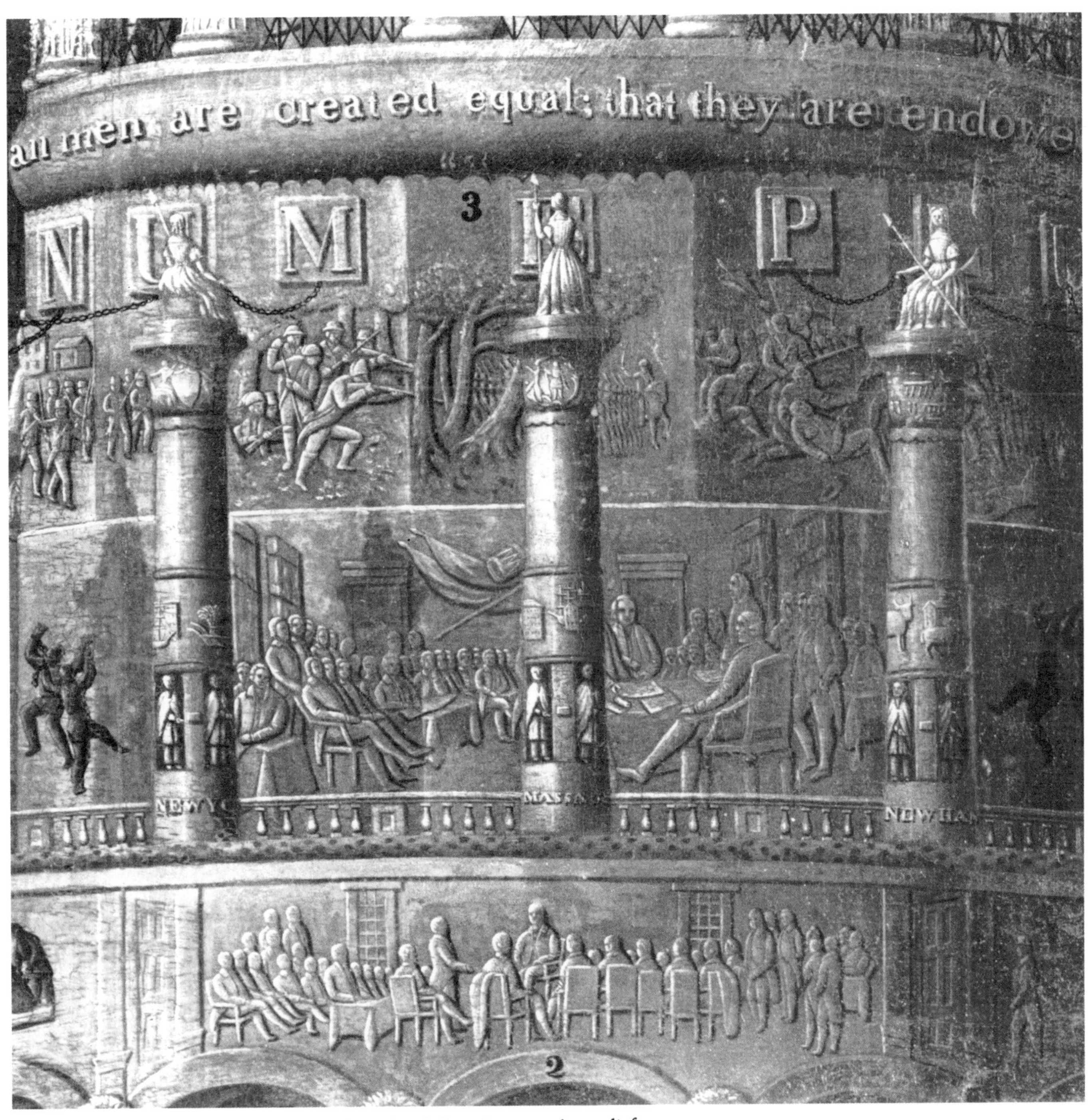

Historic Monument of the American Republic, detail, fourth tower, bas-reliefs.

In 1861 about the time that Field began painting religious and historical subjects almost exclusively, Ashley Hubbard died. His wife, Betsy, died the following year. Parker Dole Hubbard, new master of the tavern, a member of the Massachusetts Volunteers in the Civil War, was away much of the time until the mid-1860's. Nancy married and moved away. Young Caleb was probably left as the man in charge of the Hubbard house. In 1866 the tavern had a new mistress when Parker Hubbard returned bringing his bride.

Stephen Ashley Hubbard, long grown out of the yellow vest in which Field had painted him as a child, had been in Winsted, Connecticut, since 1853. In 1861 he was persuaded to move to Hartford to work on Joseph Hawley's *Evening Press*. In 1867, Hubbard moved on to the *Hartford Courant*, which had recently been purchased by Hawley and two partners.

He soon became the paper's editor, remaining in that position until his death.

Not until March, 1872, was General Hawley, publisher of the *Courant*, appointed President of the United States Centennial Commission for the fair at Philadelphia. To Field this must have seemed a gift from the angels, for Hawley was Stephen Ashley Hubbard's patron, as Hubbard was the painter's. Field undoubtedly knew the head of the Centennial Commission. If he did not, he would have counted on Stephen Hubbard to forward his interests. The idea that his vision might become the grand plan of the Centennial Fair must have filled Field's dreams by day and night. As his plans took form he added incidents to the tower walls related to the attempt to impeach President Andrew Johnson, bringing his history up to date.

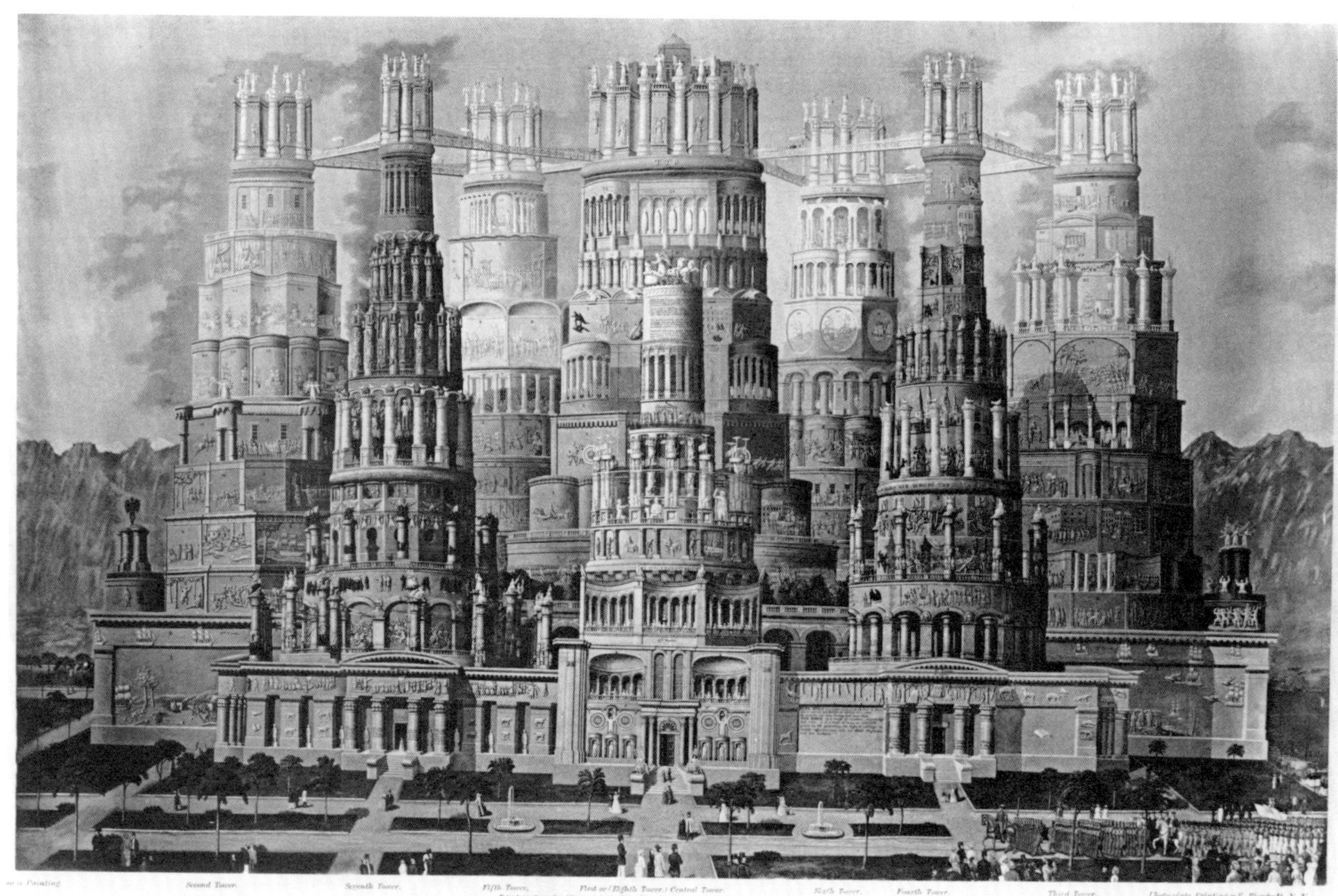

Fig. 44   *The Historical Monument of the American Republic*   (cat. no.83)

Field's hopes for exhibiting his painting at the Centennial were in vain. One can only imagine his disappointment when it was not accepted nor, as far as is known, even seriously considered for the fair. If the *Monument* was on view at the Centennial at all, it was in the form of a small albertype by Edward Bierstadt (fig. 44) and not as the final great production of Erastus Field's life.

In 1876 H.M. McCloud, Amherst printer and book-binder, was selected by Field to publish his 11-page *Descriptive Catalogue of the Historical Monument of the American Republic*. In the catalogue Field, in a labyrinth of detail, outlined the meaning of the *Monument*, both an actual and allegorical representation of the nation's history. Field's knowledge and grasp of his subject are astonishing, his ardent support of the Abolitionist movement and familiarity with scripture illustrated repeatedly.

Field's grand and extraordinary concept astounded neighbors, friends, and relations. Nothing in or out of Plumtrees equalled it and visitors came to the sun-lit interior of the red-painted Hubbard barn to watch, encourage, and commend the project. Despite the fancifulness of the *Monument* and Field's other paintings of this period, Yankee farmers respected and admired the artist's work, a vocation greatly unlike the usual ones in the island cultures of Leverett and Plumtrees.

In June Field wrote a letter to "Mr. Hubbard," almost certainly Stephen Ashley Hubbard. It concerned the *Monument* and the print that Field had made from it:

> After I returned home I opened the package I found the prints (on the) average rather better than the proof sheet, still they are not just as I would like, a number of parts are not shaded enough but other parts are. It is not Mr. Bierstadt's fault at all. It is owing to the painting. The columns that I represented in marble are taken too light, which is owing to the shading being gray as that tone always takes light, he spoke about that before he took the negative. The central tower and some others I painted too light especially the shady part, particularly the upper portion. I should know now just what to do to the painting to insure perfect prints. It would not take me but very few days to change the tone, and considering the circumstances they are the prints well done. I would like it if it will not be out of your way to see Mr. Hurlbert and state to him what I have written, and if he feel disposed to take hold of it I will go right on and make the change and take it on to New York and have another negative taken. I shall try and improve the prints by using india ink and little brown with it. I have tried some and I find I can improve them. You will please drop me a line as soon as convenient. Remember me to Mrs. Hubbard.
>
> Yours, most truly,
>
> Monday morning, since writing the above I thought it would be well to know how much royalty Mr. Hurlbert would allow before I get another negative taken. I intend at any rate to make the change in the painting with the view of having another taken as soon as I can dispose of what I have. I may go down to Amherst again in a day or two to see if there is any one that will be willing to go in company with me and share the profits. I have seen the printer and got his terms for certain numbers.[36]

The letter says so much and so little. It seems almost incredible that Field, then seventy-one years old, would have hauled the great bulk of the *Monument* to New York for photography, unless of course, he folded the canvas into a less cumbersome bundle than its size would seem to permit. It is tempting to associate "Mr. Hurlbert" with William H. Hurlbert, book publisher at 34 Park Row in New York, but if "Mr. Hubbard" is Stephen Hubbard in Hartford, it appears more likely that the Hurlbert that Field mentioned was Amandur M. Hurlbut of Hartford, neighbor of the Hubbards characterized in the Hurlbut family genealogy as having "Successfully followed the book publishing for ten years."[37]

McCloud, the printer of the catalog, is probably the man who had already given Field terms for certain numbers of prints after Bierstadt's photograph. One unassailable fact contained in the letter is that Field, with or without help, had by June 1876, already taken the *Monument* to New York City to be photographed by the brother of another American painter, Albert Bierstadt.

Field's missive tells a great deal about his ability to edit and improve his own work; his business-like association with one of his Hubbard cousins; and his determination to correct and distribute the prints he already had on hand, altogether remarkable achievements in view of his age and circumstances, but perhaps more easily understood in terms of his long and successful career as a portrait painter and photographer.

Men and women who were children at Plumtrees remember hearing their elders praise the *Monument*. But in 1933 it was found rolled up in the attic of the former home of Phineas Field's son. It was rescued by Madeline Ball Wright, Field's grand-niece, from ignominious storage in a shed behind a pig sty in Plumtrees in the mid-1940's.

While the Civil War itself barely touched Plumtrees, Leverett, and Sunderland, the issue of slavery continued to be of terrible concern to Field. In the decade following the peace almost his whole aesthetic production bore on his deep attachment to the Abolitionist cause. His emotional involvement in this issue between the North and South is suggested as the contemporary theme illustrated in an interior scene that appears to have a Biblical connotation as well (fig. 45). *Egyptian Scene,* a reunion between several groups of people, might be interpreted not only as a scene from the Bible, but also as the reunion between North and South during Reconstruction.

Between 1865 and 1880 Field executed a series of paintings illustrating the Plagues of Egypt, apparently intended as decoration for the walls of the North Amherst Church. The nine surviving examples are only part of the original series. Connecticut Valley residents recall a number of lost works that once decorated the church and that were among the paintings lining the wall of the studio. (In this century four of the remaining paintings were found laid out on the second floor of a shed behind the Cooley house.) The missing subjects include the Plagues of Frogs, Lice, Boils, Murrains, Biles, and Blains. Six of the large paintings of this series known today depict the events leading to the exodus of the Israelites from Egypt: *"He Turned Their Waters into Blood."* (pl. 26), *The Plague of Darkness* (fig. 46), *Death of the First Born* (pl. 27), *Burial of the First Born* (pl. 28), *The Israelites Crossing the Red Sea* (fig. 47), and *Pharaoh's Army Marching* (fig. 48).

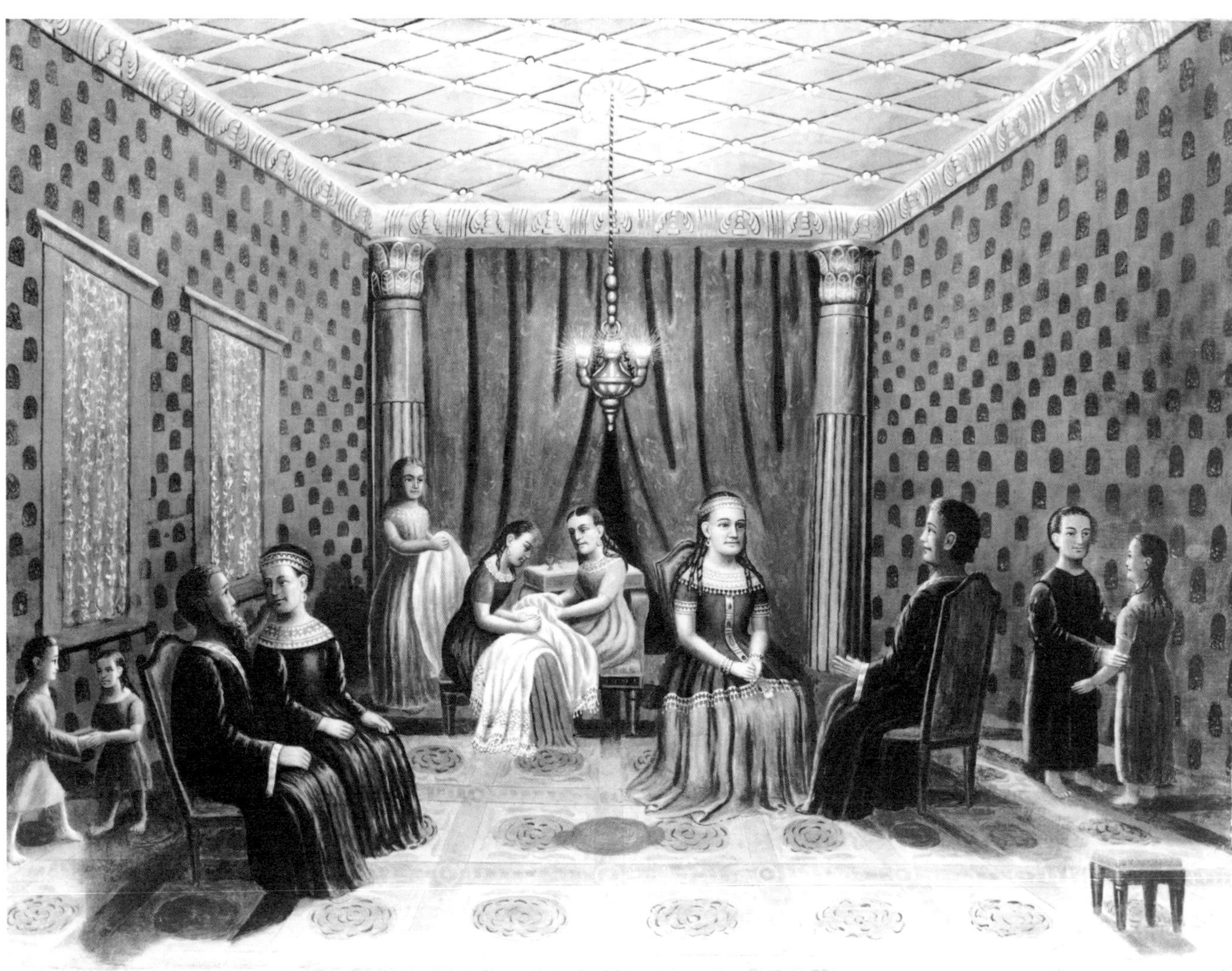

Fig. 45   *Egyptian Scene*   (cat. no.91)

Fig. 46   *The Plague of Darkness*   (cat. no.85)

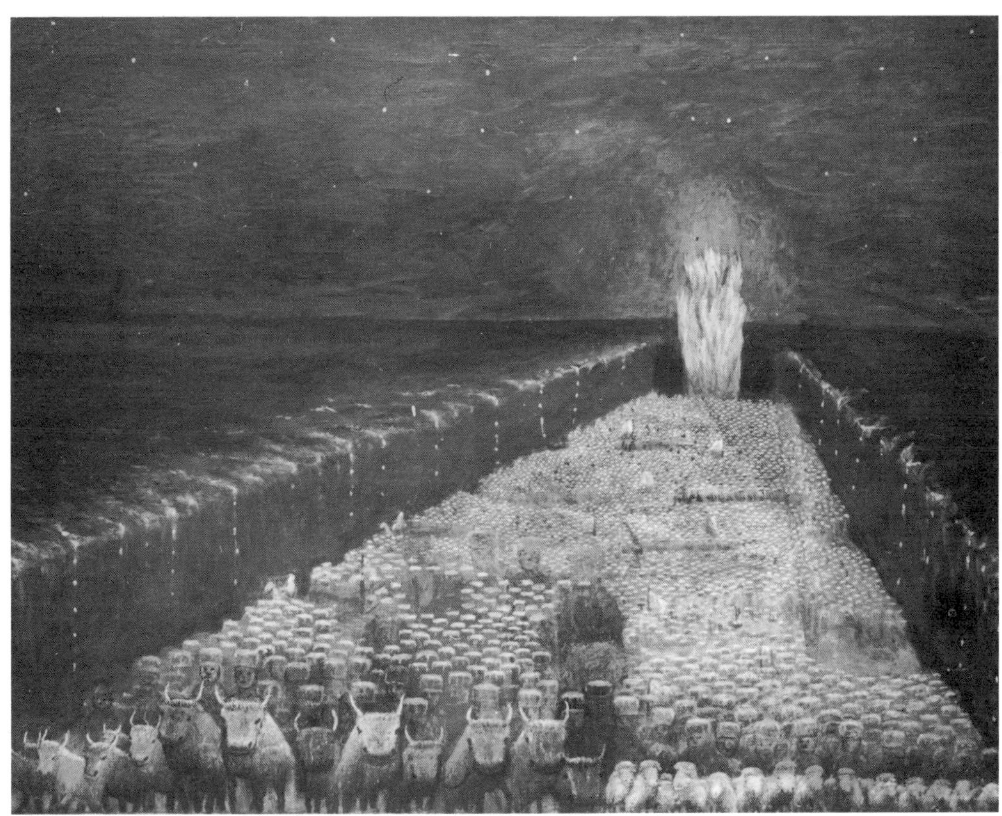

Fig. 47   *The Israelites Crossing the Red Sea*   (cat. no.92)

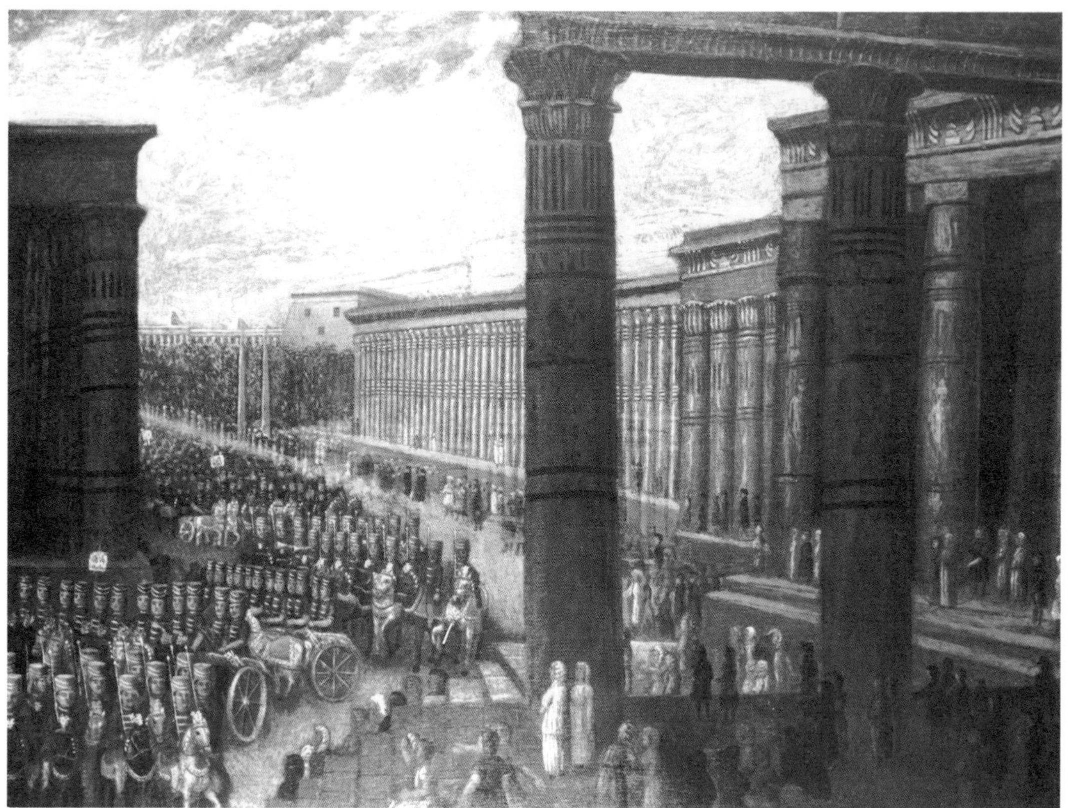

Fig. 48   *Pharaoh's Army Marching*   (cat. no.88)

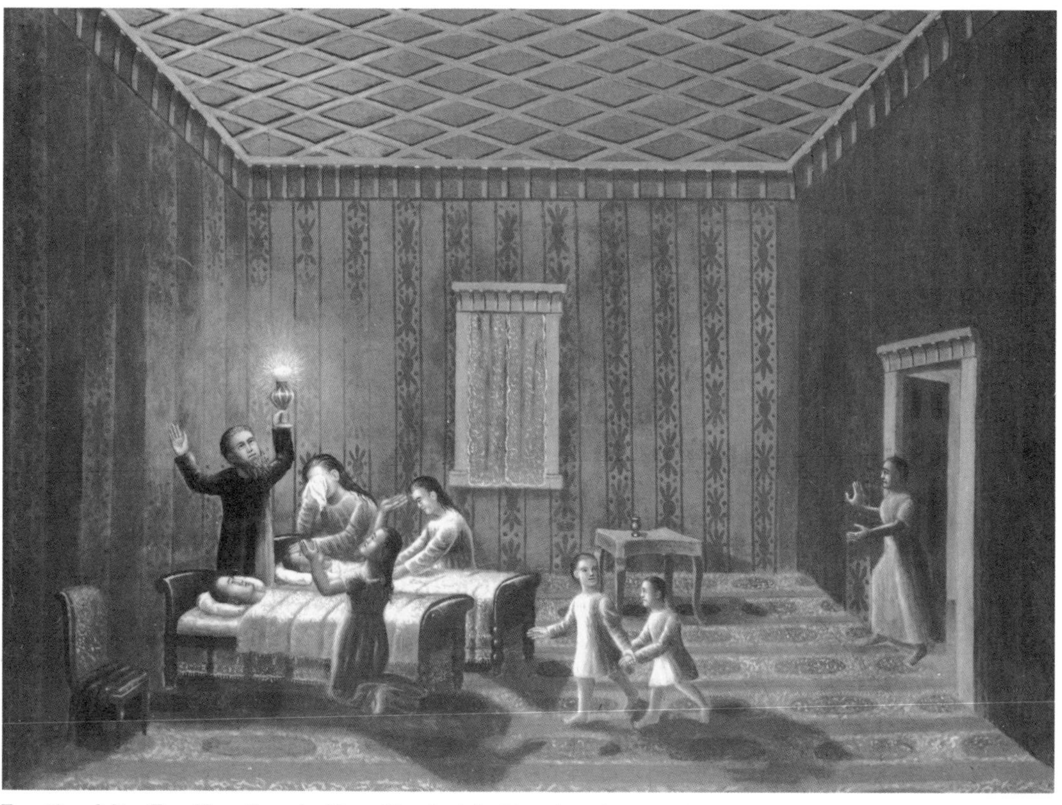

Fig. 49   *Mine Eyes Have Seen the Glory (Death of the Twins)*   (cat. no.90)

Surely Field remembered the 1842 production of *The Israelites in Egypt* or *Passage of the Red Sea*, the spectacle that he had seen more than twenty years earlier in New York. The many scenes of retribution and divine wrath probably allude to the Civil War and convey an anti-slavery message. While the two room interiors, *Death of the First Born* (pl. 29) and *Mine Eyes Have Seen the Glory (Death of the Twins)* (fig. 49), and *The Israelites Crossing the Red Sea* (fig. 47) appear to be from unidentified print sources, a number of others borrow the heroic architecture and dramatically receding space of John Martin's *Plagues of Egypt*. In adapting Martin's example to his own use, Field simplified the design and enlarged and distorted details for emphasis. Because the painting is uneven in quality, it is likely that the work was done over a period of years.

Another painting from which Field borrowed much of his imagery is *The Last Supper* of the late 1870's, based on a popular chromolithograph of Leonardo da Vinci's famous mural of the same scene (pl. 30). Walls, cornices, and ceiling are covered with decorative motifs; the table is clearly set with Plumtrees glass and pottery. The mountains, as viewed from the windows, are reminiscent of those rising from the valley floor on the west side of the Connecticut River, and the faces, bearded and astonished, might be portraits of Connecticut Valley cousins. The painting is surrounded by a frame that Field painted as part of the composition.

Long after Field died, two small boys, now grown, remember stealing into the abandoned house where the artist and Henrietta once lived. On the walls and woodwork they found fantastic decoration, pieces of tin cut and shaped as architectural ornament, combined with free-hand painted designs attached to cornices and to window and door frames in patterns simulating plaster ornaments, all created by "Mr. Field" to enrich the rooms of his small house. Now all of this is gone, the structure burned by vandals in 1939, but the decorated walls of *The Last Supper* give an impression of how it looked in Field's attempt at elegance by simple means.

In the mid-1870's Field was photographed in Hartford. Today's viewer sees the man as his neighbors and relations did, upright and vigorous. The deep-set eyes are heavy browed, and a bushy, gray beard obscures the slightly receding chin. His suit is of good fabric and fits his broad shoulders; his linen sparkles. The photograph gives the appearance that some small prosperity was his after years of struggle.

With his *Historical Monument* recorded on canvas and documented in catalogue and print, Field had reached the pinnacle of the last half of his life. The rest was a gentle decline. The pathos of the painter's old age, as the deaf, eccentric "Mr. Field of Plumtrees," was a quiet close to a long and busy life. His mind and interests continued to range beyond the hills that lined the Connecticut River on either side. His means committed him to the valley and to the charity and kindness of his relatives. But with the help of his vocation he transcended the mountains and followed his fancy beyond Mount Toby and Sugar Loaf.

Field responded to President Garfield's assassination on July 2, 1881, by quickly turning out several small bust portraits on academy board and went from house to house in Leverett and Sunderland selling them for a dollar apiece. For the Hubbards, he painted a less than life-size, full-length portrait of the dead President.

In a straight-faced allegory Field portrayed an imaginary assembly of military and political figures that dates to about this time (pl. 31). In a late 19th-century room resembling the interior of the Gothic style church in Leverett, a meeting between Washington and Lincoln is solemnly observed by Generals Burnside and Grant, and by Presidents Rutherford B. Hayes and Chester A. Arthur.

The Bible had never been far from Field's mind and hand, and from a black and white illustration, *The Ark of the Covenant* in John Brown's *Self-Interpreting Bible* (first published in New York in 1820), he painted an exact but naive rendition of the event (fig. 50).

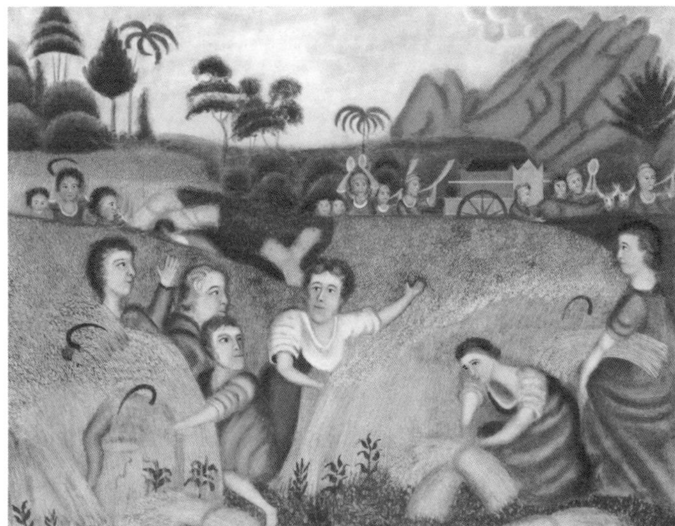

Fig. 50   *Ark of the Covenant*   (cat. no.93)

In about 1885 Field, recalling the five-mile panorama he had seen in New York so long ago, painted a panorama eighty-feet long of an imaginary trip around the world. One scene in the painting, the Brooklyn Bridge with flags flying above its roadway as they did at its opening in 1883, helps to date the work. Before reaching Brooklyn, however, Field illustrated several Massachusetts locations: the State House with its golden dome, Old North Church, the Victorian replacement for old Concord Bridge, the Bunker Hill Monument, Nix's Mate, Fort Warren, and Boston Light. After a tour of the world, Field returned by way of the American far west and Niagara Falls to end his panorama at the railroad terminal in Boston. The panorama was used to entertain small neighbors and friends; rolled up on two spindles, the painting was unwound by the artist piece by piece as he gave an account of the world's wonders.

In 1879 John Russell Young published *Around the World with General Grant*, the saga of the ex-president's tour. Soon after, one of its black and white illustra-tions, *Grant Entering Agra*, provided Field with the source for *The Visit of Ulysses Grant to India* (fig. 51). Field's interest in Grant's visit to India was surely heightened by Grant's visit to Hartford in 1880, a ceremonial occasion for which Stephen Ashley served as chairman of arrangements.

The Taj Mahal appears in several pen, ink, and pencil sketches, as well as in oil paint at this same time (figs. 52, 53). While the versions are almost certainly based on prints or book illustrations, the exact sources have not been discovered. The draftsmanship in the sketches is precise and accurate. The paintings, on the other hand, are less detailed, poorly drawn, and garish in color. Among Field's exotic subjects, the Taj Mahal, the temple to a beloved wife's memory, may be associated with the deaths of family and friends, occuring now with bewildering frequency. Several other paintings of about 1880, a tabernacle and a design for a sarcophagus, were also modeled on Indian designs (figs. 54, 55). One of the reliefs from the Arch of Titus gave Field a third composition (fig. 56).

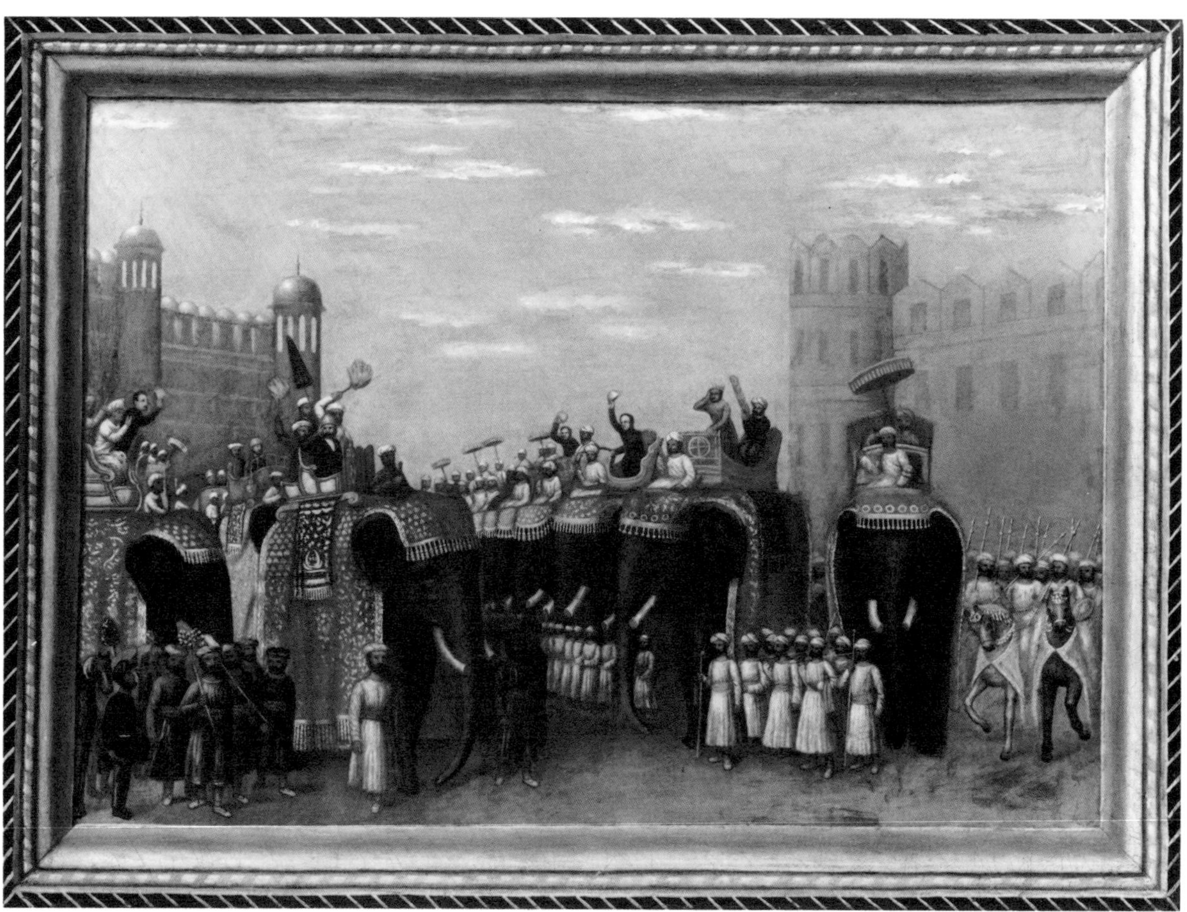

Fig. 51   *The Visit of Ulysses Grant to India*   (cat. no.95)

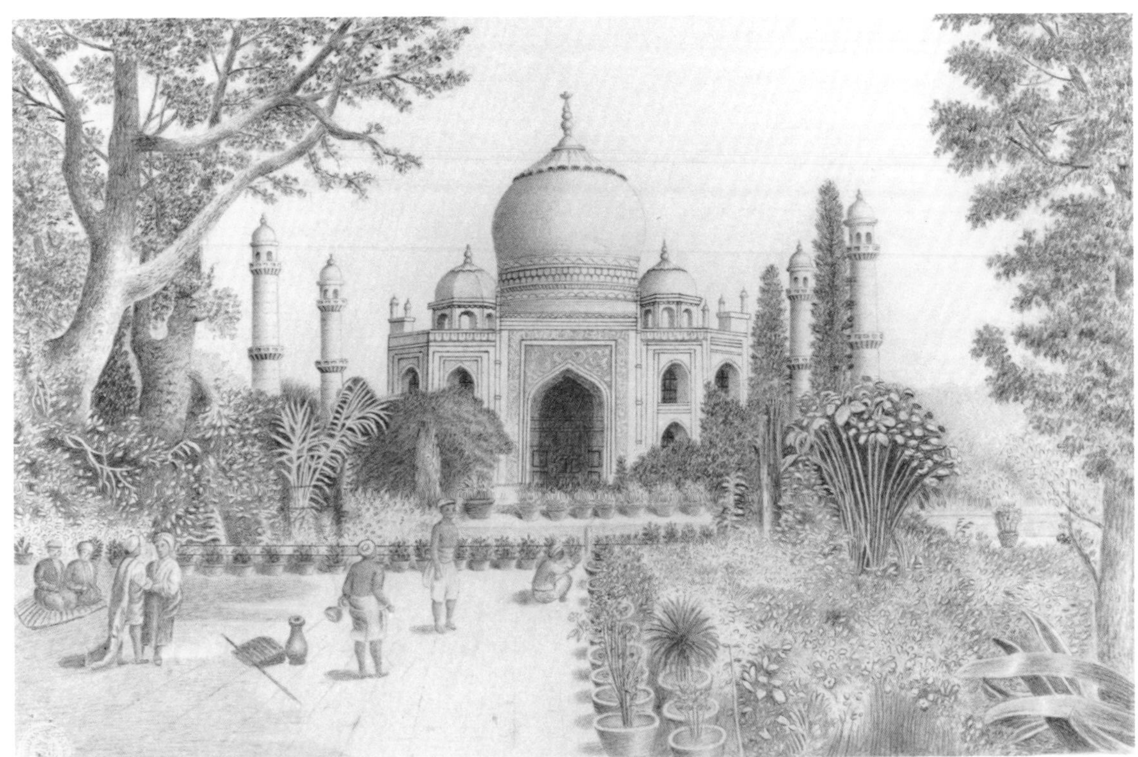

Fig. 52   *The Taj Mahal and Its Gardens*   (cat. no.99)

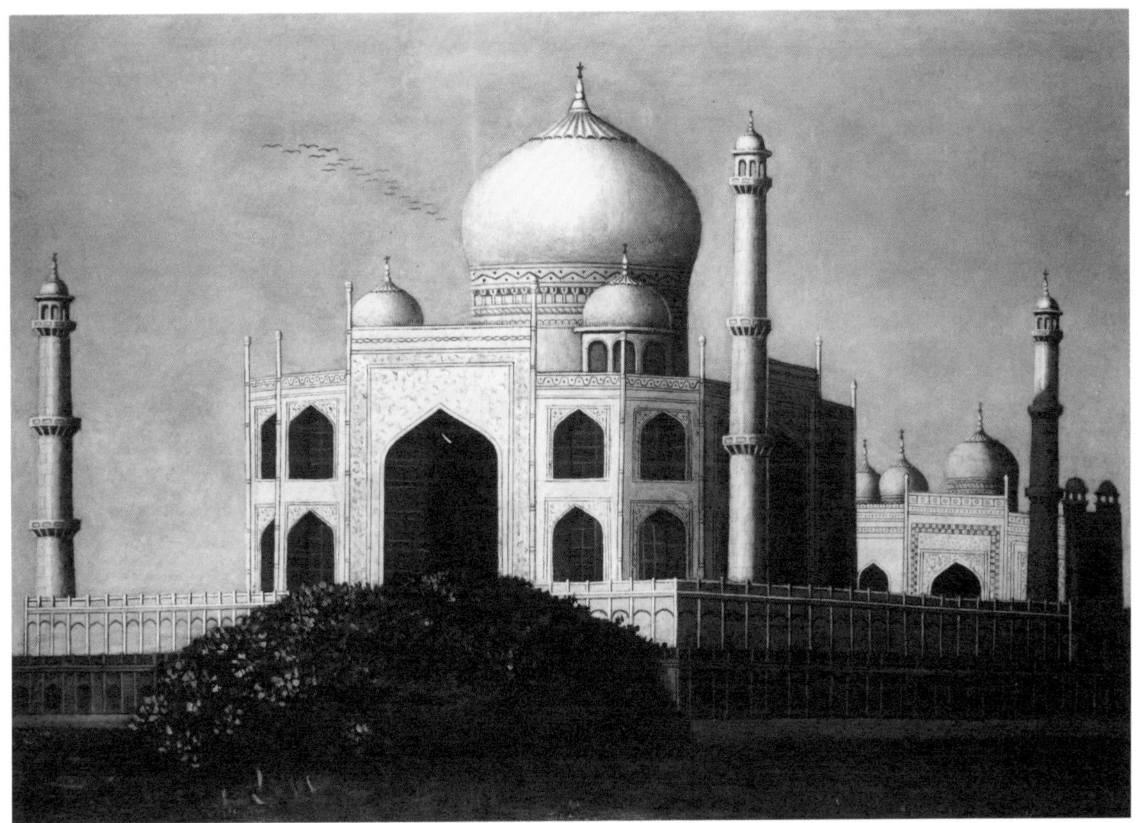

Fig. 53   *The Taj Mahal*   (cat. no.96)

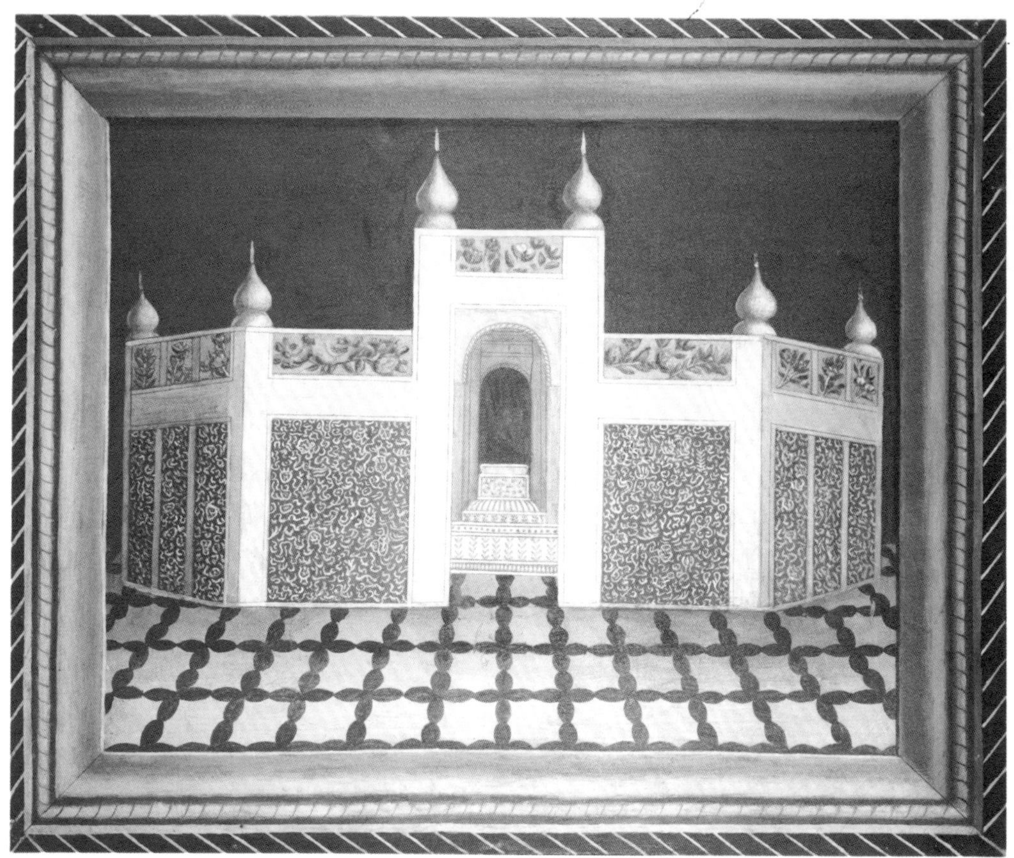

Fig. 54   *Design for a Tabernacle,*
India   (cat. no.102)

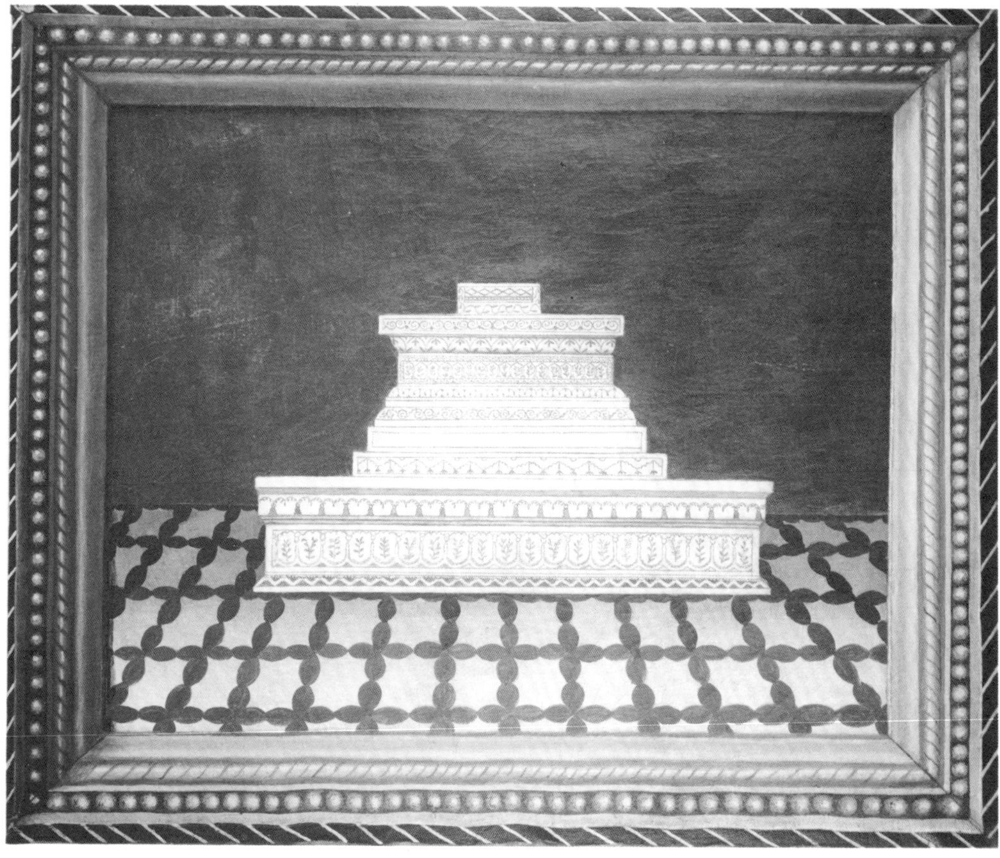

Fig. 55   *An Egyptian Sarcophagus*
(cat. no.104)

A portrait of the artist as an old man may be drawn from the accounts of men and women who knew him when they were boys and girls at Plumtrees. The school there was attended by young Cooleys and Hubbards and by members of a large Irish family. At recess they would climb the hill to the studio and sit enthralled at the artist's description of the works which lined the walls. In the summer Plumtrees children would be joined by other small relations from Leverett and Amherst. The paintings that they saw and heard described included the series, *Christ's Temptations in the Wilderness* (now lost), The Plagues, and *The Last Supper.*

Field gathered sap from his small sugar bush, sometimes adding sap from other trees, and in early spring a big kettle of syrup simmered on the little stove in the back room of the studio. Later in the year he would walk the long uphill road to the family wood lot in Leverett, where he chopped wood for the house and studio stoves. He had no horse and one of his nephews, Adin Field, Stillman's son, would cart the wood back to Plumtrees with his wagon and team.

Field was an independent, proud old Yankee. Sunday after Sunday, dressed in his best black suit and long dark cloak, wearing a tall hat and cowhide boots, and carrying an umbrella or cane, he would walk the two miles from Plumtrees to North Amherst Church, refusing rides for both himself and for Henrietta (in her best ringlets and rings), because, he said, the switching of the horse's tail and the jangling of the harness disturbed his thoughts. He was a contemplative old man, and his paintings illustrate that he had much to think about. His days, broken only by the visits of the school children and much younger relations and friends, were spent in the studio or puttering in his garden. His voice was harsh and gutteral, the tones those of a man long deaf.

Bent and bearded, and old as he was, he still slipped a beautifully carved and polished maple yoke over his shoulders every morning and walked to the Hubbards for water. One load for the house and one for the studio and the day's work began. A letter he wrote three days after Christmas in 1886 provides clues to his home situation:

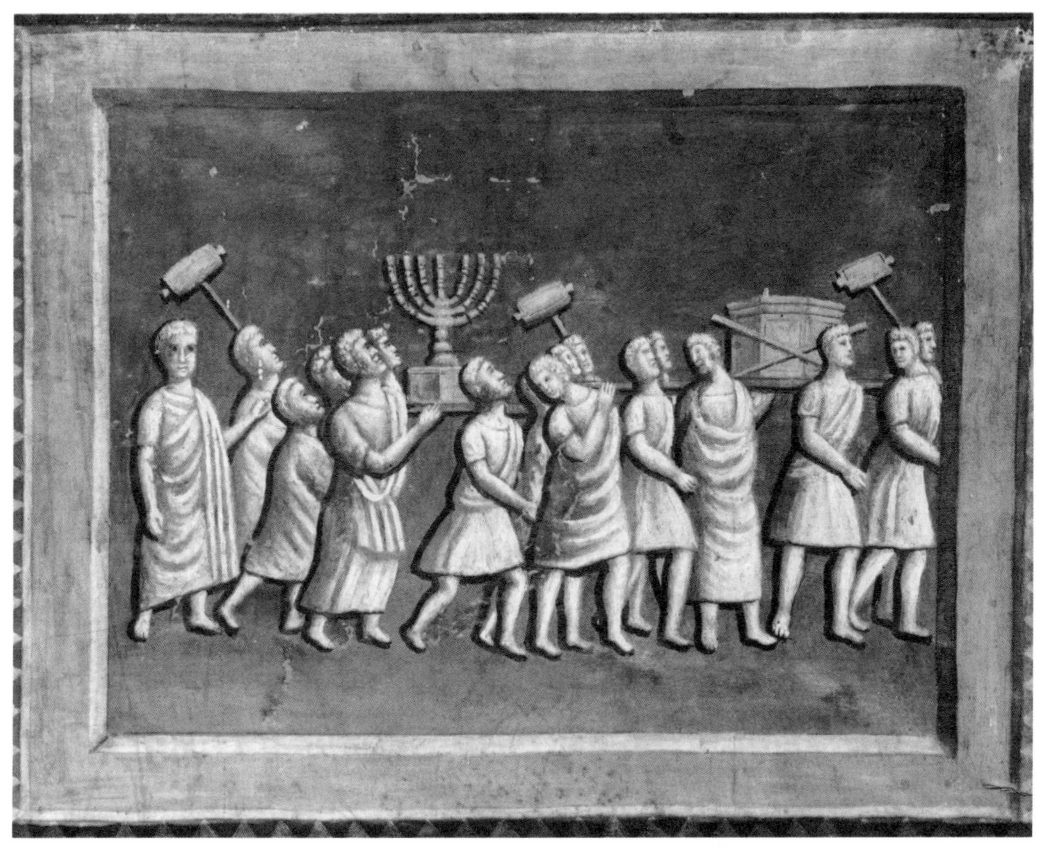

Fig. 56   *Relief from the Arch of Titus*   (cat. no.105)

After Etta wrote to you I concluded to write a line not
knowing whether she gave the true reason or not, In the
first place when she spoke about going to Hartford I said
if I am to live and well as usual I should want to leave
for home about the middle of March. She was not in-
clined to consent to it, I said then if I cannot have the
consent to come home about the middle of the month I
should prefer not to go. She then said I shall write Shall
I you prefer not to come. I said yes (supposing she would
give the true reason) Whether she did or not I can not
say. Now Mrs. Hubbard I can say that I have always enjoyed myself through the winters with you but when
March comes in I then have a strong desire to be at
home for certain reasons You and Mr. Hubbard have
always been remarkably kind and free hearted to both of
us for which I feel very grateful and never shall forget it.
Excuse the miserable writing.[38]

Stephen Ashley Hubbard and his wife continued as
the free-hearted patrons of Field's old age; and it was
to their pretty little Neo-Gothic cottage on Asylum
Street in Hartford that the painter and his daughter
went for the worst of the winter months. But Field's
"strong desire" to be at home "when March comes in"
shows spirit and Yankee pride.

Living was hard, there was no doubt of it, a dollar
here and there for small portraits had to be sup-
plemented by produce from garden and farm, wood
from the family lot, syrup from the trees, and by
"Etta's" earnings from dressmaking and piano lessons.
Whether Field was at home in 1888, when the great
blizzard took place, is not known. The studio would
have been drifted over, but snow banks mattered little
to these hardy farmers who endured bad weather
every winter of their lives.

In the last decade of his life Field is remembered as
a shy, quiet, unassuming man, confident of his small
world of relatives, and secure in the faith that the
"The Lord will provide." Aided by friends and cousins,
the Lord did. Field's many interests kept him young
for his years, and his independence kept him active.

In 1890 Stephen Ashley died in Hartford. Field's
sisters, Julia Ann Field Sears and Emily Field Gaylord,
died in 1893 and 1895. His Connecticut Valley home
was being deserted by his contemporaries, leaving
behind younger cousins, nephews, and nieces whom
the old man had seen grow from infants to middle age.
By the end of the century, only he and Thankful remained in his generation of Fields and Hubbards.

In the last decade of the 19th century, change was
in the air. Young great-grand-nieces and nephews came
on bicycles, instead of on horseback to see him. He
may have seen an automobile; Ford's first was completed in 1893. In 1898 he journeyed to Springfield
where he sat to A.C. Moore at Gill's Art Building for
a photograph. He looked like Rip Van Winkle still
sleepy from his long nap. In 1900 he cast his vote in
the state election just before his ninety-fifth birthday
as one would expect this Yankee among Yankees to do.

In the *Atlantic Monthly* of April and May, 1899, appeared a devastating criticism of late 19th century life
in a Connecticut River village, written by Rollin
Lynde Hartt, who was for one year a resident in "A
New England Hill Town." Hartt named this town
Sweet Auburn, "half a century behind the times," but
his true subject seems to have been Leverett and its
people.[39] Their devotion to religion, as much for entertainment as for moral value, was roundly blasted by
Hartt. "Ethically considered, Sweet Auburn is not a
town; it is a misfortune. Its religion is fanciful, its
morality artificial, its social atmosphere morbid."[40]
The women of the town, thriving on domesticity, were
"superior to their husbands," whose small scale lives
were warped because "masculine character spoils if it
is shut up too long."[41]

While Field's faith in the Calvinist principles of his
ancestors was strong, he had once left the enveloping
atmosphere that began to invade his hill town at mid-
century, and possibly he escaped the flawed character
of the men that Hartt criticized. The children of the
community perceived the painter as an accessible and
loveable eccentric; their observations probably
reflected the view of their parents.

While Hartt seems not to have had Field in mind
as the source of the trouble that he saw in this small
Eden, substitution of the Field family name for Glenn
in the following passage identifies the source of the hill
town's woes:

> The mountains limiting communication with neighbor-
> ing villages, Glenns have married Glenns from time im-
> memorial. Hence a complete and inert solidarity. We
> have a single hearthstone seven miles long, eighty farms
> sit musing at the ingleside, our ancient rooftree shelters
> three hundred and fifty complicated kinsmen. Saving
> only the random stranger within our gates, we are a clan
> in the narrowest sense of the word. The town is own
> cousin to itself.[42]

In May's *Atlantic Monthly* castigation of the town
continued. "You can find 'natives' in Sweet Auburn
who have never ventured beyond the visible horizon . . .

The civil war called a stalwart half dozen into the South; three or four of our men took up claims in the West and returned disappointed."[43] Hartt's pique sought out every aspect of village life for criticism, claiming "There is not one good picture in our whole village, no, not one" as the villagers rhapsodize over a "Madonna reproduced on glass with a rococo edging of filmy gilt and a prop to stand up by." Lest it be thought that Field's later works were overlooked, the *Monument* or the Plagues seem to be intended by Hartt's outburst, "And what of the long and narrow etchings by the indefatigable Field! We cross ourselves before them with pious adoration."[44]

Despite this corruscating outside criticism of Leverett and surrounding settlements, its resident painter was praised in an article, "Old Folks of the County," appearing on the 9th of June in the local *Greenfield Gazette and Courier.*

> Although Mr. Field was an all-around painter of the old school, his work which has been most appreciated is that of portrait painting; his likenesses of people of past generations are as nearly correct as can well be made in oil, and give to posterity faithful ideas of the personal appearance of their ancestors.

He was the oldest man in Franklin County and recognition of his work by his Connecticut Valley peers was barely in time. This June the studio door, with its wooden latch polished by much use, remained closed. Field was slipping quietly and inevitably away from Plumtrees. For a few weeks he hovered between dreams of the hosts in the Leverett graveyard and the glories of the world beyond the mountain wall. On Saturday, the 28th of June, Field dropped beyond the dreams into eternity.

His obligation to his own people had been fulfilled. By the insight of his portraits and naive visions illustrating historical and religious themes, he had demonstrated that a life spent as a painter, even in a close knit agrarian society, could be an enriching influence.

For the 20th century, Field's paintings are windows that open to the character, taste, and appearance of his society in 19th-century America. Even more important, the little man seated at his easel before his patron of the moment preserved each Yankee subject just as he saw him emotionally, spiritually, and aesthetically. It is a good legacy.

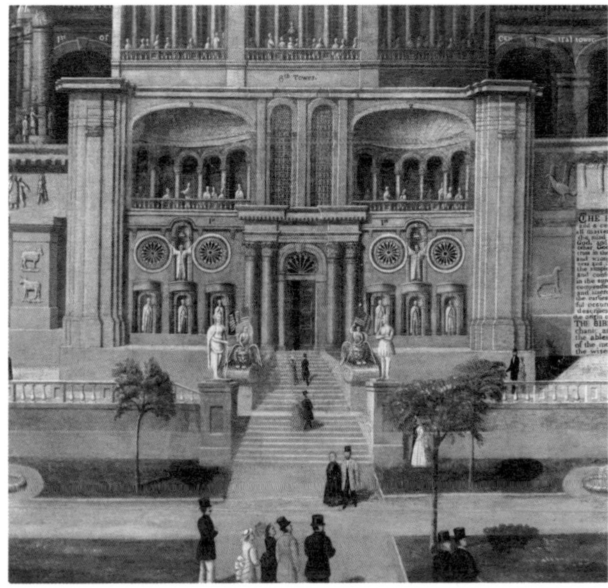

The Historical Monument of the American Republic, (detail)

Endnotes

1. Commemorative plaque, Pocumtuck Valley Memorial Association, Deerfield, Massachusetts.

2. This grandfather was born in the summer of 1745 at Sunderland, just north of Plumtrees on the east bank of the Connecticut River. In about 1770, he married Dorothy Kellogg of Amherst, daughter of Ephraim and Dorothy (Hawley) Kellogg. (She died in August 1773, two weeks after the birth of the painter's father.) For a brief period during the Revolution he served as a private in Captain Reuben Dickinson's company of minutemen. Receiving the alarm of a battle between British troops and patriots, the Connecticut Valley militia marched toward Lexington and Concord on April 19, 1775, and saw service for 16 days. Demonstrating the intermittent pattern of military service that characterized the patriot army, William Field reenlisted in the fall of 1777, and served in the company of Captain Joseph Slarrow for 26 days, "on an expedition to the Northward." Following these two short terms of duty, this grandfather returned to his hill town farm and held a variety of town offices.

3. Seven months later, the town voted "to lend our minds in writing to the Provincial Congress by a Committee." Ashley and four others were charged with carrying out this instruction. His absence from the town rolls as selectman in 1776 and 1777, his return to this office from 1778 to 1782, another absence in 1783, and another return from 1784 to 1785, are, along with the military rank of Captain, likely indications of his service in the Massachusetts militia during the Revolution.

4. William Dunlap, *History of the Rise and Progress of the Arts of Design in the United States*, ed. James T. Flexner, New York, 1969, II, 292. Harding was abroad from 1823 to 1826; he settled in Springfield, Massachusetts, in 1830.

5. Stock's journal and accounts are in the collection of the Connecticut Valley Historical Museum, Springfield, Massachusetts. See *The Paintings and the Journal of Joseph Whiting Stock*, ed. Juliette Tomlinson, with a checklist of Stock's works compiled by Kate Steinway, Middletown, Connecticut, 1976.

6. Information on Goodell is from Cynthia Seibels, recorded by Ruth Pinwonka and Roderic Blackburn, *A Visible Heritage, Columbia County, New York, A History in Art and Architecture*, Kinderhook, New York, 1977, 123.

7. The career of Augustus Fuller is documented by Agnes Dods, "Connecticut Valley Painters," *Antiques*, XLVI, no. 11, October 1944, 207-209. For George Fuller see *George Fuller, His Life and Works: A Memorial Volume*, ed. Josiah B. Millet, Boston and New York, 1886.

8. "Old Folks of the County," *Greenfield Gazette and Courier*, June 9, 1900.

9. From Erastus Field to Samuel Morse, October 13, 1824, Samuel F.B. Morse Papers, Library of Congress.

10. Prospect House Register, May 28, 1824, cited by Jill A. Hodnicki, "The Connecticut Valley in Literature," in *Arcadian Vales: Views of the Connecticut River Valley*, ed. Martha J. Hoppin, George Walter Vincent Smith Art Museum, Springfield, Massachusetts, 1981, 25.

11. *Samuel F.B. Morse, His Letters and Journals*, ed. Edward Lind Morse, Boston and New York, 1914, I, 258.

12. *Ibid.*, 257-258. Field's fellow student, Frederic S. Agate, became a portrait and history painter. "Henry" was Henry Cheever Pratt, another painter who had studied with Morse in 1817 and had traveled with his teacher as his assistant in Charleston, South Carolina in 1819, in Washington in 1821, and back to Charleston the following year.

13. Correspondence from Mrs. Carey Stillman Hayward to Mary Black, 1958-1960, in the files of the Abby Aldrich Rockefeller Folk Art Center, Williamsburg, Virginia.

14. In the files of the Abby Aldrich Rockefeller Folk Art Center, Williamsburg, Virginia.

15. From Erastus Field to his son, Erastus Salisbury Field, July 28, 1827, in the files of the Abby Aldrich Rockefeller Folk Art Center, Williamsburg, Virginia. If the town had been larger, the school, under a brand new Massachusetts law, would have been tax supported. In any case, the study of United States history was required. Required or not, it is certain, from the small library of this family that remains intact, that history was a subject that appealed to Erastus Salisbury Field, his father, and his brothers.

16. His first appearance on the town's tax list was in May, 1797.

17. From Erastus Salisbury Field to his father, Erastus Field, June 28, 1828, in the files of the Abby Aldrich Rockefeller Folk Art

Center, Williamsburg, Virginia.

18. William Ashley married twice, and both his wives, Nancy Pomeroy and Jerusha Leonard, came from towns near Leverett. By Nancy (who died about 1801) he had four children: William, Jr., who died at sea, and Chester and Elisha, who before 1825 had both settled in Little Rock, Arkansas; his daughter Mary married William Van Alstyne of nearby Shodack Landing.

19. Letter from Mrs. James Spencer, cited in Mary Black, "Erastus Salisbury Field's Portrait of his Cousin Lauriette Ashley," *Museum Monographs I*, Saint Louis Art Museum, 1968, 51-62.

20. Surviving into this century were drafts of a letter that Lauriette wrote to Abraham Lincoln condemning slavery. She never married and lived until 1870. The place she held in her family's affections is illustrated in the naming of two nieces, one on each side of the family: Elisha Ashley's oldest daughter, born in 1819, was given the name; and Phineas, Erastus' brother, named his daughter Lauriette Ashley Field.

21. Genealogical information concerning the Hulberts is from the Bassett family history supplied by Henry Holt, a descendant who resides in Essex Fells, New Jersey.

22. According to Clara Sears, *Some American Primitives*, Boston, 1941, 156, Field also painted a Mrs. Dyer of Somerville, Massachusetts (Fruitlands Museums). The portrait dates to about 1838 and may mean that Field visited the Boston area; or he may have painted it in Westminster, as Sears suggests a link between Mrs. Dyer and Mrs. Joslin.

23. Alfred Frankenstein, *The San Francisco Chronicle*, newspaper clipping in the files of the Abby Aldrich Rockefeller Folk Art Center, Williamsburg, Virginia. In 1887 John, Elizabeth, and Mina Pearce were farming land in Hadley, and the portraits represent, in all likelihood, members of the same family.

24. The steeples of the churches and the large brick buildings extending to docks on the river might be a free rendition of the Connecticut capital at the end of the 1830's. If it is Hartford, it is generally the view seen in an 1840 engraving of the city.

25. *Samuel F.B. Morse, His Letters and Journals*, II, 160.

26. Unidentified newspaper clipping, present location unknown.

27. *Carey Hayward*, The Springfield Sunday Union and Republican, May 14th, 1939, 8E.

28. From Nancy (Minnie) Hubbard to her sister, September 27, 1855, in the files of the Abby Aldrich Rockefeller Folk Art Center, Williamsburg, Virginia.

29. See Mary Black, "Erastus Salisbury Field and the Sources of his Inspiration," *Antiques*, LXXXIII, no. 2, February 1963, 201-204.

30. This notice was discovered by Betsy Jones, Associate Director of the Smith College Museum of Art, Northampton, Massachusetts.

31. Erastus S. Field, *Descriptive Catalogue of the Historical Monument of the American Republic*, Amherst, Massachusetts, H.M. McCloud, 1876, 4.

32. The contemporary and not always accurate account of Trumbull's contribution to the rotunda decoration is contained in Dunlap, *History of the Rise and Progress*, I, 375-393.

33. For Morse's *Old House of Representatives* and *Gallery of the Louvre* see Paul Staiti and Gary A. Reynolds, *Samuel F.B. Morse*, Grey Art Gallery, New York, 1982.

34. *Samuel F.B. Morse, His Letters and Journals*, II, 267-268.

35. Field, *Descriptive Catalogue*, 3.

36. Erastus Salisbury Field to Mr. Hubbard, June 25, 1876, in the files of the Abby Aldrich Rockefeller Folk Art Center, Williamsburg, Virginia.

37. Letter from William L. Warren to Mary Black, March 7, 1965.

38. Erastus Salisbury Field to Mrs. Stephen Ashley Hubbard, December 28, 1886, in the files of the Abby Aldrich Rockefeller Folk Art Center, Williamsburg, Virginia.

39. Rollin Lynde Hartt, "A New England Hill Town," *The Atlantic Monthly*, LXXXIII, no. 498, April 1899, 562.

40. *Ibid.*, 564.

41. *Ibid.*

42. *Ibid.*, 566.

43. Rollin Lynde Hartt, "A New England Hill Town," *The Atlantic Monthly*, LXXXIII, no. 499, May 1899, 712.

44. *Ibid.*, 717.

Bibliography

BOOKS

Balston, Thomas, *John Martin, His Life and Works*, London, 1947.

Black, Mary, "Erastus Salisbury Field's Portrait of His Cousin Lauriette Ashley," *Museum Monographs I*, St. Louis, 1968, 51-62.

__________, "Erastus Salisbury Field, 1805-1900," in *American Folk Painters of Three Centuries*, ed. Tom Armstrong and Jean Lipman, New York, 1980.

__________ and Jean Lipman, *American Folk Painting*, New York, 1967.

Ford, Alice, *Pictorial Folk Art, New England to California*, New York, 1949.

History of the Town of Amherst, Amherst, Massachusetts 1896.

Holdridge, Barbara and Harry, with an introduction by Mary Black, *Ammi Phillips, Portrait Painter, 1788-1865*, New York, 1968.

Howells, William Dean, "Sketch of George Fuller's Life," in *George Fuller, His Life and Works, A Memorial Volume*, ed. Josiah B. Millet, Boston and New York, 1886.

Hubbard, Florence G., "Erastus Salisbury Field," in *History of the Town of Sunderland, Massachusetts*, ed. George M. Smith, Greenfield, 1899.

Little, Nina Fletcher, *The Abby Aldrich Rockefeller Folk Art Collection*, Boston, 1957.

Noble, Louis L., *The Course of Empire, Voyage of Life, and Other Pictures of Thomas Cole, N.A., with Selections from His Letters and Miscellaneous Writings, Illustrative of His Life, Character, and Genius*, New York, 1853.

Pierce, Frederick B., *Field Genealogy*, 2 vols., Chicago, 1901.

Robinson, Frederick B., "Erastus Salisbury Field," in *Primitive Painters in America, 1750-1950, An Anthology*, ed. Jean Lipman and Alice Winchester, New York, 1950.

Samuel F.B. Morse, His Letters and Journals, ed. Edward L. Morse, 2 vols., Boston and New York, 1914.

Sears, Clara Endicott, *Some American Primitives: A Study of New England Faces and Folk Portraits*, Boston, 1941.

Smith, George M., *History of the Town of Sunderland, Massachusetts*, Greenfield, 1899.

Temple, J.H., *History of the Town of Palmer, Massachusetts*, Palmer, 1889.

Walker, Alice M., *The Story of a New England Church*, Amherst, Massachusetts, 1901.

__________, *Historic Homes of Amherst*, Amherst, Massachusetts, 1905.

CATALOGUES AND PERIODICALS

Black, Mary, *Erastus Salisbury Field, 1805-1900*, The Abby Aldrich Rockefeller Folk Art Collection, Williamsburg, Virginia, 1963.

__________, "Erastus Salisbury Field and the Sources of His Inspiration," *Antiques Magazine*, LXXXIII, no. 2, February, 1963, 201-204.

__________, "Rediscovery: Erastus Salisbury Field," *Art in America*, 54, no. 1, January-February, 1966, 49-56. Adapted from the 1966 Colonial Williamsburg film, "Erastus Salisbury Field of Plumtrees."

Cahill, Holger, *American Folk Art, The Art of the Common Man in America*, New York, Museum of Modern Art, 1932.

Catalogue Containing a Correct List of All the Articles Exhibiting at the Annual Fair of the American Institute of the City of New York, New York, 1841-1849.

Dods, Agnes M., "Connecticut Valley Painters," *Antiques Magazine*, LXVI, no. 11, October, 1944, 207-209.

__________, "A Checklist of Portraits and Paintings by Erastus Salisbury Field," *Art in America*, 32, no. 1, January, 1944, 32-40.

__________, "Erastus Salisbury Field (1805-1900) A New England Folk Artist," *Old-Time New England*, XXXIII, October, 1942, 26-32.

__________ and Reginald French, "Erastus Salisbury Field," *Connecticut Historical Society Bulletin*, XXVIII, no. 4, October, 1963, 97-144.

Exhibition of Paintings by Erastus Salisbury Field, Department of Fine Arts, Amherst College and the Amherst Historical Society, Amherst, Massachusetts, 1947.

Field, Erastus Salisbury, *Descriptive Catalogue of the Historical Monument of the American Republic*, Amherst, Massachusetts, 1876.

Jenkins, Frank J., "Some Nineteenth-Century Towers," *Journal of the Institute of British Architects*, February, 1958, 2ff.

Maytham, Thomas N., "Two Faces of New England Portrait Painting," *Bulletin of the Museum of Fine Arts, Boston, Massachusetts*, LXI, 1963, 31ff.

New York City Directory, New York, 1841-1848.

101 Masterpieces of American Primitive Painting from the Collection of Edgar William and Bernice Chrysler Garbisch, New York, 1961.

Piwonka, Ruth and Roderic Blackburn, *A Visible Heritage, Columbia County, New York, A History in Art and Architecture*, Kinderhook, New York, 1977.

Robinson, Frederick B., "Erastus Salisbury Field," *Art in America*, 30, October, 1942, 244-253.

__________, *Somebody's Ancestors, Paintings of Primitive Artists of the Connecticut Valley*, Museum of Fine Arts, Springfield, Massachusetts, 1942.

__________, "The Eighth Wonder of Erastus Field," *American Heritage*, XIV, no. 3, April, 1963, 12-17.

NEWSPAPERS

Allen, O.P., "Painters of Portraits," *Palmer Journal*, May 12, 1913.

Brown, W.R., "Painter Field," *The Amherst Record*, June, 1947, editorial.

Hampshire Gazette and Northampton Courier, May 28, 1867.

Hartt, Rollin Lynde, "A New England Hill Town," *Atlantic Monthly*, LXXXIII, nos. 498-499, April and May, 1899.

"Old Folks of the County," *Greenfield Gazette and Courier*, June 9, 1900.

Wright, Madeline Ball, "Search for Connecticut Valley Primitives Leads to Many a Rustic Adventure," *Springfield Sunday Union and Republican*, February 1, 1942.

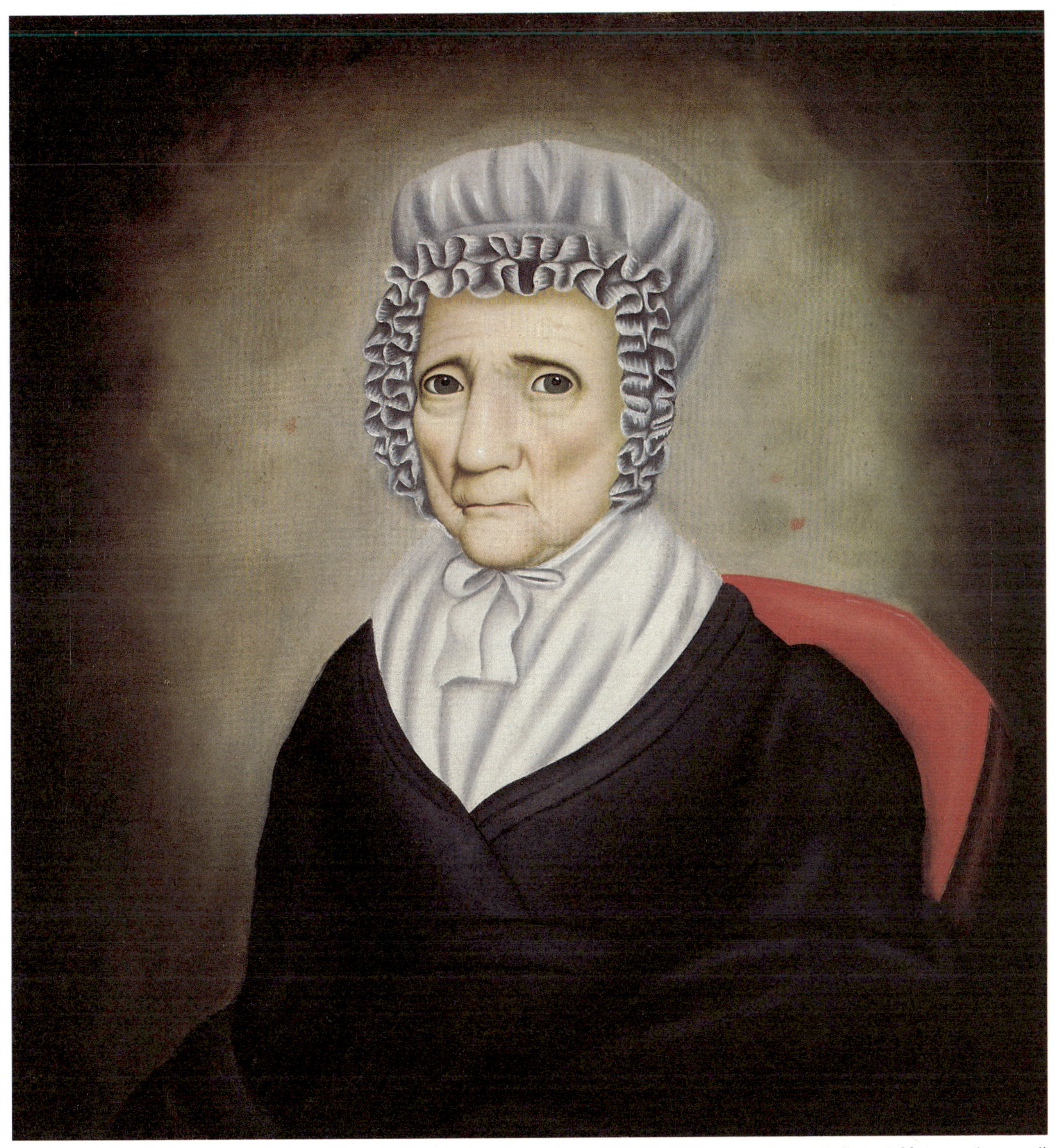

Pl. 1   *Elizabeth Billings Ashley*   (cat. no. *1*)

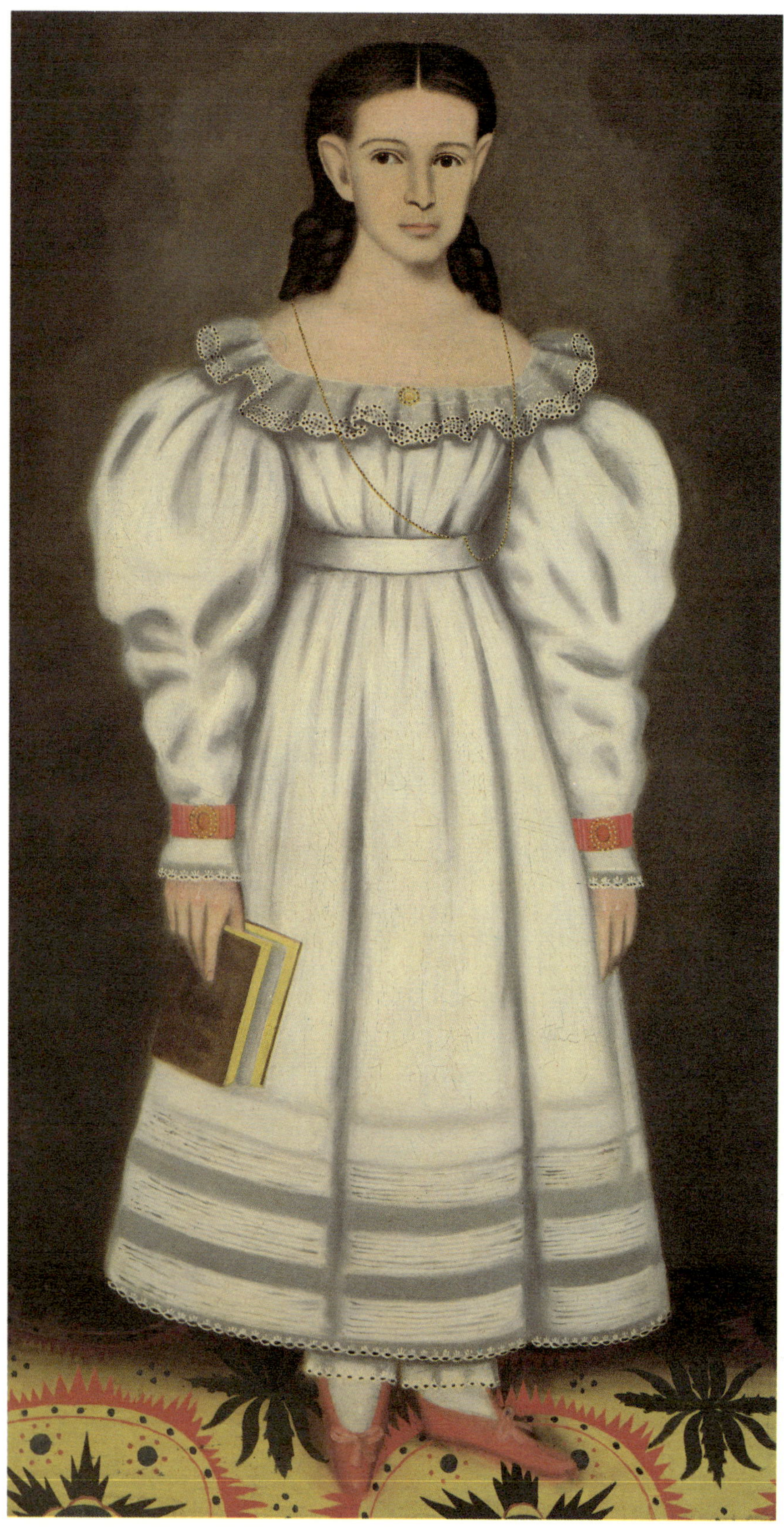

Pl. 2   *Mary Werner Bangs?*   (cat. no.9)

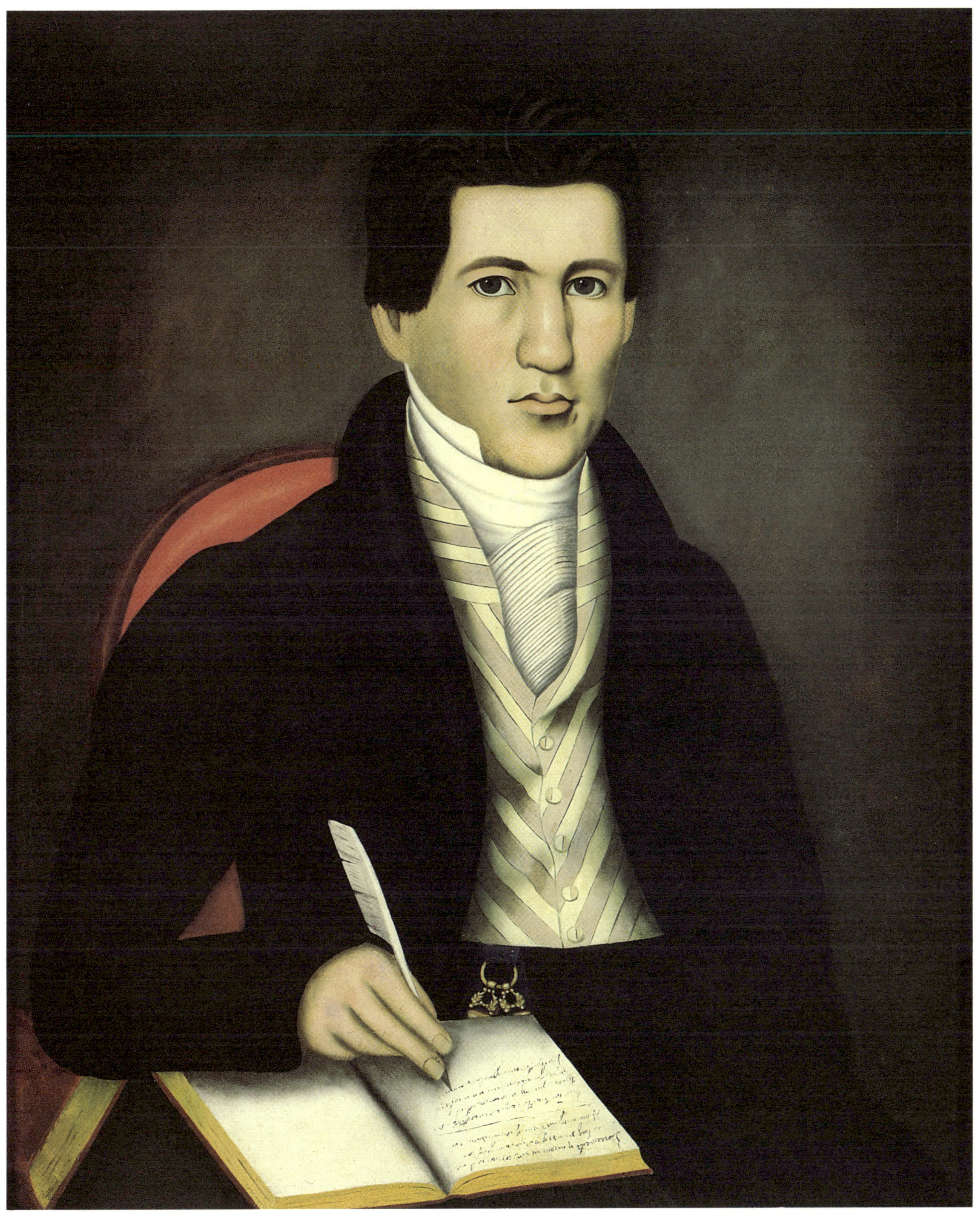

Pl. 3   *Phineas Field*   (cat. no.13)

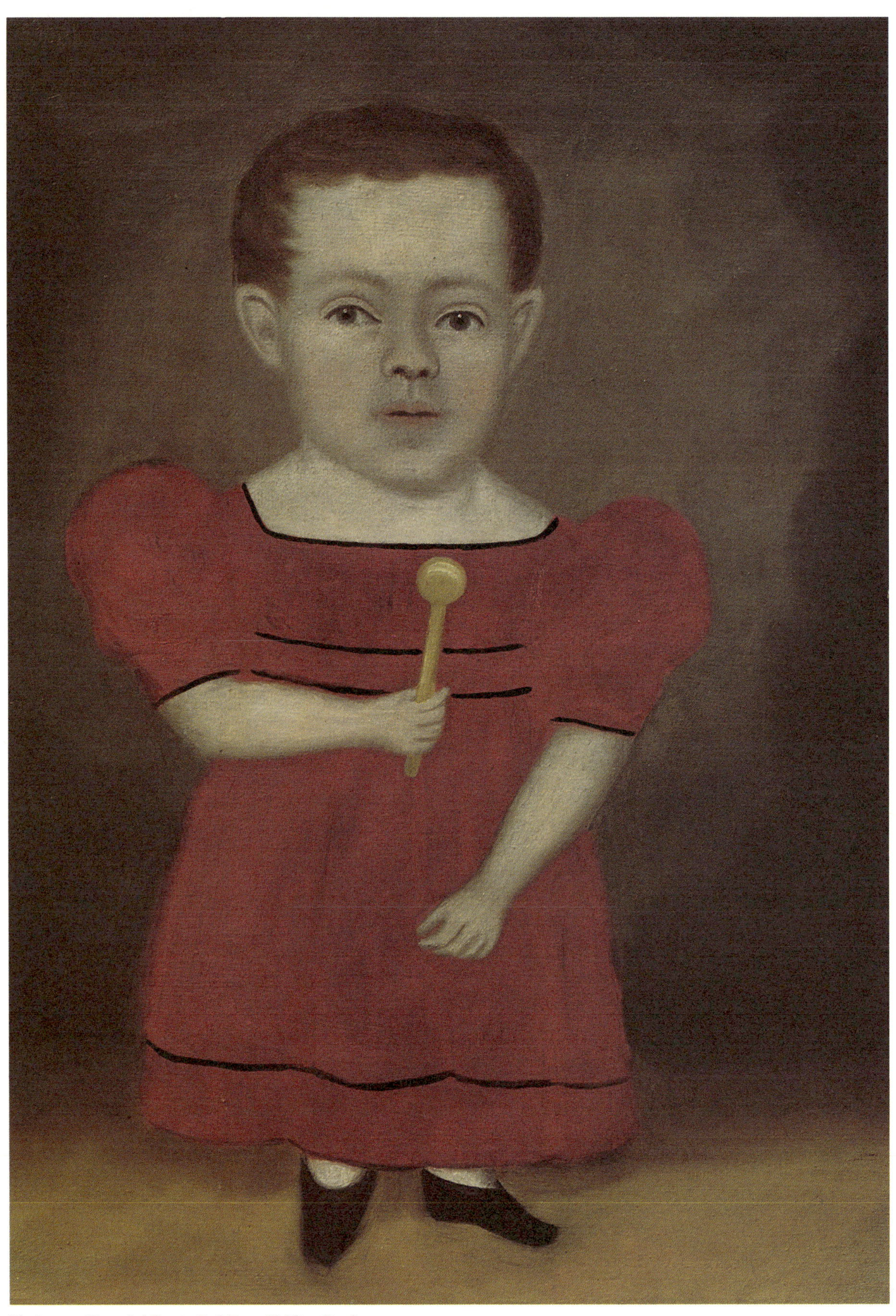

Pl. 4   *Dwarfed Boy in Red Dress Holding Rattle*
(cat. no.14)

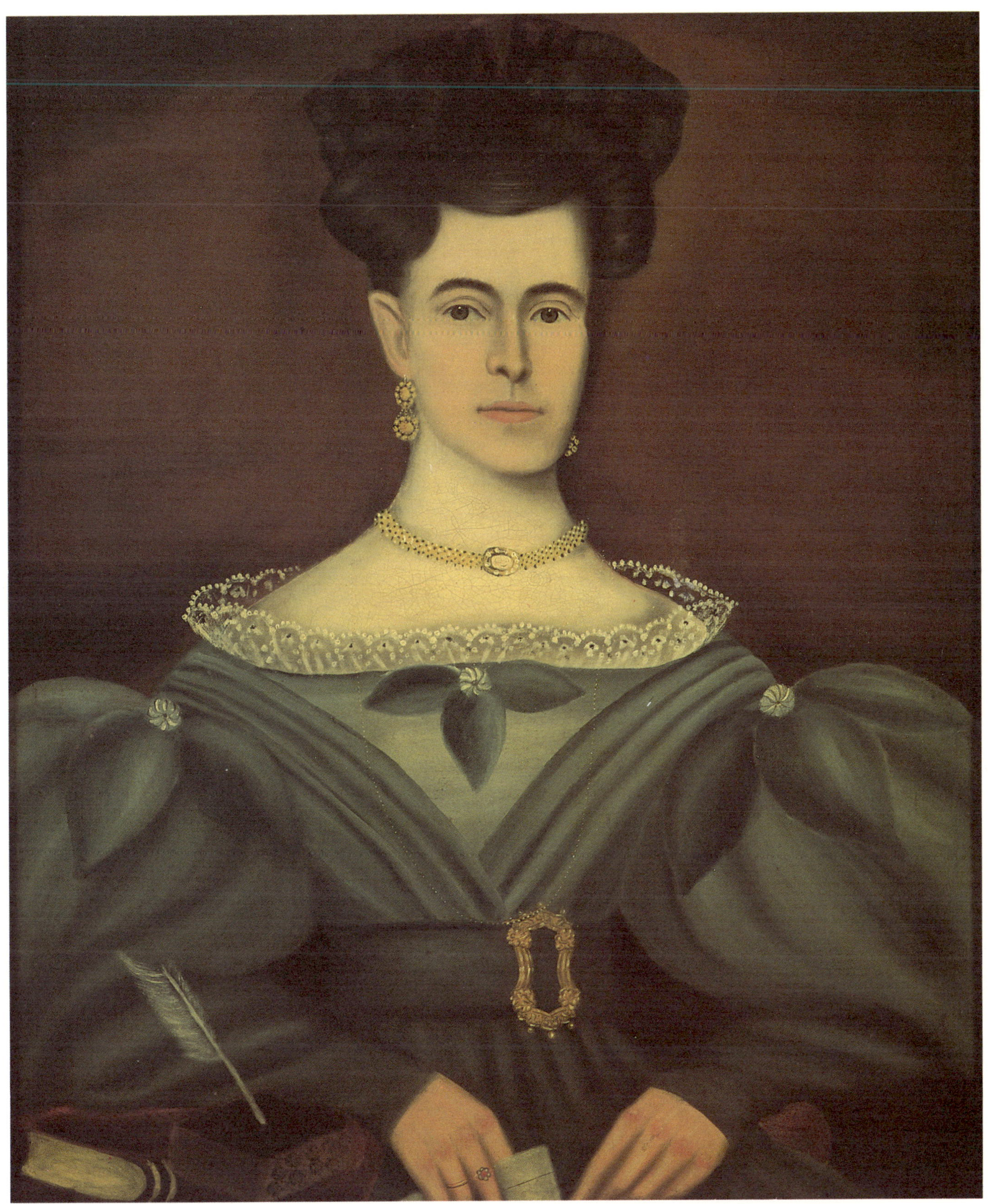

Pl. 5   *Portrait of a Young Woman*   (cat. no.15)

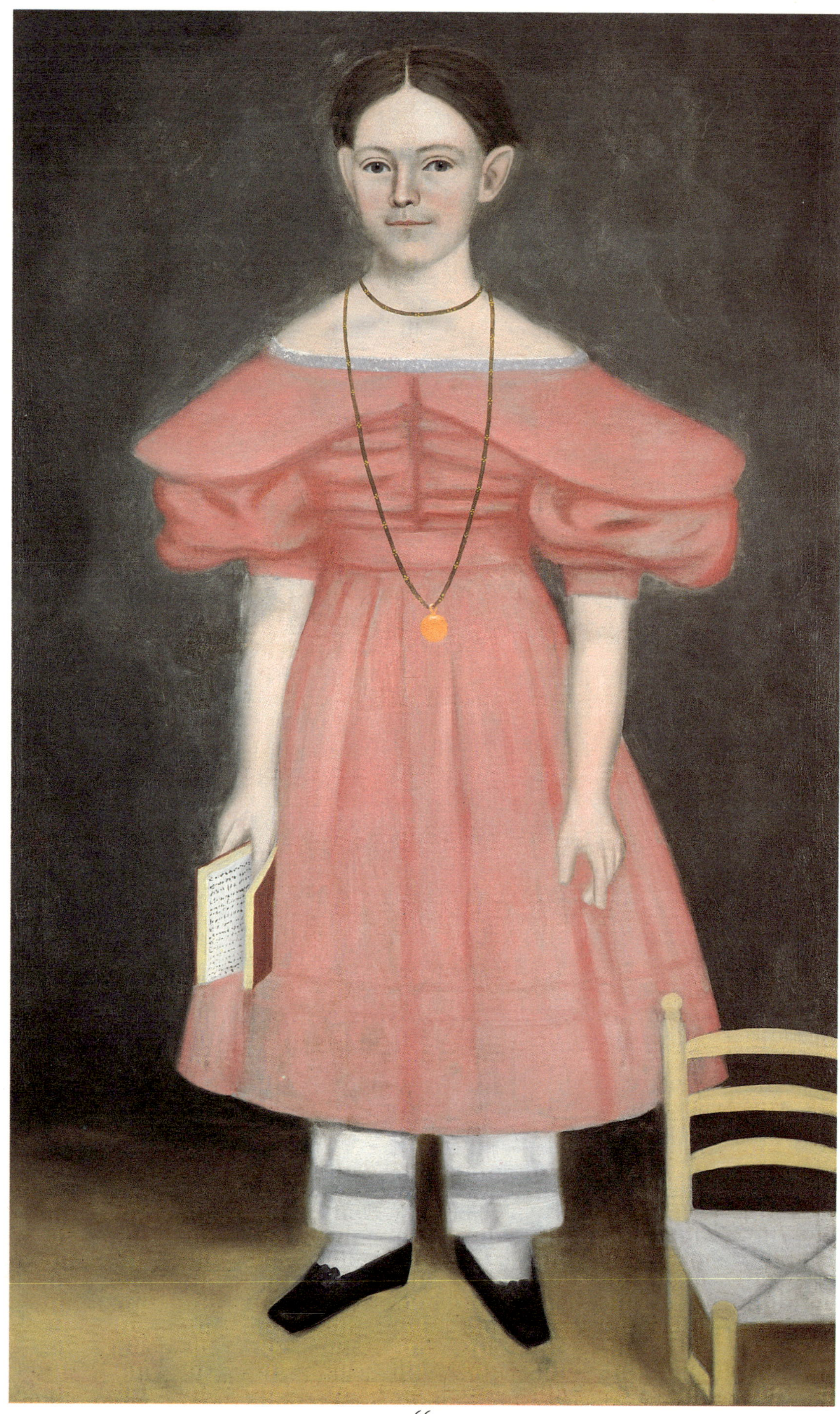

Pl. 6   *Elizabeth Camilla Jillson*
         (cat. no.24)

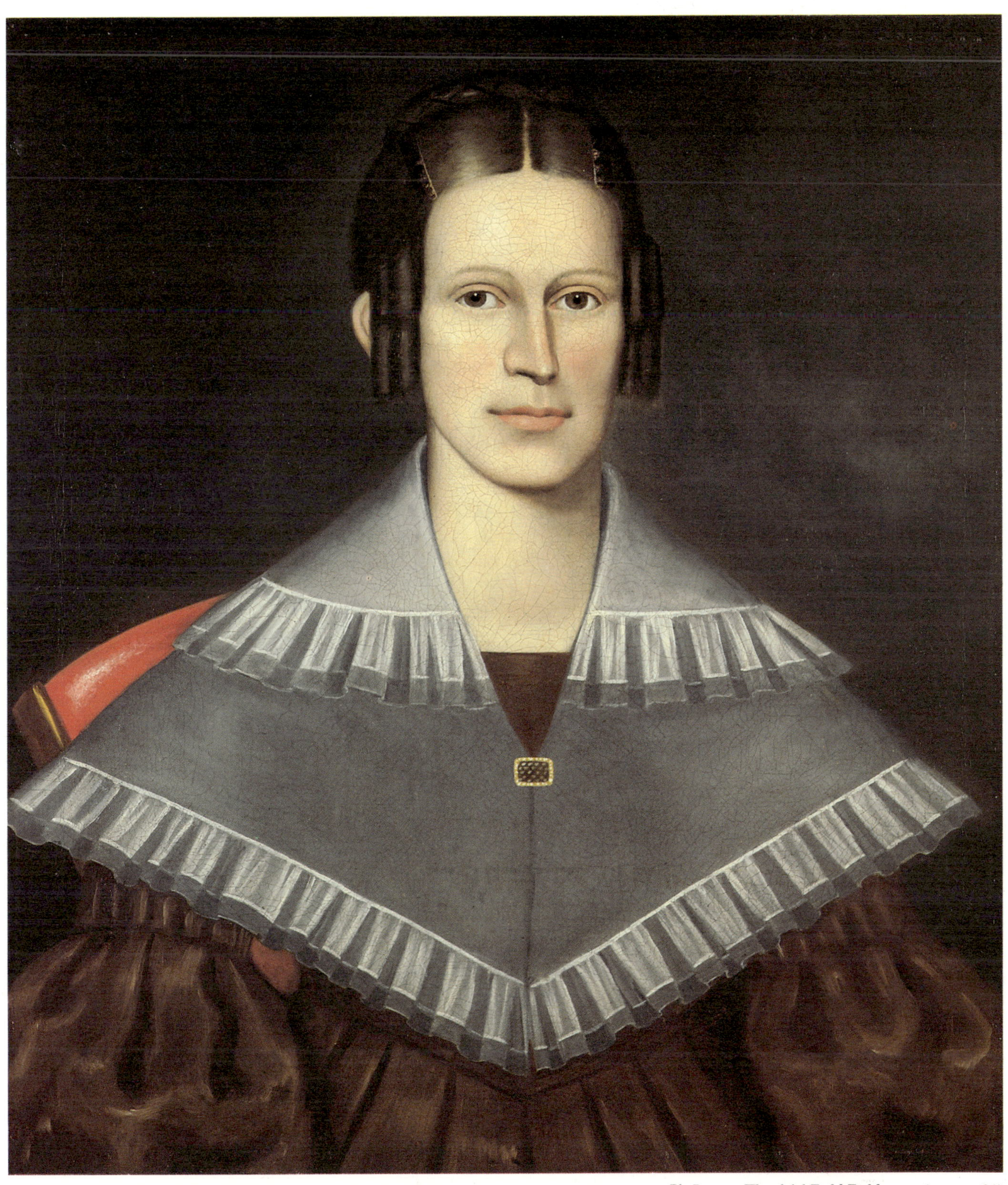

Pl. 7   *Thankful Field Field*   (cat. no.28)

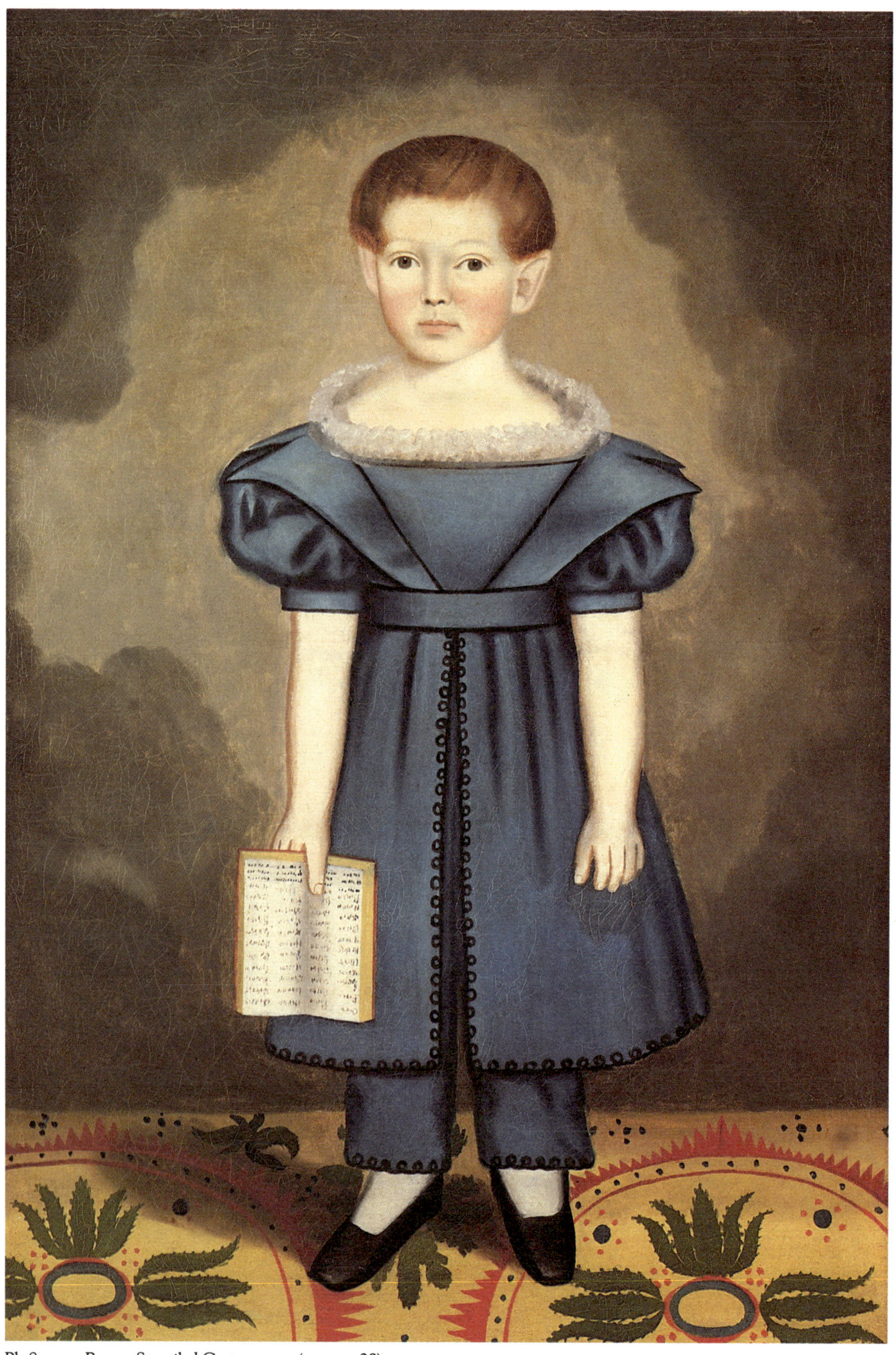

Pl. 8   *Boy on Stenciled Carpet*   (cat. no.29)

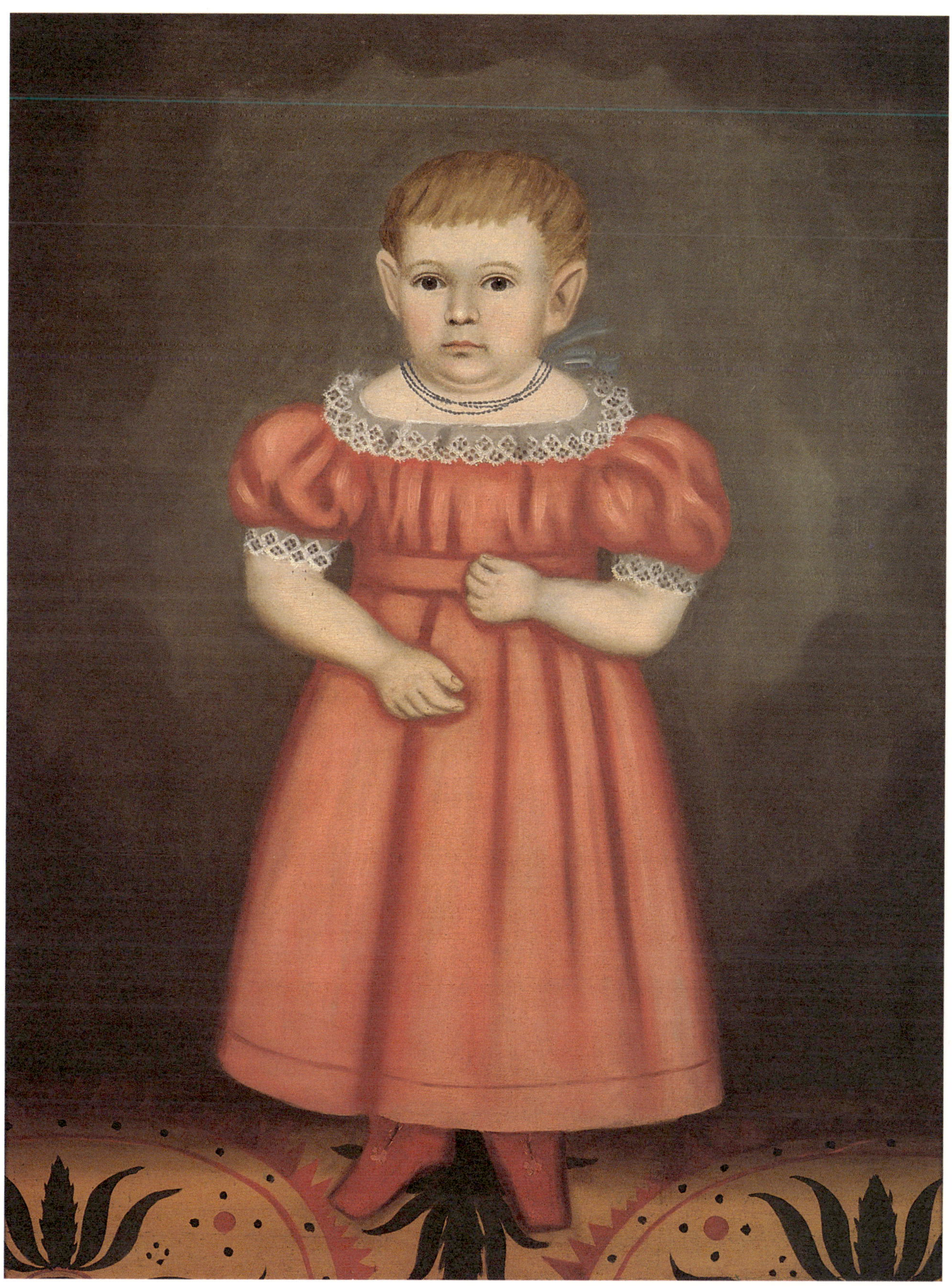

Pl. 9　　*Young Girl in Pink Dress*　　(cat. no.30)

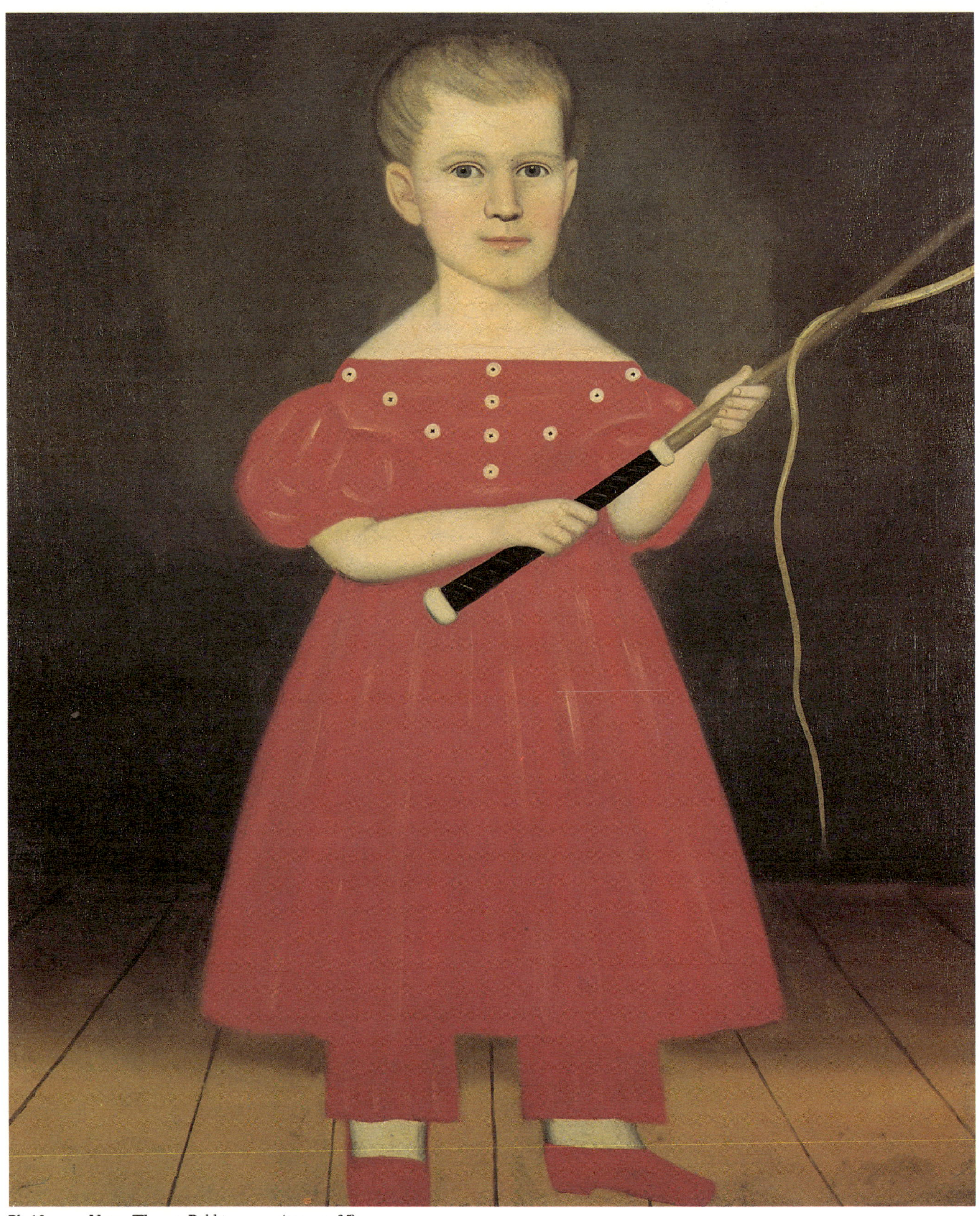

Pl. 10   *Henry Thomas Robbins*   (cat. no.35)

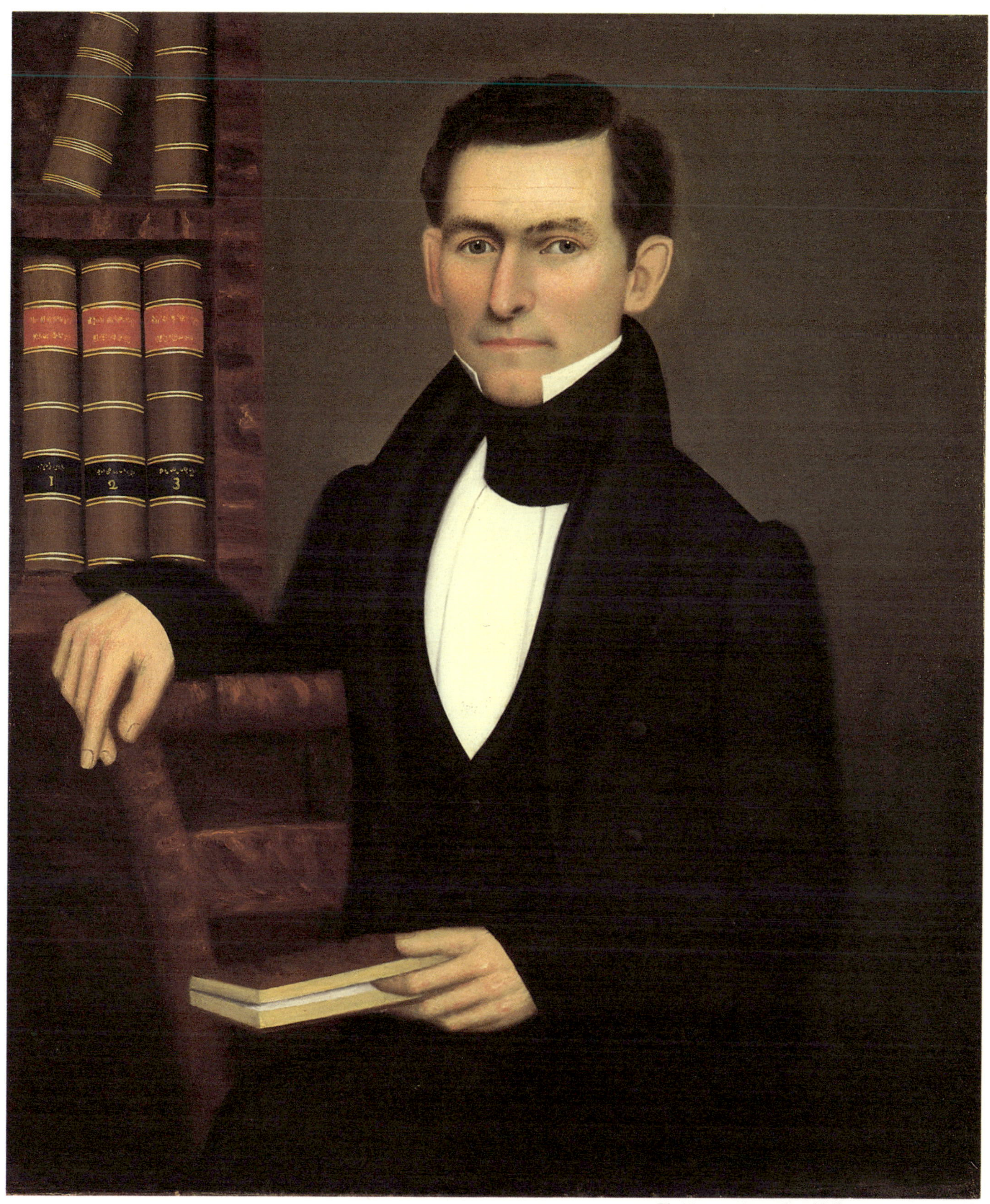

Pl. 11   *Amos Geer Hulbert*   (cat. no.38)

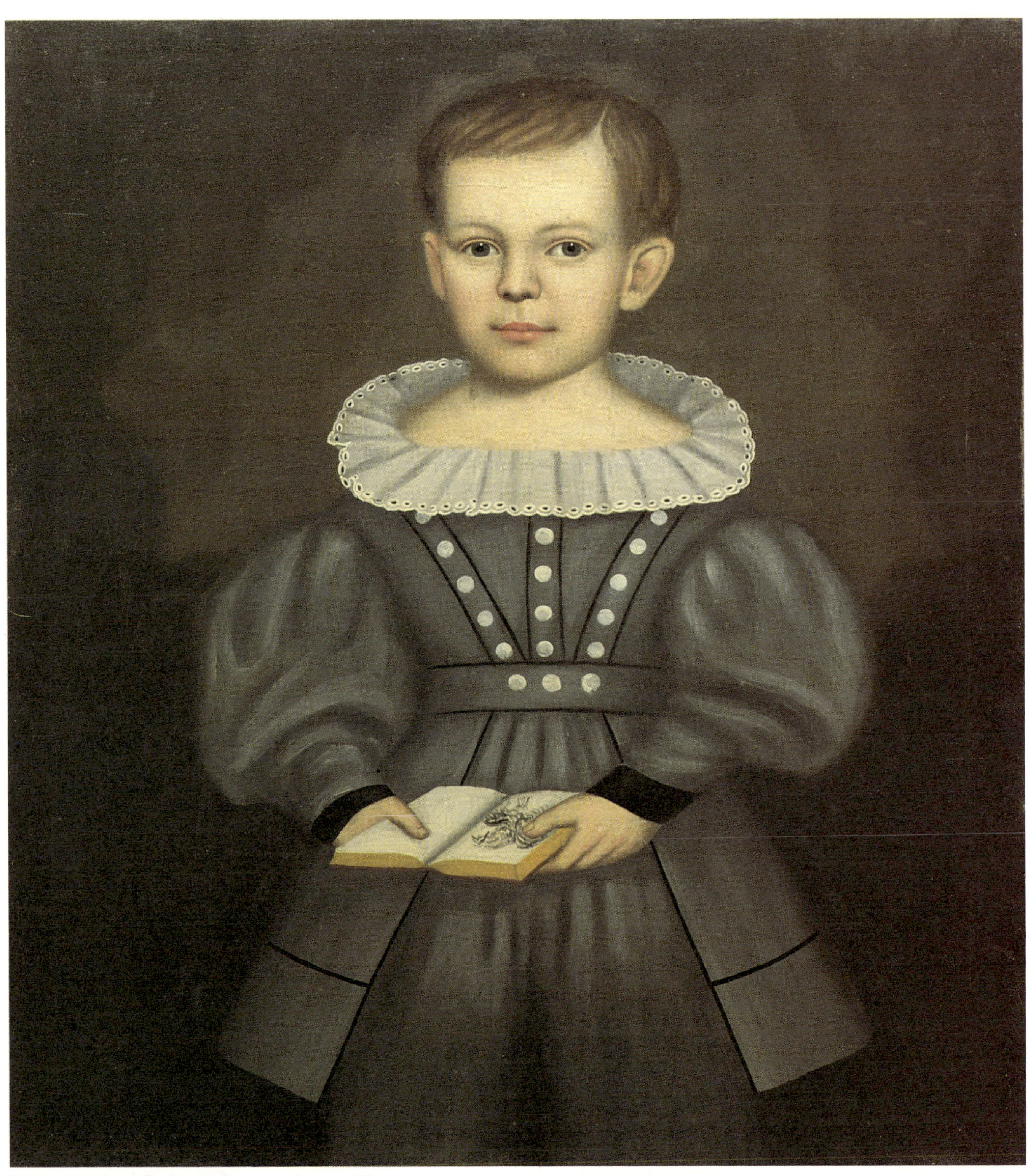

Pl. 12   *Henry Carlton Hulbert*   (cat. no.39)

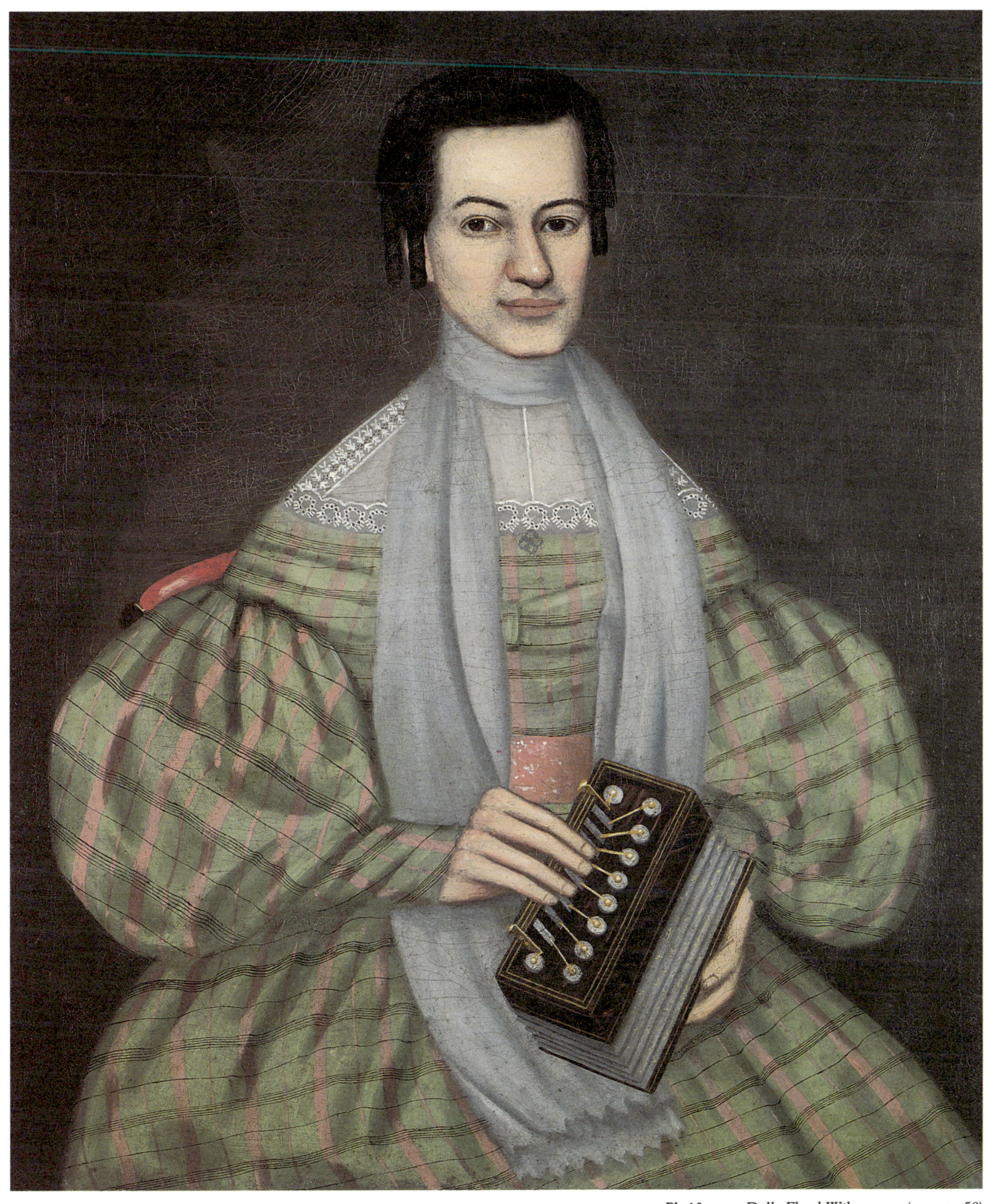

Pl. 13   *Dolly Floyd Wiley*   (cat. no.50)

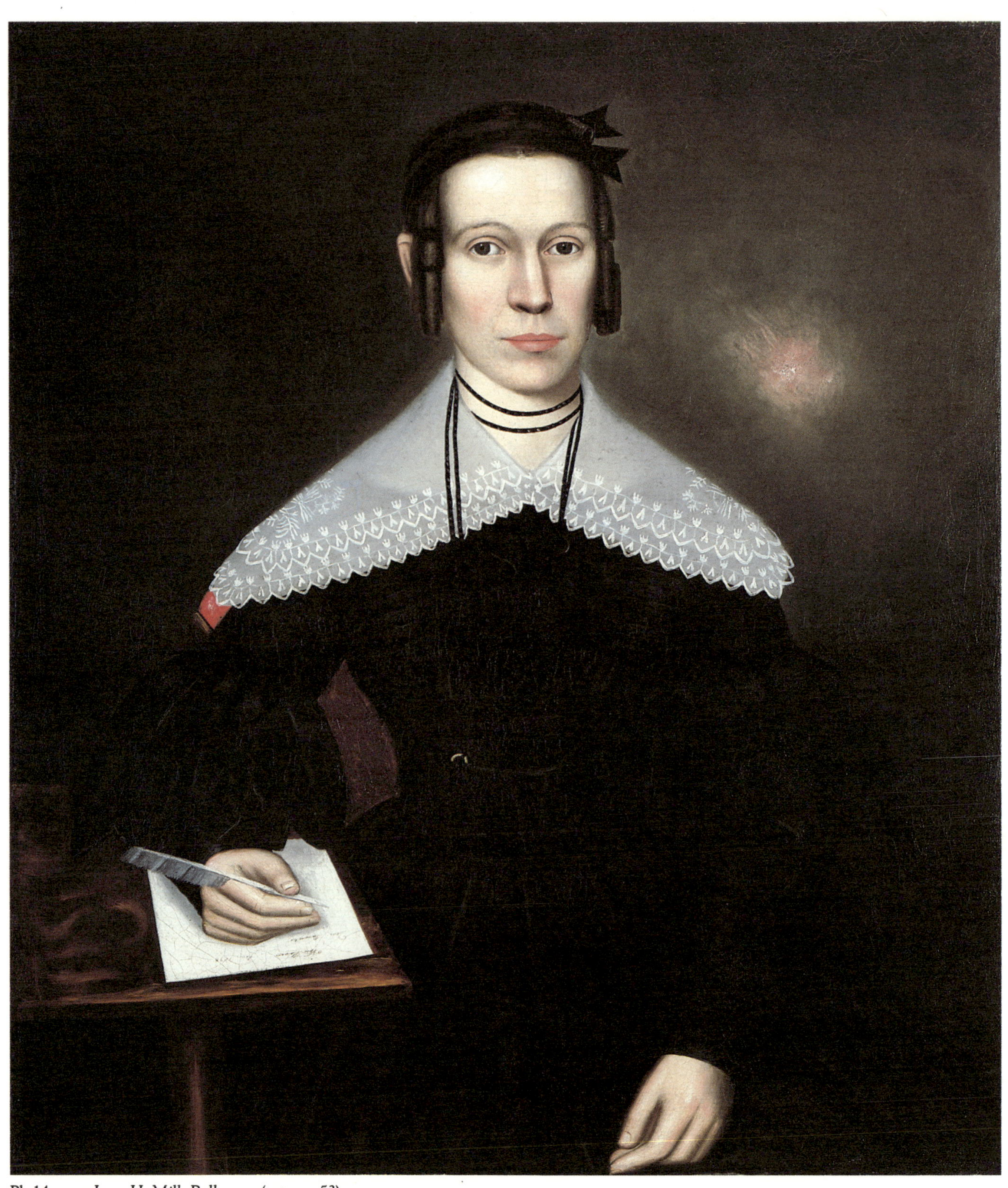

Pl. 14   *Lucy H. Mills Ball*   (cat. no.53)

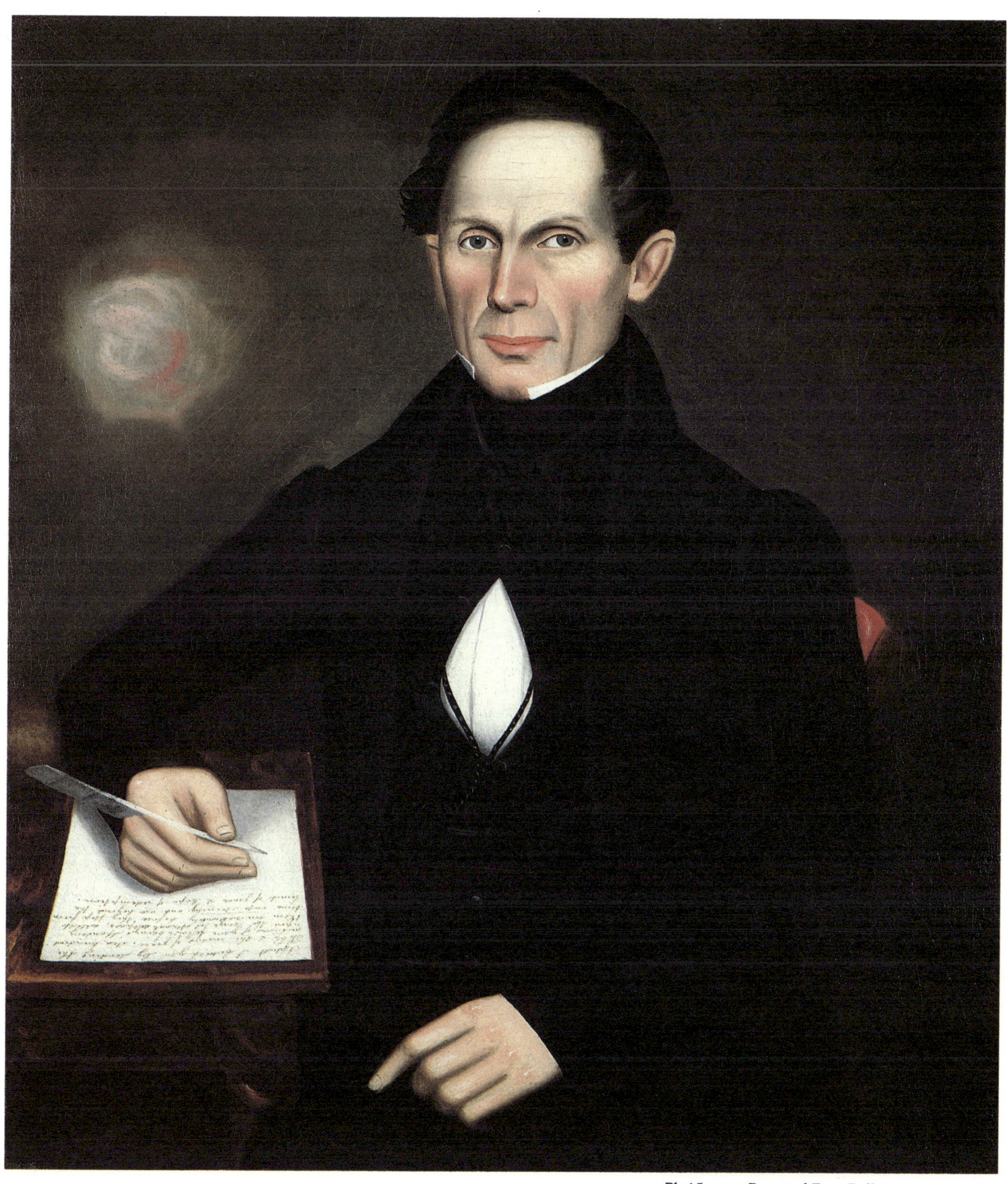 Pl. 15   *Reverend Dyer Ball*   (cat. no.52)

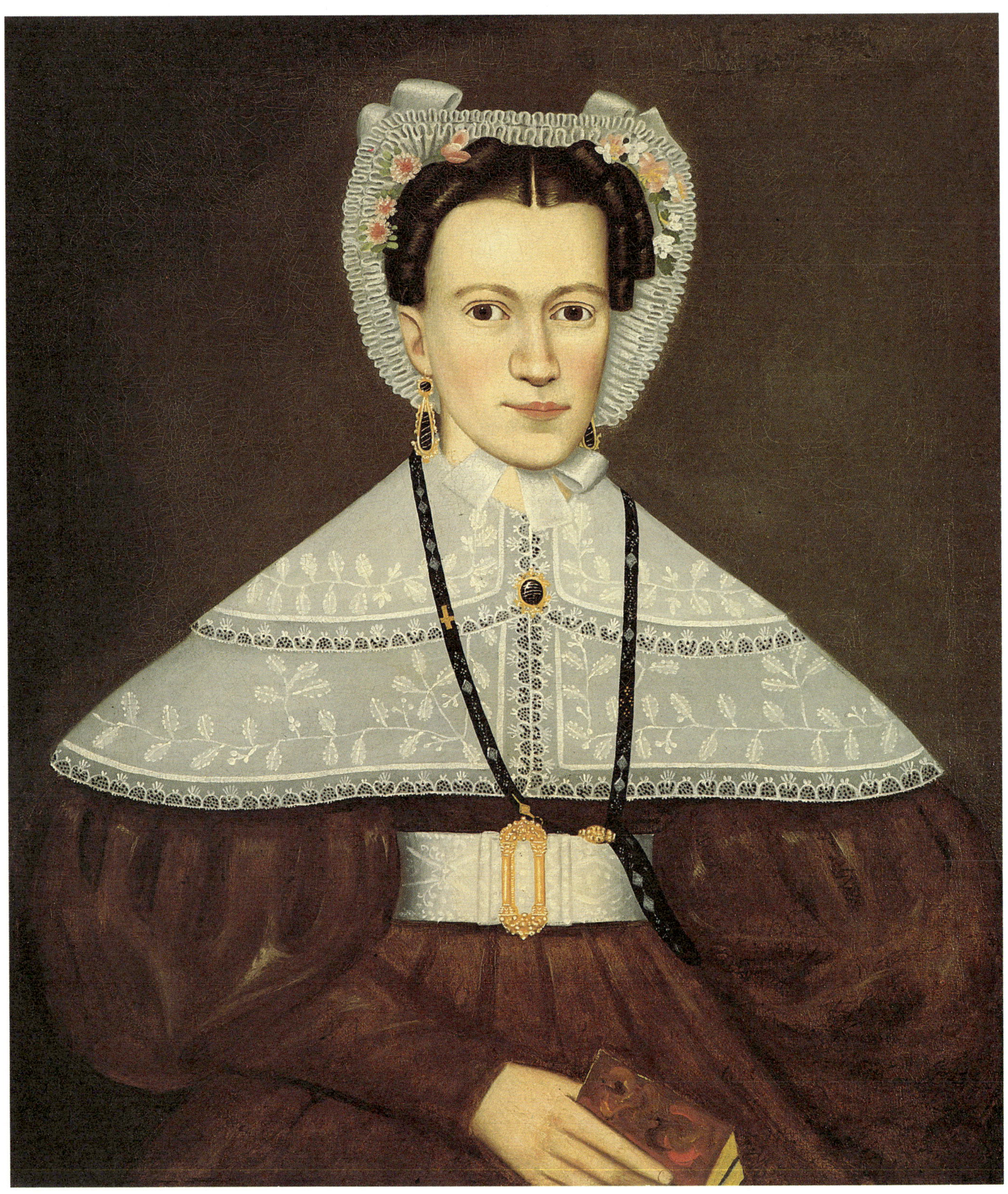

Pl. 16   *Mrs. Pearce*   (cat. no.58)

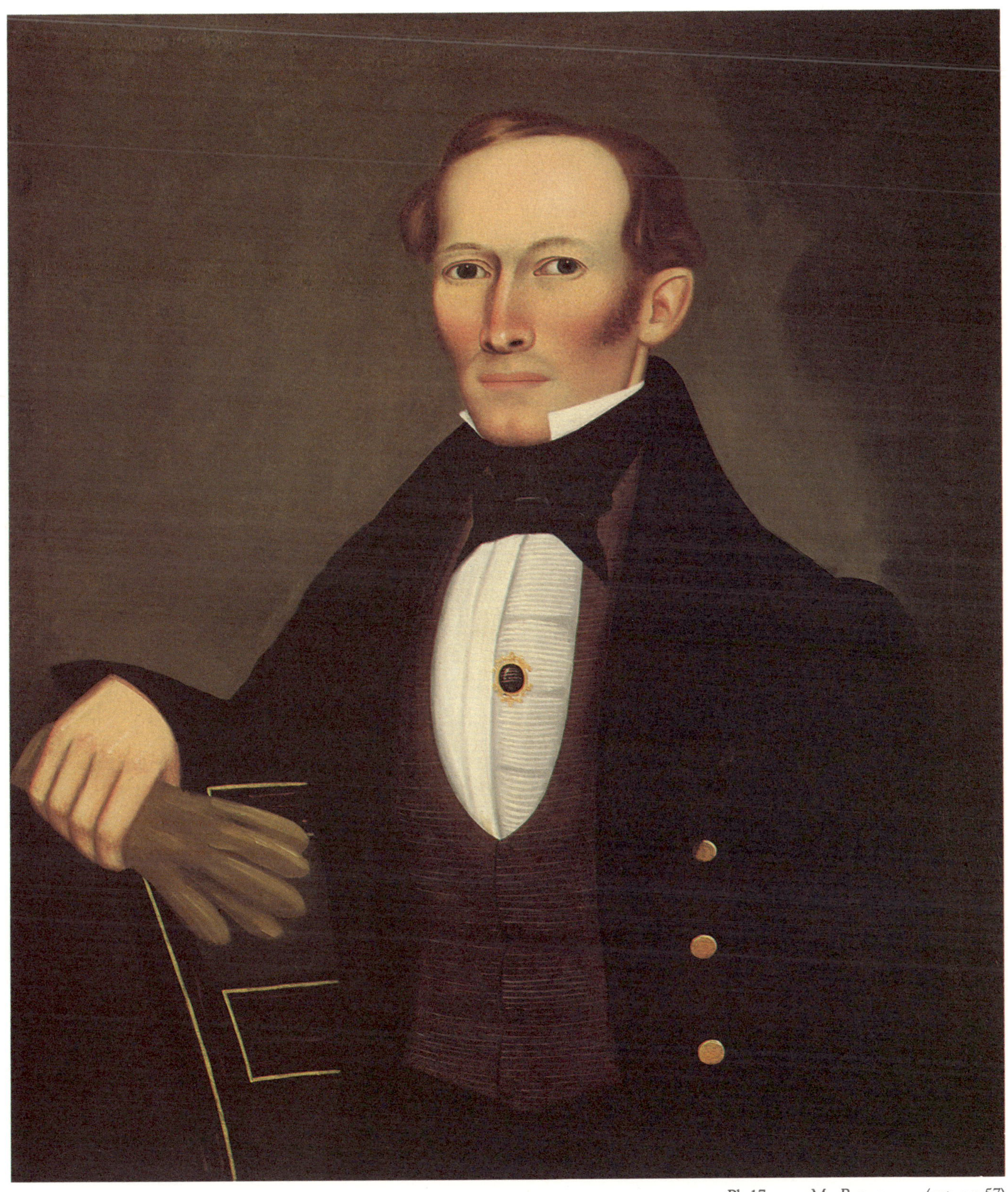

Pl. 17   *Mr. Pearce*   (cat. no.57)

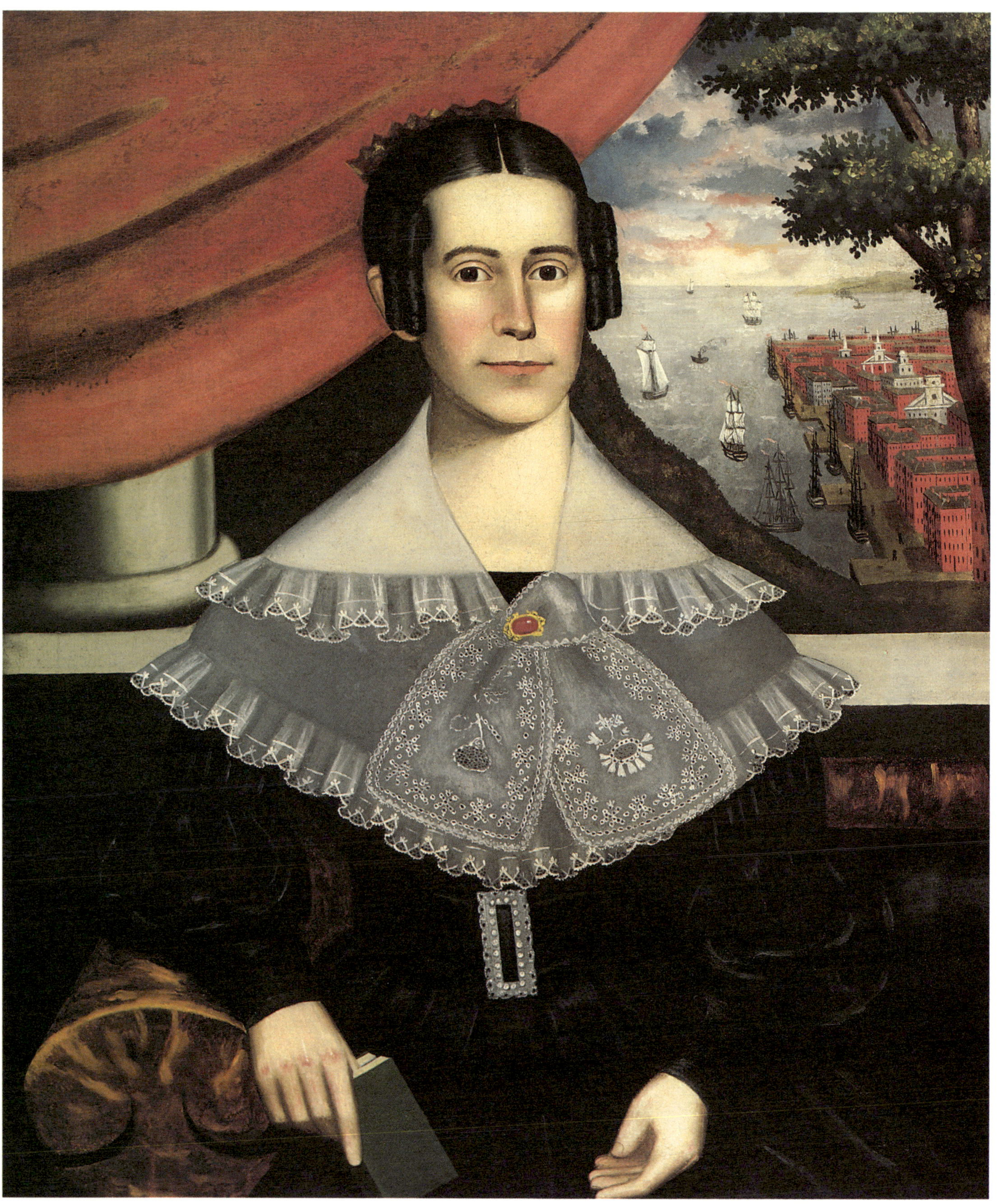

Pl. 18   *Louisa (Clarissa?) Gallond Cook*   (cat. no.63)

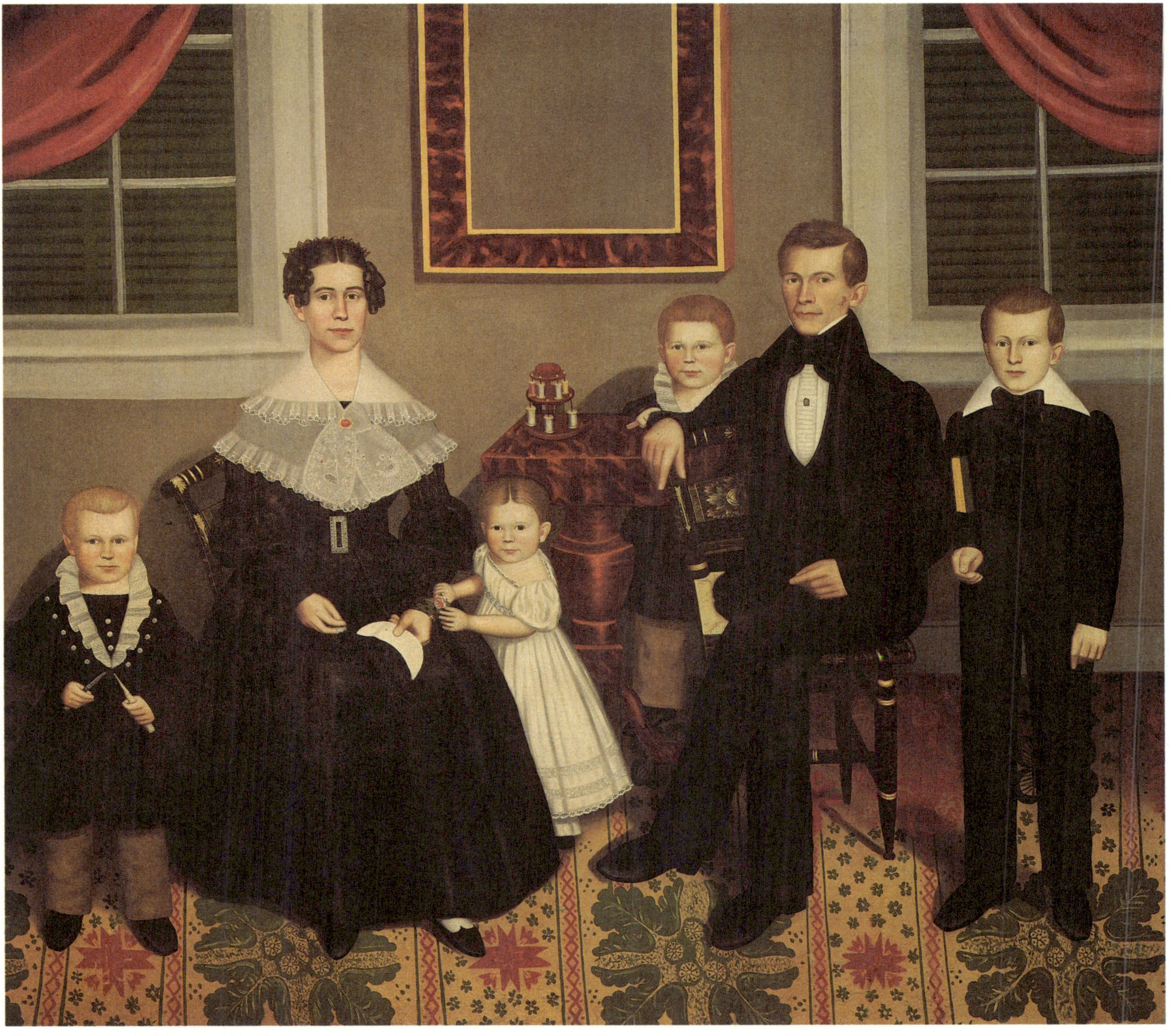

Pl. 19   *Joseph B. Moore and Family*   (cat. no.64)

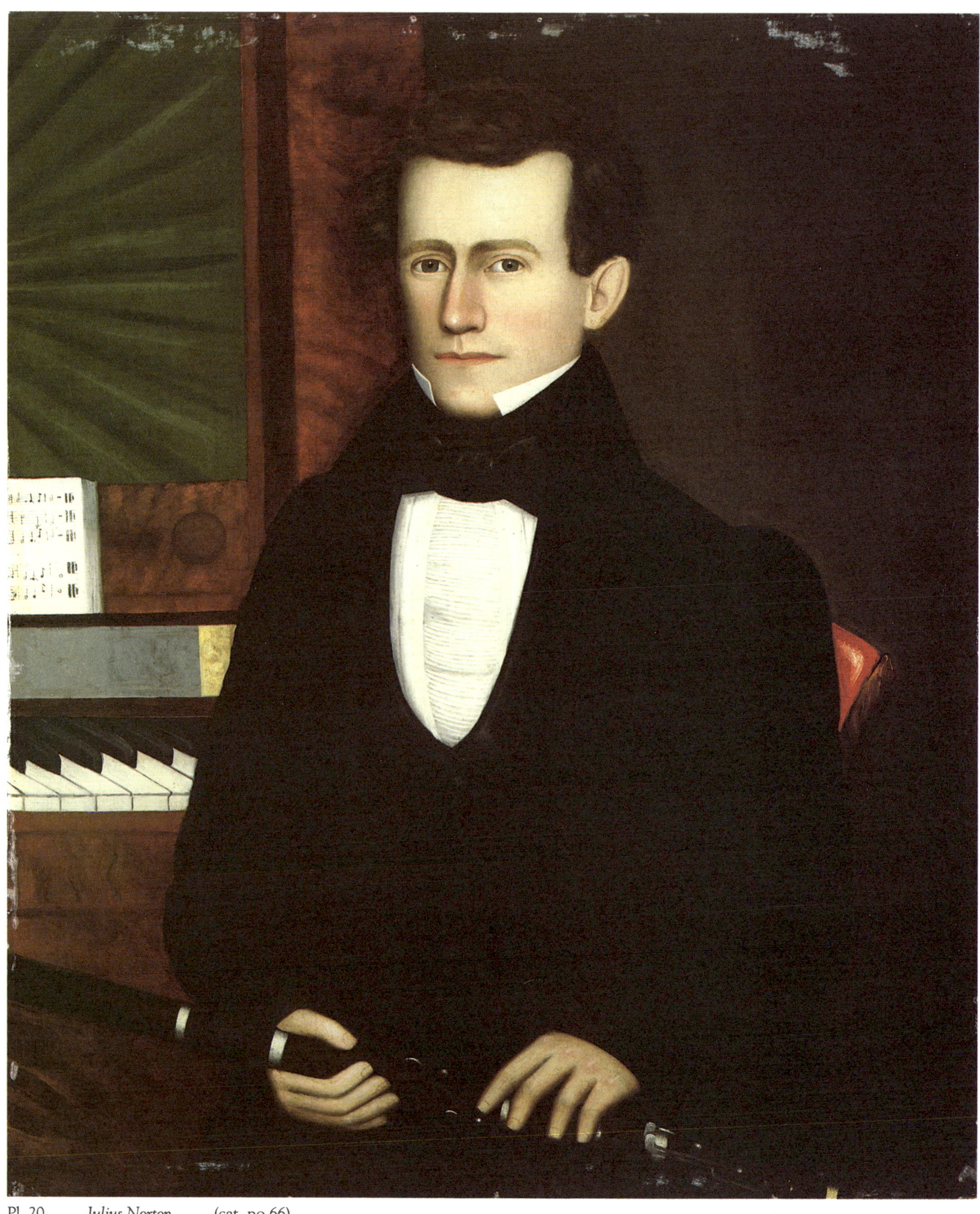

Pl. 20   *Julius Norton*   (cat. no.66)

Erastus Salisbury Field
1805 ∽ 1900

Erastus Salisbury Field was born in 1805, in Leverett, Massachusetts, a small agrarian community just north of Amherst. Leverett was isolated from centers of artistic activity so Field would not have seen major art exhibitions that might have inspired his ambitions to become an artist. However, nineteenth century New England was steeped in the crafts tradition, and Field's exposure to the wealth of decorative art produced by local artisans might have helped foster his early interest in painting. Apparently Field's parents encouraged his childhood experiments and supplied him with painting materials. His self-taught efforts must have brought him local success and the confidence to further his career through professional training.

In 1824, when he was nineteen years old, Field made the long trip to New York City and entered the studio of the famous artist and inventor Samuel F.B. Morse. Morse was a trained artist and painted some of the celebrated personalities of the early nineteenth century. The visit of General Lafayette to Morse's studio during Field's apprenticeship left an indelible impression on the young artist. Later in the century he depicted this event in a painting that chronicled the history of the United States. Field's stay in New York was brief. After three months Morse's wife died and Field returned to Leverett. Shortly after his return in 1825 he painted the portrait of his grandmother, Elizabeth Billings Ashley. This painting is Field's earliest known work and marks the beginning of his career as a portraitist.

The popularity of portraiture in England and America during the eighteenth century continued well into the nineteenth century. Many academic artists (those who had received extensive training in a formal setting) painted exclusively for the wealthy classes, while self-taught itinerant artists satisfied the demand for portraiture by rural middle class citizens. Traveling from town to town with their painting supplies, some of these artist-entrepreneurs made portrait painting a lucrative profession.

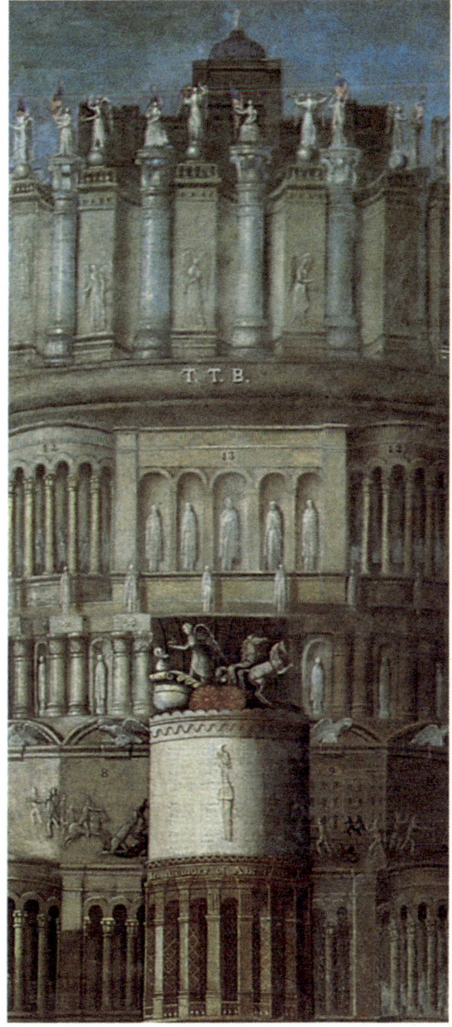

The Historical Monument of the American Republic, 1867 and 1888 (detail, tower 8) The Morgan Wesson Memorial Collection, Springfield Museum of Fine Arts

Itinerant artists usually worked quickly, using a minimum of brushwork to convey details of clothing and nuances of facial expression. Rapid workmanship and an adherence to certain compositional conventions resulted in stylistic similarities among portraits painted by different itinerant artists. The style is commonly referred to as folk portraiture.

The portrait of Elizabeth Billings Ashley demonstrates many of the stylistic characteristics of folk portraiture. Field depicted his subject in an ambiguous space defined as neutral grey background that darkens toward the edges of the canvas. He carefully outlined her facial features and dress and filled them in with color. The folds in her scarf and the creases in her dress are modeled to create the appearance of depth, yet their harsh outlines form distinct patterns. The shallow space behind the figure and the limited use of shading make the portrait appear flat, a feature commonly found in folk portraiture.

Field's brief apprenticeship with Morse helped him polish his rudimentary skills of representation, but he never attained a thorough knowledge of anatomy. The figure of his grandmother seems stiff and the folds of her clothing do not fall naturally to reveal the structure of her body. Field may have chosen the format of a small bust portrait to avoid painting her hands, a difficult problem for him throughout his career.

Field's strengths as an artist are demonstrated in the expressive representation of his grandmother's facial features. Emphasizing her large, deep set eyes, Field created a compelling image of an older woman. The focus on her eyes gives the portrait a spiritual intensity, which is enhanced by the shaded grey background. The muted tones of the painting are offset by the red upholstered chair, which became a standard prop in Field's portraits. The symmetrical composition, with its linear patterns and minimal but effective use of color, reveals a decorative sense of design that Field was to refine and develop in his later portraits.

In the years from 1825 to 1840 Field was steadily employed as a portrait painter. During this period his representational skills improved and he was able to paint rapidly, often completing a large portrait within a day. His prices varied, but in 1837 he usually charged $4.00 for a large portrait of an adult and $1.50 for smaller ones of children. Although these were substantial sums of money by nineteenth century standards, a comparison of Field's prices with those of academic artist Thomas Sully suggests that formal training elevated the status of an artist. In 1837 Sully received $300 for a portrait of an adult similar in size to those customarily painted by Field. The same year Sully charged $300 for portraits of children.

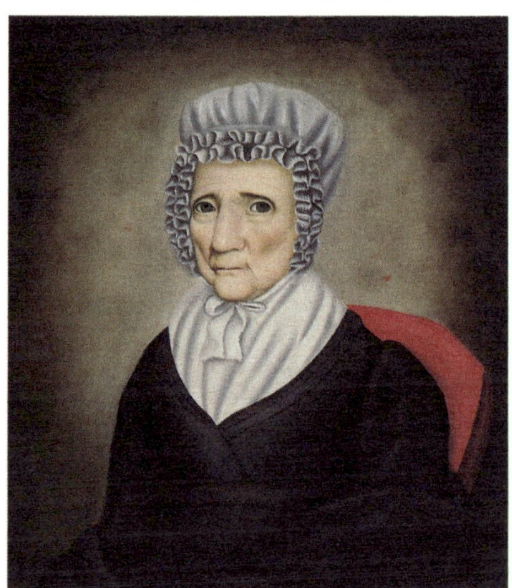

Elizabeth Billings Ashley c. 1825
The Morgan Wesson Memorial Collection,
Springfield Museum of Fine Arts

In 1831 Field married Phebe Gilmur of Ware, Massachusetts. It was unusual for inhabitants of small rural towns like Leverett to marry into families outside their immediate community, but Field's vocation as a traveling artist might have freed him from the restrictions of local custom. In 1832 Field's only child Henrietta was born in Monson, Massachusetts.

In the next years, Field, like many other itinerant artists, left home to go out on painting expeditions. Many of Field's family members and friends had settled in different parts of New England, creating a network of patrons for his practice as a portraitist. Field's family connections contributed to the financial success that enabled him to buy property in Three Rivers, Massachusetts, in 1833.

The portraits Field painted in the years 1836 to 1840 are considered to be his best work, as the companion portraits of the Reverend Dyer Ball and his wife Lucy Mills Ball demonstrate. The Ball portraits show some similarity in composition to the painting of Elizabeth Billings Ashley. Each figure is set squarely in the center of the canvas and is slightly turned, so that a corner of a red upholstered chair can be seen. The three-quarter format of the Ball portraits indicates that he had overcome some problems in representing the figure, although his incomplete knowledge of anatomy still hampered his ability to portray his subjects naturalistically.

The Balls were a recently married couple about to embark as missionaries on a voyage to China. It has been sug-

gested that the swirls of reddish light that appear in the characteristic neutral grey background symbolize spiritual power. Whether or not that is true, it is clear that Field wanted to convey the importance of his subject's vocation. Without the restraints dictated by academic training, Field, like other folk artists, could manipulate spatial relationships or the representation of objects to convey a message. The table upon which the Reverend rests his arm is tilted toward the viewer at a higher angle than the table in the companion portrait of his wife so that the script of his message can be read:

> Assist, I beseech you, by sending the Bible and the means of Grace, six hundred millions of your fellow beings standing on the verge of eternal despair, assist them immediately before they step from time into eternity and far beyond the limits of Grace and the hope of redemption.

Field's depiction of the Reverend's ascetic features conveys the character of a man imbued with religious purpose. His portrait of Lucy Ball is less dramatic; even the reddish ball of light behind her seems muted and indistinct, and the letter on her table is inscribed simply with the salutation "Dear Parents." Field clearly wanted to emphasize the individuality of each sitter. His ability to convey character in the portraits of this period was paralleled by his skill at representing their material finery. The lace collar of Lucy Ball's dress is expertly rendered with economical strokes of white paint over a solid background, and the folds of her dress are modeled with fluid brushwork. Field had developed a technique of simulating mahogany veneer with deft brushstrokes, evidenced by the tables in the portraits.

In the thirteen years that had elapsed between Field's portrait of Elizabeth Billings Ashley and the Ball portraits, Field had perfected his expressive style and rapid method of workmanship. It is not known what prompted him to return to New York City at this point in his career. Perhaps, feeling that he had achieved some skill as a portraitist and tired of continual travel, he decided to settle in a large urban center to practice his profession.

While Field was living in New York, he could have been exposed to artistic developments that prompted his exploration of subject matter. In the years since Field had first been in New York, landscape and genre painting had replaced portraiture in popularity. Early in the century, history painting was advocated by academically trained artists like Field's former teacher Samuel Morse as the highest form of artistic expression. Again, in the 1840's, history paintings with religious, mythological, or literary themes were being widely exhibited as art academies.

After he arrived in New York, Field listed himself in the 1841 city directory as a portrait painter, but in the 1842-43 directory he listed himself as an artist, a significant change of title that perhaps reflected these new influences.

The changing tastes in art were also affected by the technical innovation of photography. In 1839, daguerreotypy, a photographic process utilizing a silver-coated plate, was introduced to America from Europe. In a short period of time, daguerreotype studios specializing in portraiture had opened up all over the country and were phenomenally suc-

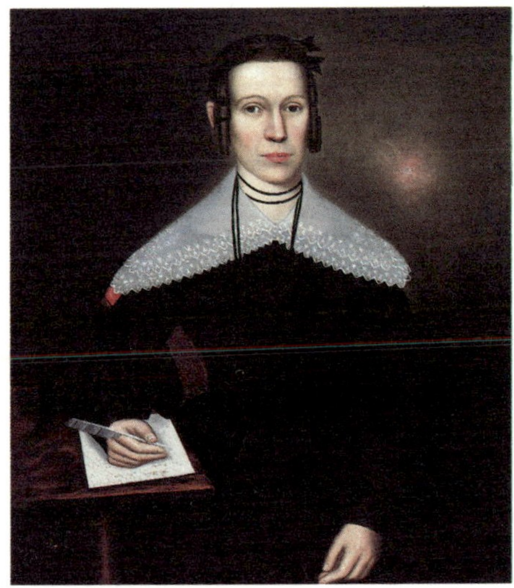

Lucy H. Mills Ball

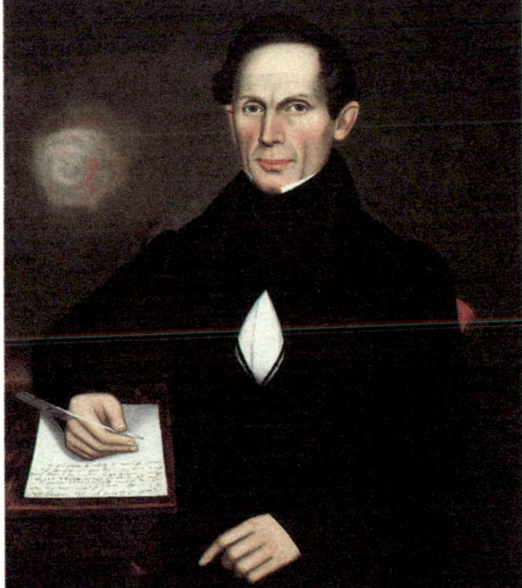

The Reverend Dyer Ball 1838

The Morgan Wesson Memorial Collection, Springfield Museum of Fine Arts

Erastus Salisbury

Museum of Fine Arts, Springfield, Massachusetts; National Portrait Ga
Museum of American Folk Art and The Metropolitan Museum of Art,

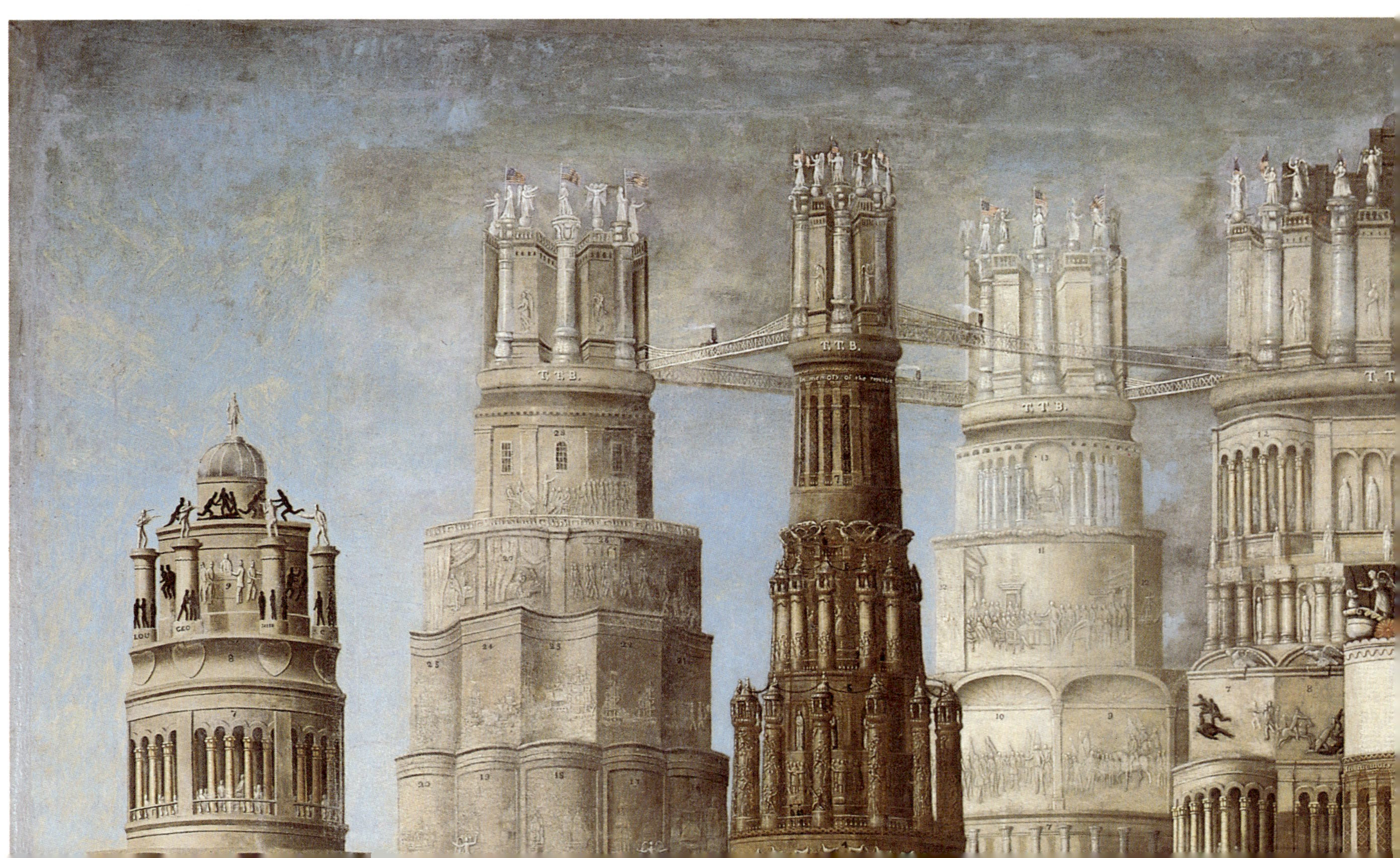

Field: 1805~1900

llery and National Museum of American Art, Washington, D.C.;
New York City; Marion Koogler McNay Art Institute, San Antonio, Texas

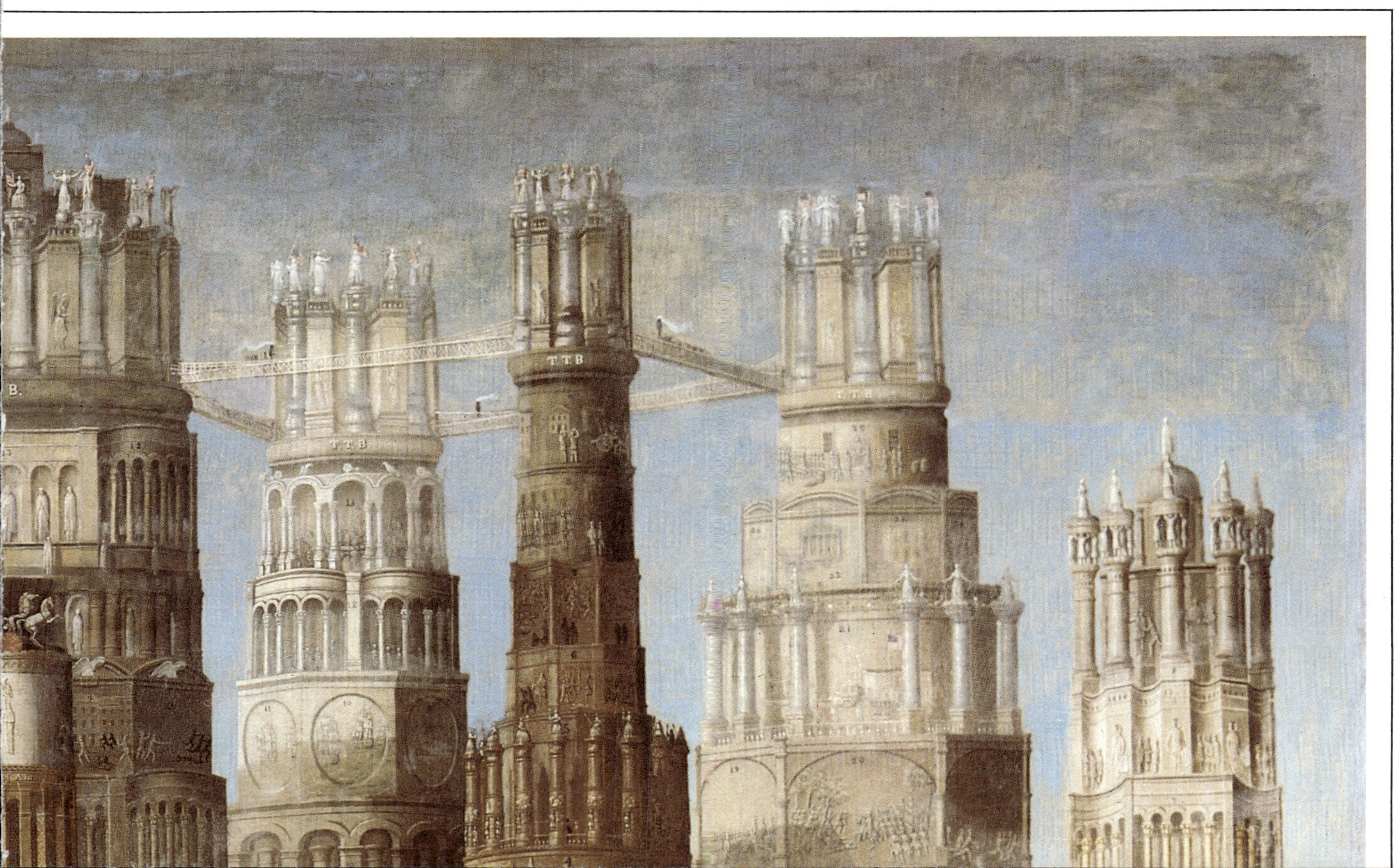

Robin de Campi
SPRUCEHAVEN FARM
Chester Heights, PA 19017
April 19, 1999

Dear Mr. Tillou,

I've seen your name a number of times in connection with your knowledge of Erastus Salisbury Field's paintings. I trust I am not imposing on your profession and am thus perfectly willing to reimburse you for your expertise.

Enclosed is a photo of a painting I bought about one year ago in North Brookfield, Massachusetts. It is unsigned (I'd removed the frame to look for a signature) and the canvas measures 40" wide x 28 3/4" tall. The stretcher wood is 4" top & bottom and 3" both sides, mortised and an old dark brown stain. The canvas that's wrapped around the stretcher may be painted but not intended for a self-border, I'd judge. The frame is slightly large all around for the canvas and doesn't look original to or comtemporary with the painting.

I took it to a reputable restorer I use on the Main Line, but they prefer not to deal with primitives. The painting obviously needs cleaning and has a difficult area around the sails that shows (what I'd call) crazing, as well as in the shadows on the lower left, and would need a goodly amount of inpainting, the restorer advised.

I have Mary Black's book on Field and the brochure put out by the Springfield Museum. There appear to be some aspects similar to Field's other landscape phantasies (touches of red highlights, treatment of trees, small figures). But it may be Continental, perhaps Italian? I am no authority.

If you can't tell much without actually seeing it and if you have interest in seeing it, we frequently drive to New Hampshire (where we're building a house) and could arrange to stop by in Litchfield at a mutually convenient time. I have enclosed a stamped, self-addressed envelope.

I'm appreciative of your attention.

Robin de Campi

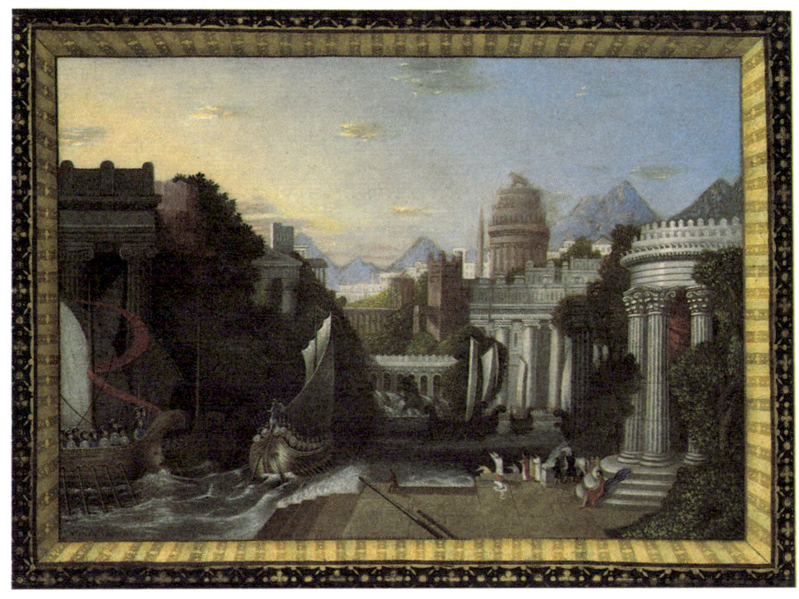

The Embarkation of Ulysses
c. 1844
The Morgan Wesson Memorial Collection, Springfield Museum of Fine Arts

cessful. Daguerreotypes were inexpensive in comparison to painted portraits, resulting in a drastic drop in the demand for work by itinerant portraitists. Many portraitists opened up daguerreotype studios to compensate for their lack of work, while more established artists used photographs as models for their paintings. Field did little portrait painting in the latter part of his career, but when he did, he painted from photographs. The portraits Field painted from photographs lack the expressive characterizations and decorative power of his early work.

Whether or not Field was influenced by the work of other artists living in New York City, or had lost commissions for portrait painting because of the growing popularity of daguerreotypes, he nevertheless started painting subject pieces while he was living in New York in the 1840's. His first known subject piece, *The Embarkation of Ulysses*, was based on a print by J.W. Appleton entitled *A City in Ancient Greece*. In the nineteenth century copying the work of other artists was a common and not dishonorable practice. Although the scene is taken from a print, the color scheme was Field's creation and clearly demonstrates the decorative sense of design that characterized his work as a folk portraitist.

The painting shows a careful patterning of light and shade. The group of buildings in the background contrasts with the terracotta buildings in the middle ground. In the foreground, the buildings are composed of tones of grey and white. Field characteristically included some red highlights in the composition, which can be seen in the banner of the ship on the left, the draperies of the figures on the landing, and between the columns of the building on the right. Close examination reveals that Field did not use an actual picture frame for the painting, but instead painted the edge of the canvas to simulate one.

Field's subject paintings in the late nineteenth century exhibit his preoccupation with religious and patriotic themes. The composite portrait of *Lincoln with Washington and his Generals* shows from left to right: James Birdseye McPherson, Abraham Lincoln, George Washington, Ulysses S. Grant, George C. Meade, and Ambrose Burnside. Field's purpose in painting the portrait was to express his philosophical beliefs about abolition. His grouping of Lincoln with Washington as the father of our country shows the artist's support of Lincoln in the Civil War.

The painting demonstrates many of the characteristics associated with Field's work. The figures seem stiff and oddly proportioned and the perspective is distorted. The floor is tilted toward the viewer, giving the figures the appearance of hovering in an ambiguous space. Field included the familiar red upholstered chair in the interior. He might have used photographs as models to paint the faces of Lincoln and his generals.

Field's interest in religious and political themes during the latter part of his career is reflected in his painting *The Historical Monument of the American Republic*. Painted in the same style, the *Monument* exhibits the symmetrical composition, linear patterning and interest in decorative design that characterized his work as a portraitist and painter of subject pieces.

Field started painting his grandiose history of the United States in the final years of the Civil War. The painting represents a huge structure with ten towers connected at the top by steel bridges supporting steam engines. On the ten towers Field visually narrated, in painted imitation of raised carving, the history of the Republic from the early days of its settlement to post Civil War. He selected incidents that reflected his own moral and philosophical beliefs, which he imparted to viewers through a detailed guide entitled *Descriptive Catalogue of the Historical Monument of the American Republic*, published in 1876. When the painting was first completed in 1867, it showed eight towers. Before the publication of the guide in 1876 Field added details, and in 1888 he added two end towers, left and right, and made other minor changes.

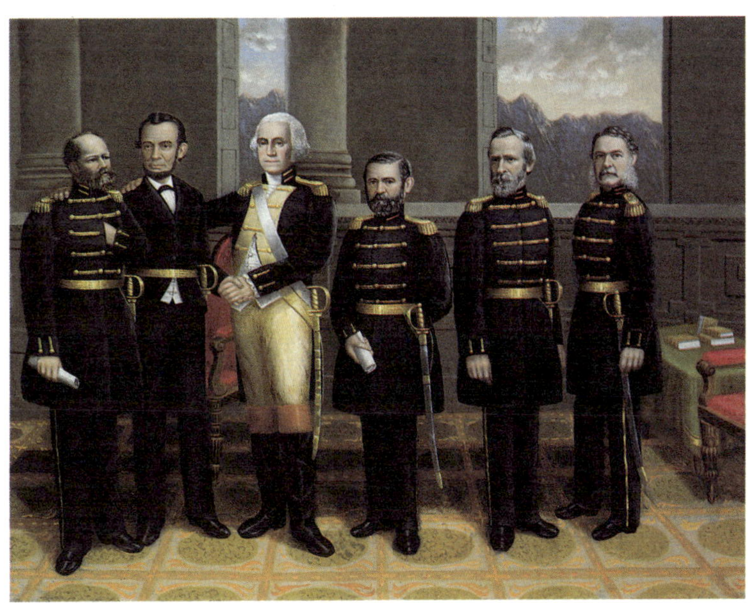

Lincoln with Washington and his Generals 1881
The Morgan Wesson Memorial Collection, Springfield Museum of Fine Arts

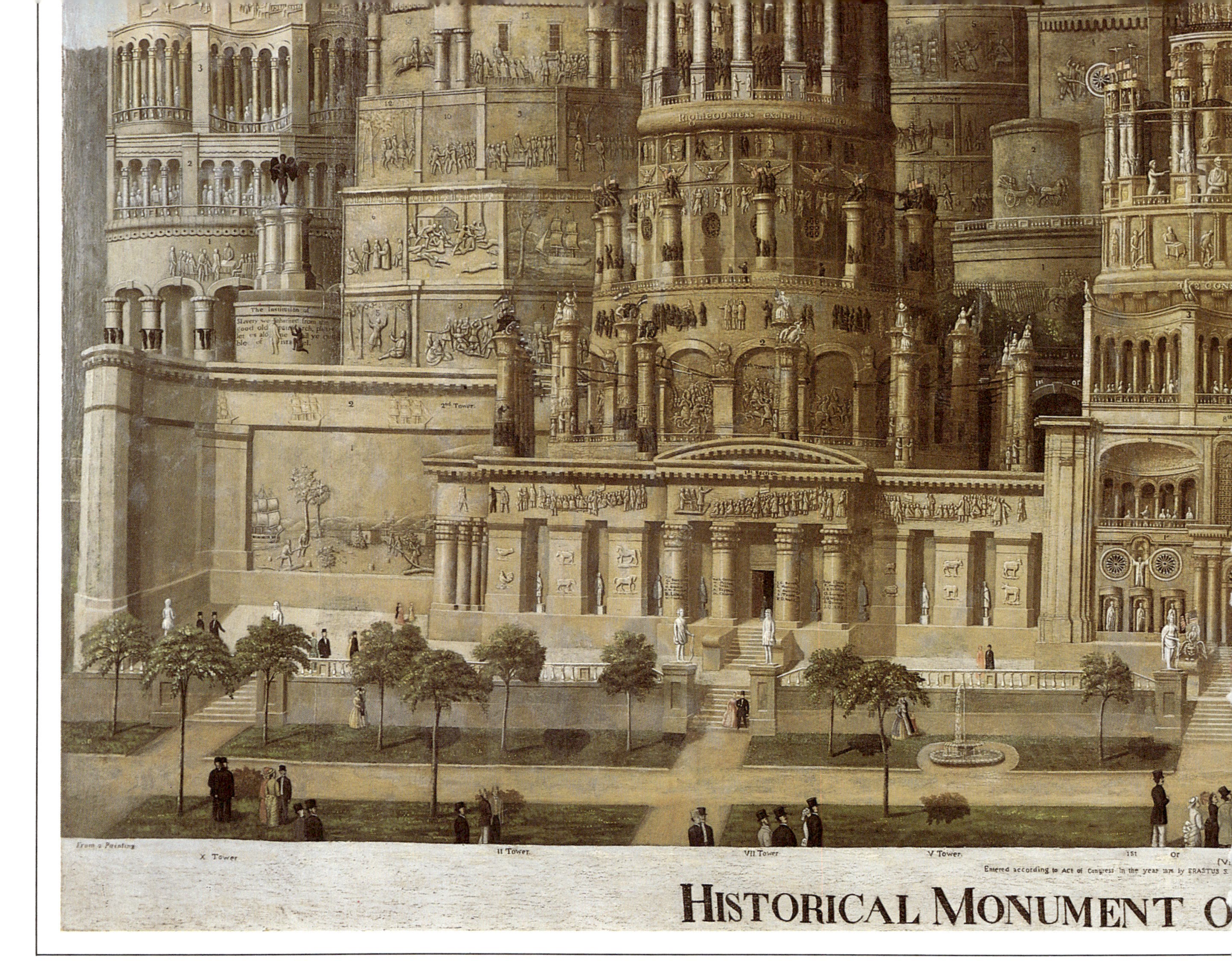

Erastus Salisbury Fie[ld]
Historical Monument of the A[merican Republic]
oil on canva[s]
The Morgan Wesson Me[morial Collection]
Museum of Fine Arts, Sp[ringfield]

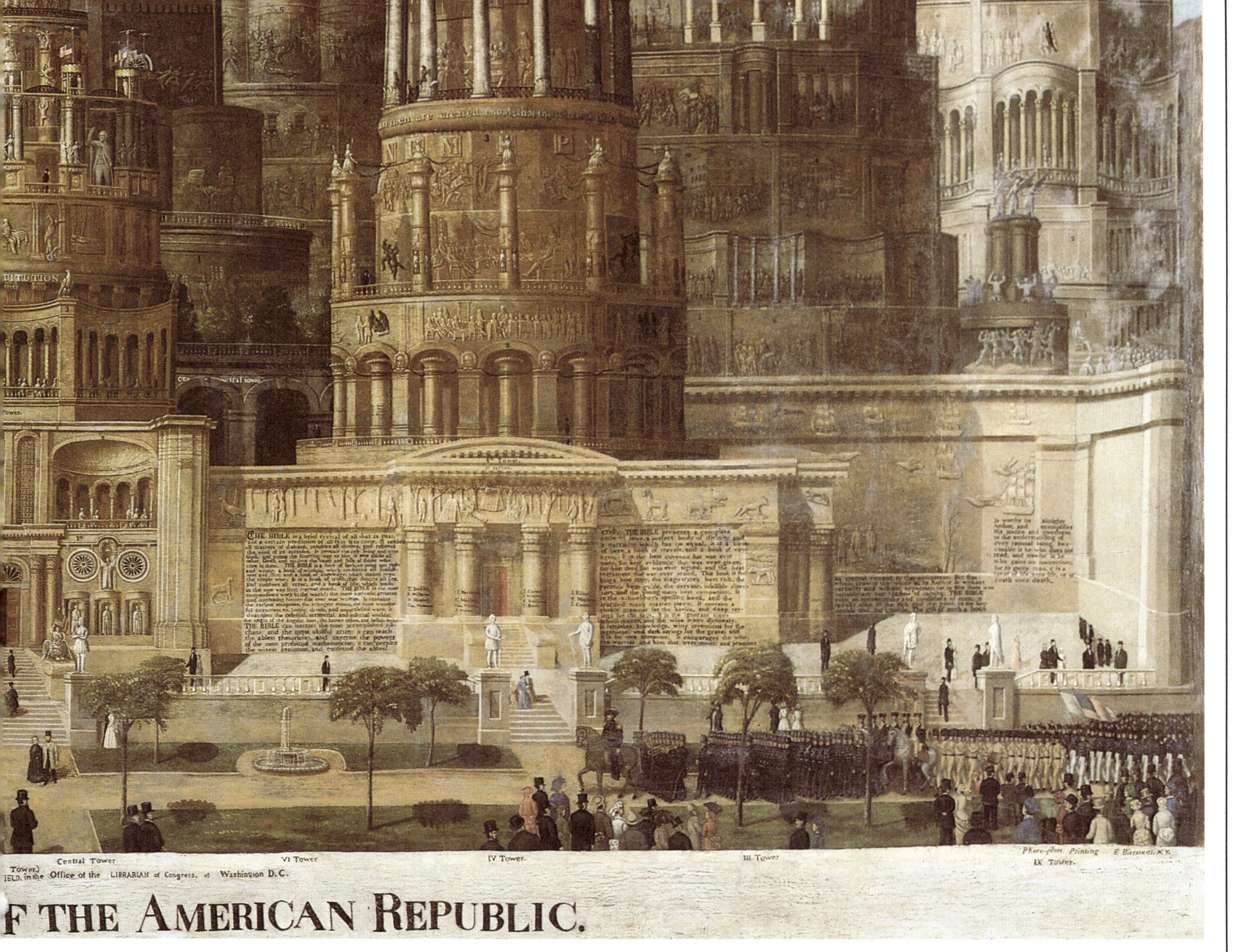

d, American, 1805-1900
merican Republic 1867 and 1888
s, 9'3"x13'1"
norial Collection (60.16)
ringfield, Massachusetts

When Field completed his first version of the *Monument,* a notice appeared in a local newspaper that described the work and announced the artist's intention to have it publicly displayed around the country, accompanied by a lecture. It was common for artists to exhibit large scale history paintings with an explanation of their meaning. Samuel Morse was among the first to initiate this practice in America; and many artists found they could collect substantial revenues if their paintings were well received by the public. The immense size of the canvas, Field's symbolic use of classical architecture, and his written guide link the *Monument* to a long tradition of history painting.

In the same year the *Descriptive Catalogue* was published, Field had the *Monument* painting photoengraved in New York City by Edward Bierstadt. A passage from the opening comments of his *Descriptive Catalogue* suggests Field intended that the Monument be built. Had it been built, it would have been an enormous structure, with towers both circular and polygonal rising 500 feet in the air, a height that would dwarf the Washington Monument. In the painting, Field situated the *Monument* in a pleasant park, where sightseers stroll around the gigantic structure. On the main towers at the level of the train trestles, the initials T.T.B. can be seen. In his guide, Field explained that these initials stand for The True Base. An inscription about the Bible is written on the foundation of the towers, perhaps indicating that he felt that religious principles were the basis for the founding of the country.

The main theme of the painting is the conflict between the northern and southern states that culminated in the Civil War. The first and eighth towers represent the war and its aftermath. The towers on the left represent the southern states and the towers on the right show events from the history of the northern states. A cluster of columns rising from the base of the second tower is topped by a figure of Satan, indicating Field's attitude toward slavery. At the right on the base of the third tower a cluster of columns is surmounted by angels. Apparently, Field saw the events as a battle between good and evil, with God on the side of the northern states. The long inscription about the Bible as

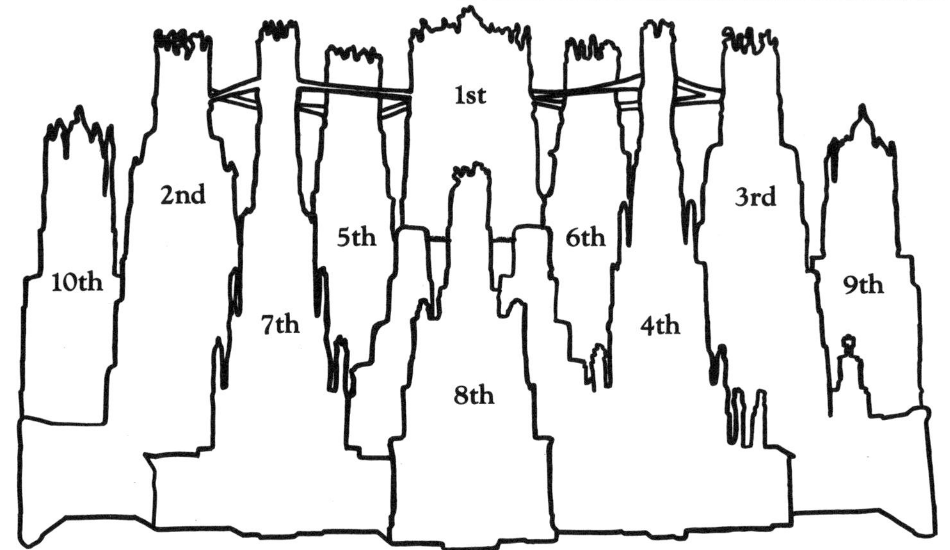

1st Tower
The first tower represents the events which occurred after the assassination of Lincoln and during the beleaguered presidency of Andrew Johnson. At the top Field painted a scene of the Centennial celebration.

2nd Tower
The lower scenes chronicle events beginning with the founding of Jamestown, Virginia, in 1607 and ending with Bacon's Rebellion in 1675. Upper levels show scenes from the French and Indian wars and the War of 1812. Scenes of the fiftieth anniversary of the nation's independence and deaths of Presidents Adams and Jefferson in 1826 are surmounted by a depiction of Andrew Johnson making his 1833 proclamation against nullification.

3rd Tower
The base of the tower represents the landing of the Pilgrims in 1610 and is followed by scenes from the earliest days of the northern colonies. Events from pre-revolutionary Boston depicted on the middle of the tower include the Boston Massacre of 1770 and the Boston Tea Party of 1773. Scenes of the inauguration of George Washington and the Whiskey Insurrection of 1794 are followed by the representation of the arrival of General Lafayette to Castle Garden, New York, in 1824. Higher up on the tower is a scene representing Samuel Morse inventing the telegraph. The figures of George Washington and Ulysses S. Grant appear on the top of this tower.

4th Tower
The fourth tower is devoted to the freedom of the American people. Scenes showing the Continental Congress of 1774, the Declaration of Independence of 1776, and the convention that wrote the Con-

stitution in 1787 are followed by scenes from the Florida and Mexican wars. Scenes on the top of the tower illustrate the political conflict over the status of Kansas as a slave or non-slave state.

5th Tower
The lower scenes show early settlements of the southern colonies in Maryland, North Carolina, South Carolina, and Georgia. Scenes from the French and Indian wars are followed by the surrender of Cornwallis at Yorktown. The depiction of Robert Fulton's steamboat is surmounted by a scene showing Daniel Webster delivering his famous speech to the Senate in 1830.

6th Tower
The first scenes show the settlement of New York in 1610 and William Penn's Treaty with the Indians in 1682-84. Upper levels show scenes that illustrate the Stamp Act and incidents from the War of 1812. The top of the tower shows a scene representing the signing of the Fugitive Slave Law.

7th Tower
The scenes represent events that preceded and occurred during the Civil War.

8th Tower
The eighth tower celebrates the actions of Lincoln during the Civil War. On the base of the tower Lincoln can be seen turning the wheels of government. On a higher level a scene of Lincoln's assassination is topped by an illustration of Lincoln ascending to heaven in a fiery chariot.

9th and 10th Towers
The key for these two towers, which were added in 1888, has never been located.

a source of truth and righteousness appears on the base of the columns representing the north. The work reflects the artist's belief that the optimism of the early days of the Republic, despite the disillusionment of the Civil War, could be renewed if faith in religion was restored.

The *Monument* is a product of Field's evolution as an artist. In his career as a portraitist, he perfected a method for quickly producing stylized, colorful compositions, characteristic of folk painting. The decline in the demand for portraiture and Field's exposure to history painting while he was living in New York City might have increased his interest in painting religious and historical subject matter. A logical successor to this development, *The Historical Monument of the American Republic* is a religious allegory of the political and ideological conflicts that resulted in the Civil War. A complex interplay of history and folk painting, the *Monument* is a summary of the influences that shaped his career.

A publication of the Education Department, Museum of Fine Arts, Springfield, Massachusetts

Text - Kay Nichols
Design - Deborah Hewitt
Photography - David Stansbury

This brochure is supported by a grant from the National Endowment for the Arts.

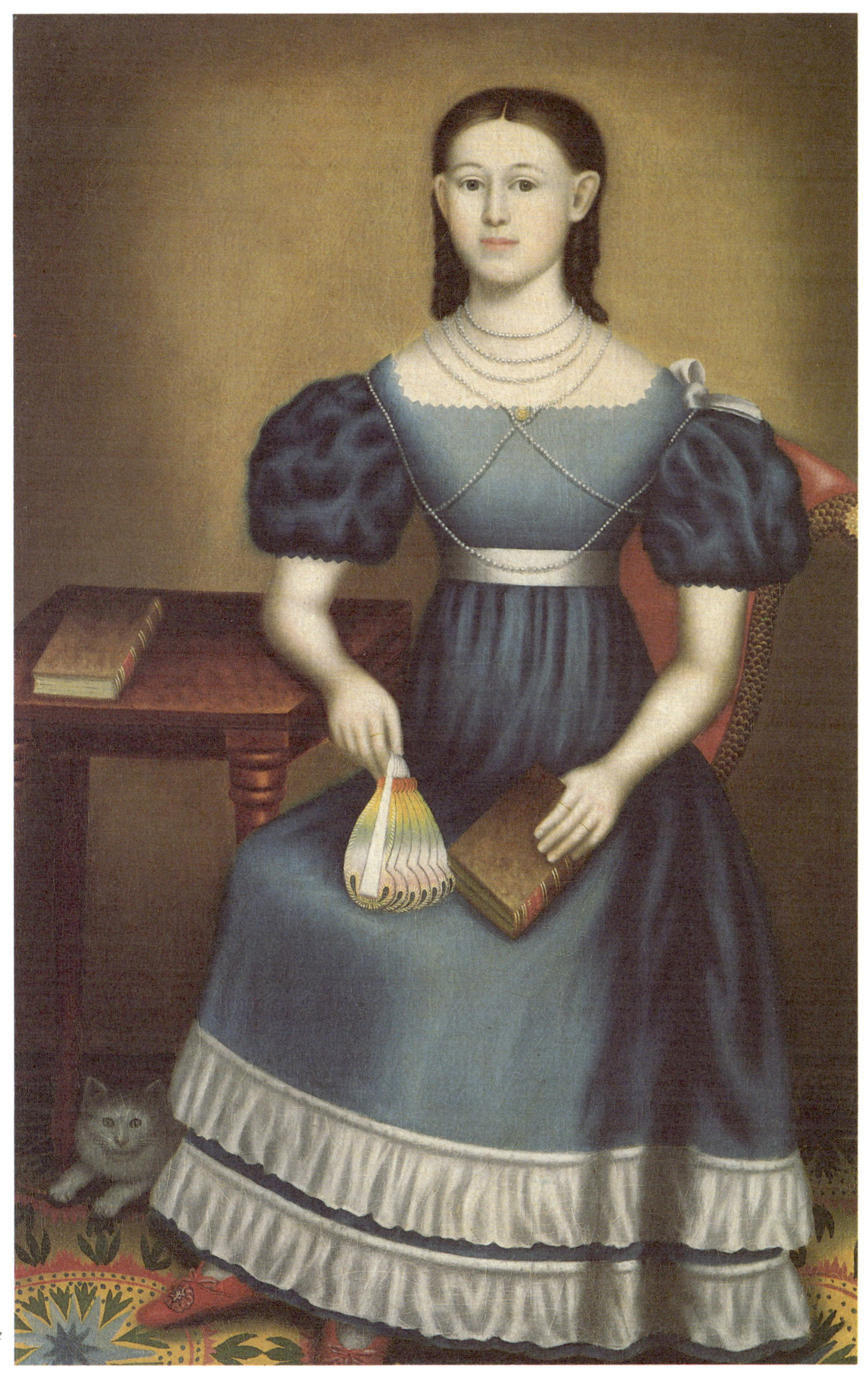

Pl. 21 *Margaret Gilmore*
(cat. *no.70*)

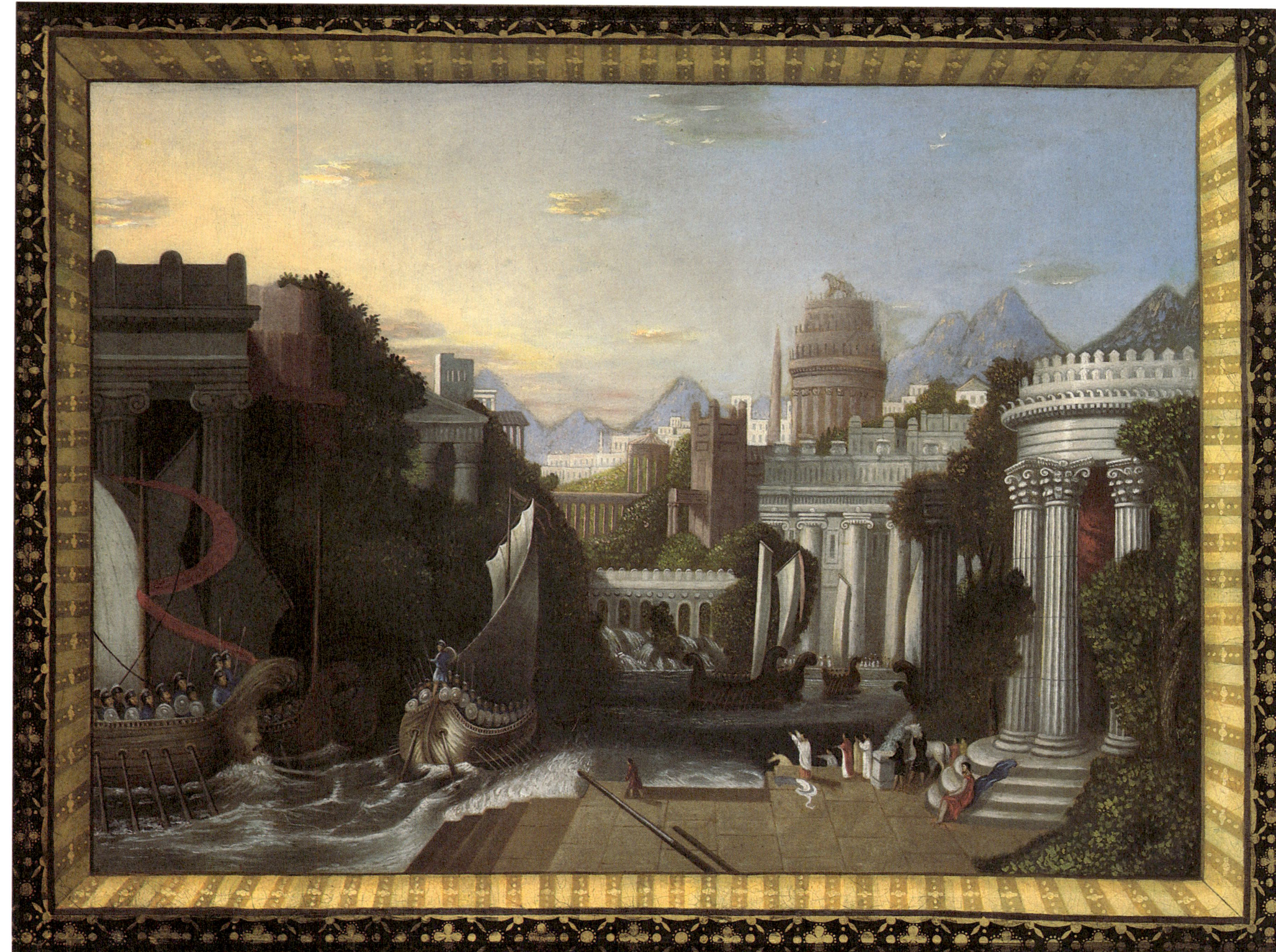

Pl. 22   *The Embarkation of Ulysses*   (cat. no.68)

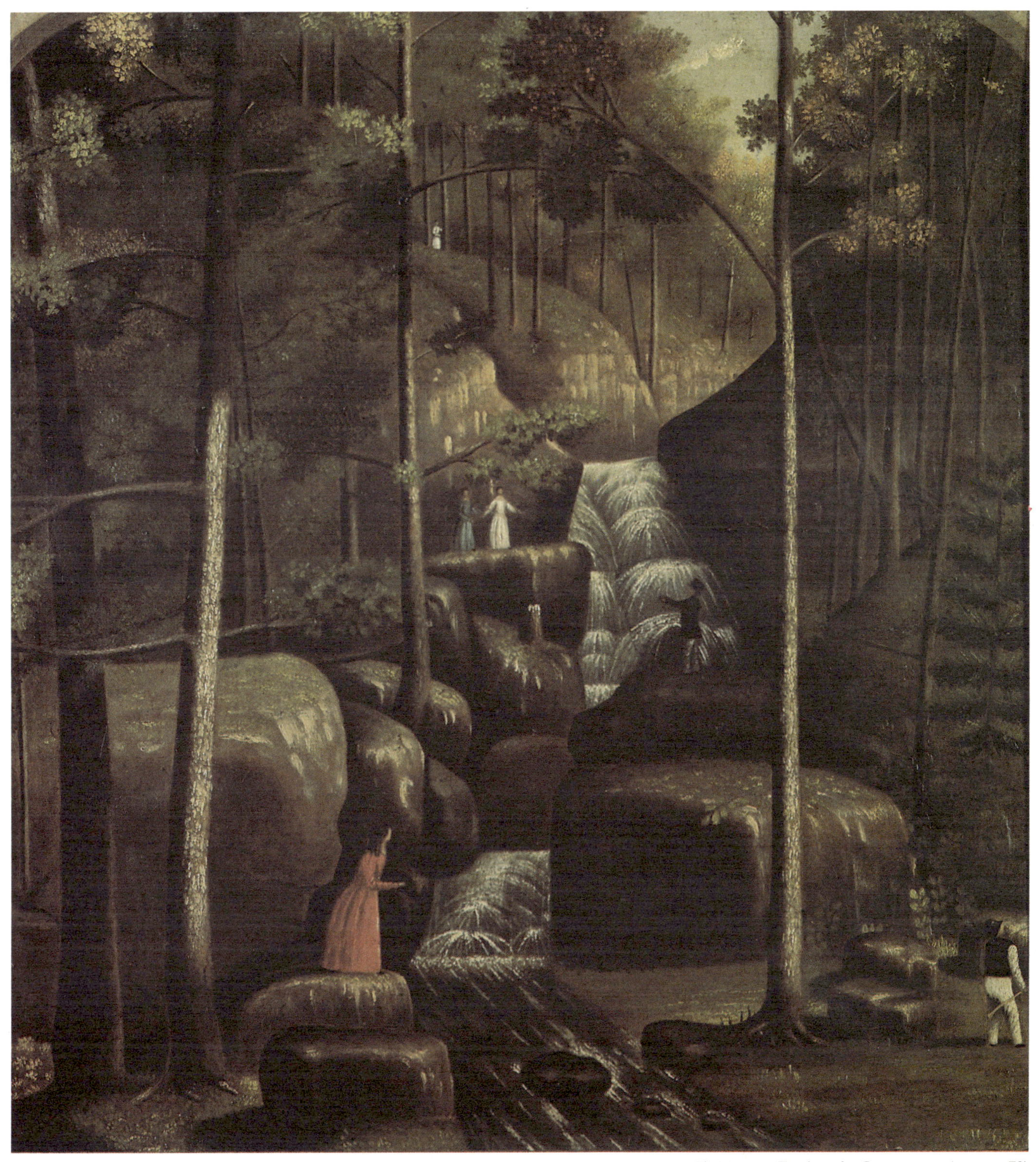

Pl. 23   *Rattlesnake Gutter*   (cat. no.72)

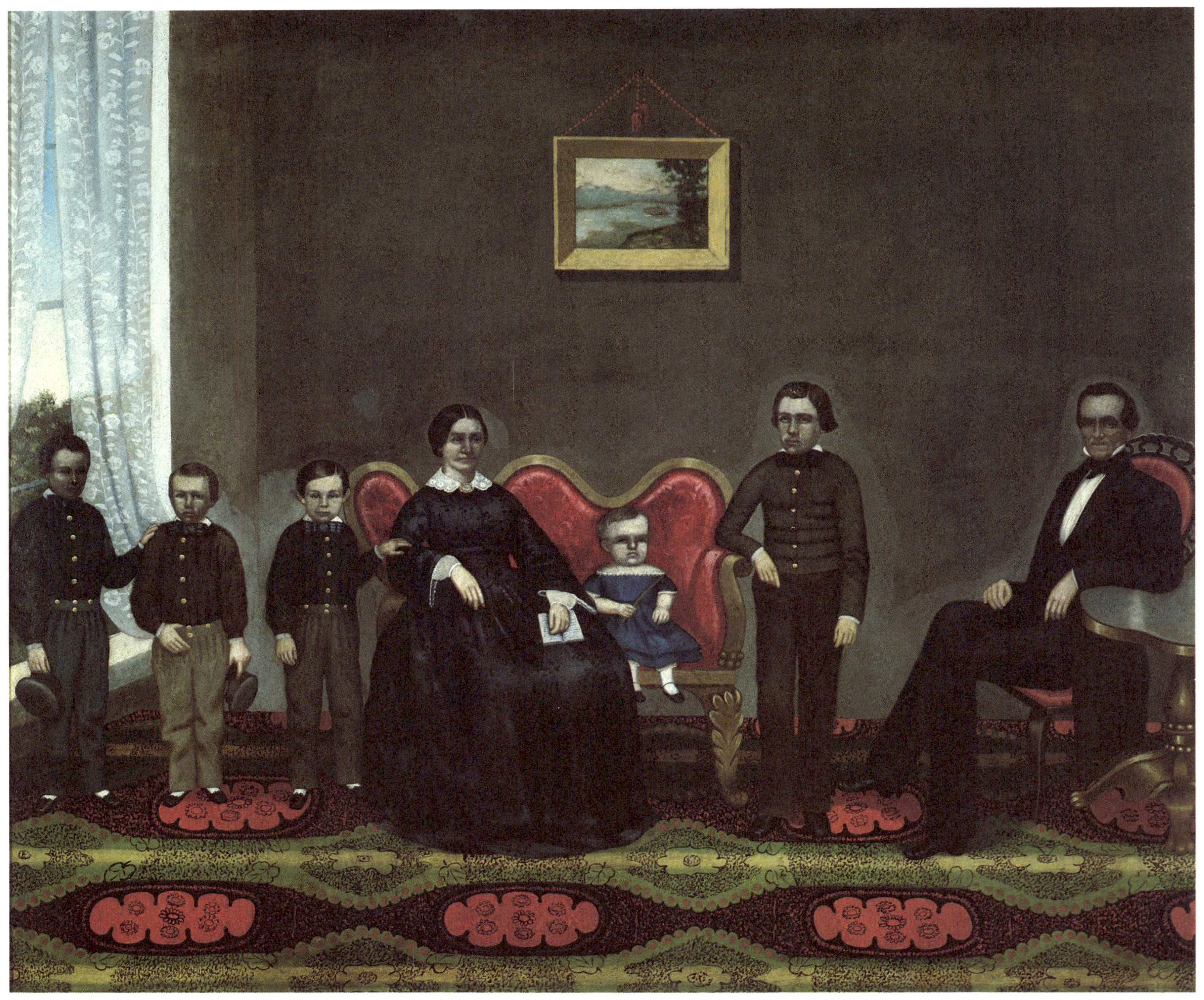

Pl. 24   *The Family of Deacon Wilson Brainerd*   (cat. no.74)

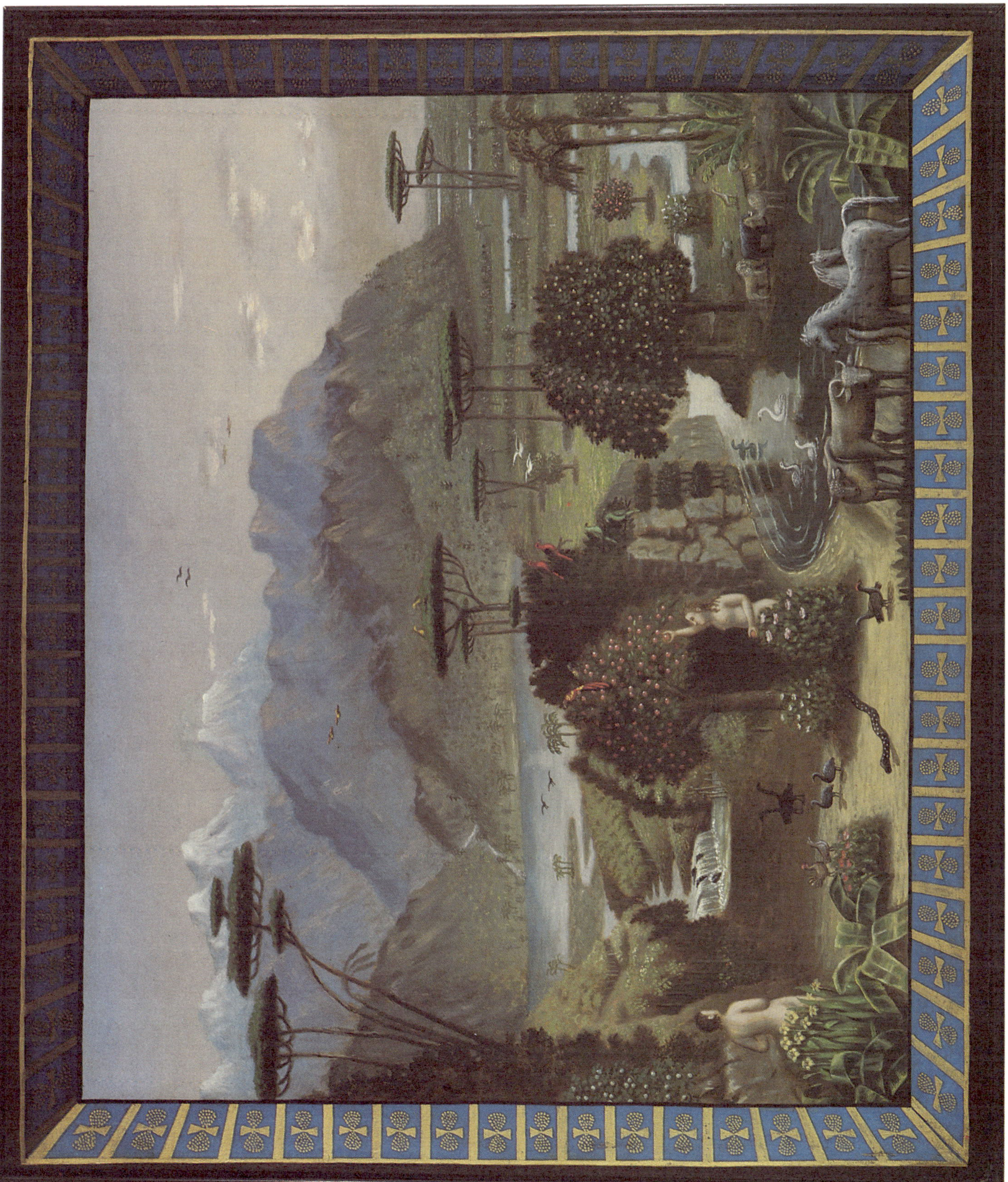

Pl. 25   *The Garden of Eden*   (cat. no.77)

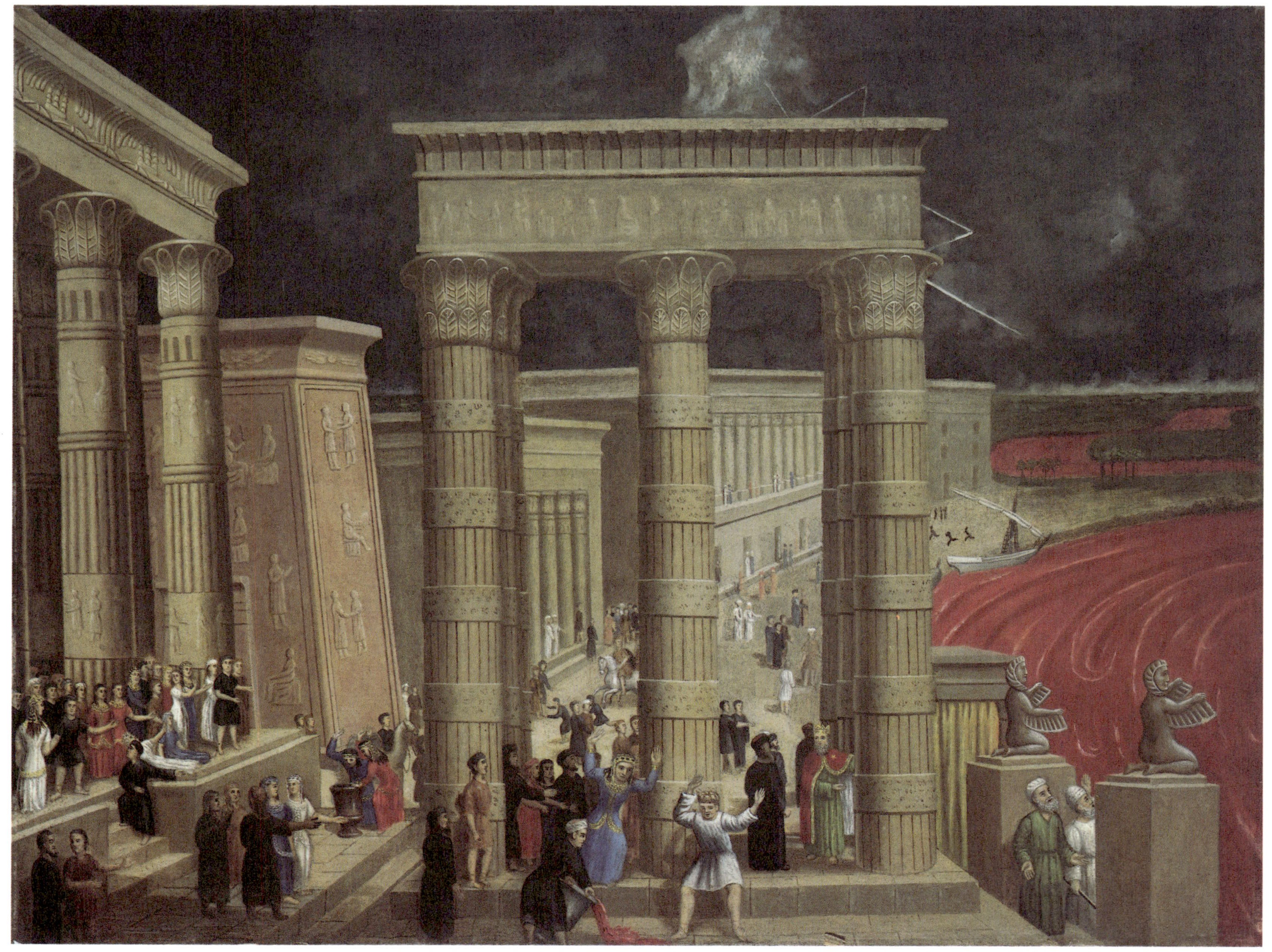

Pl. 26   "He Turned Their Waters Into Blood"   (cat. no.84)

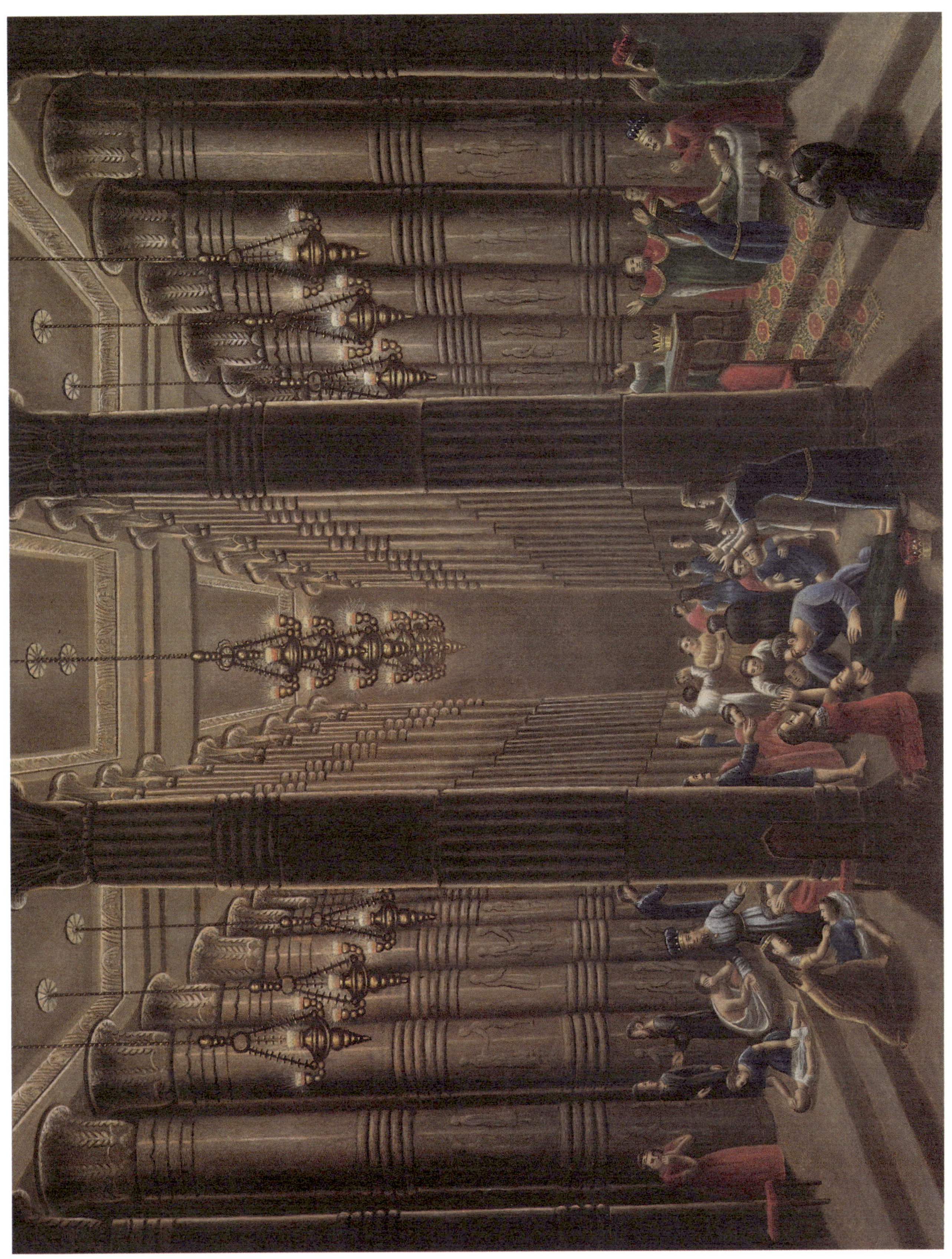

Pl. 27   *Death of the First Born*   (cat. no.86)

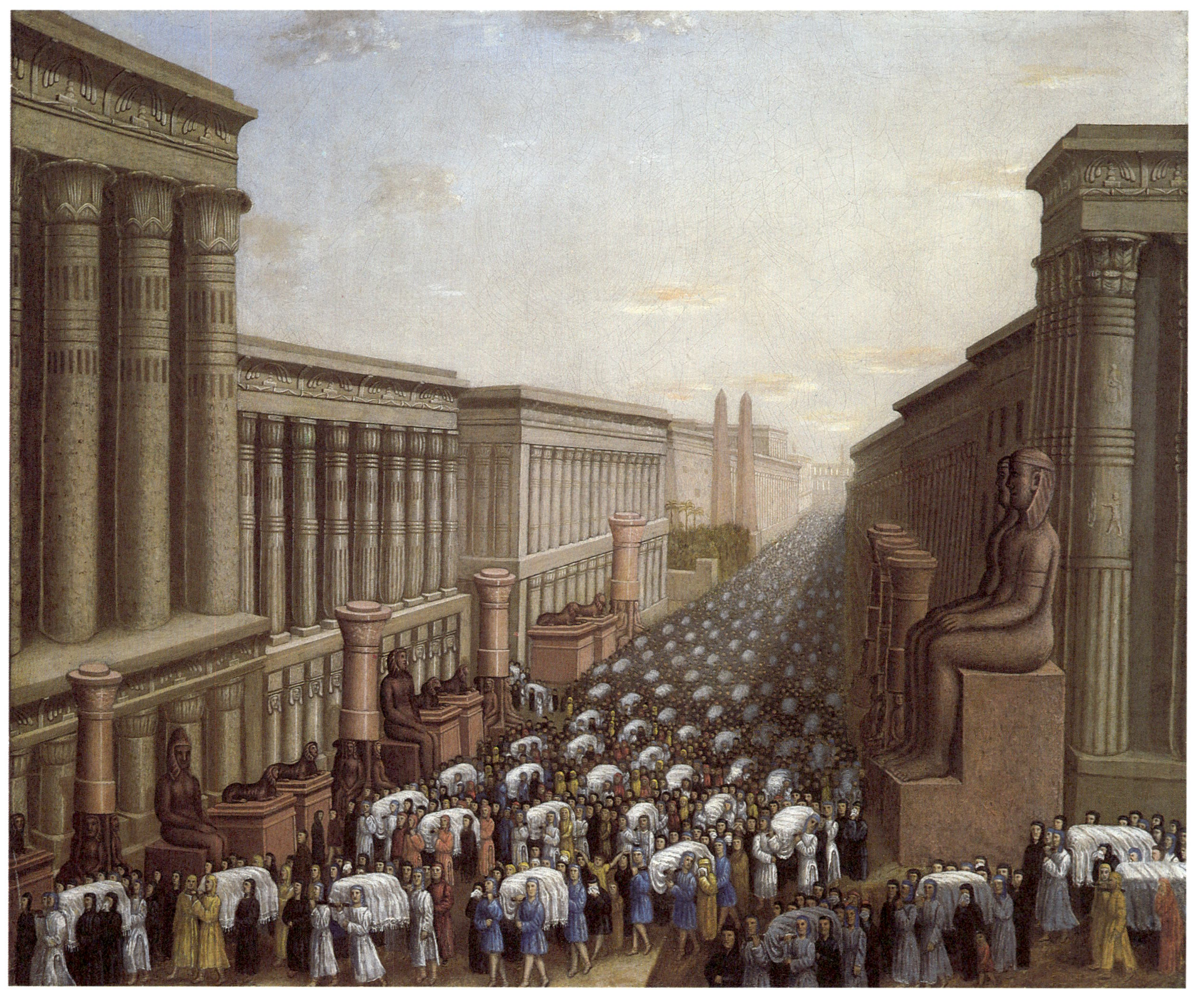

Pl. 28   *Burial of the First Born*   (cat. no.87)

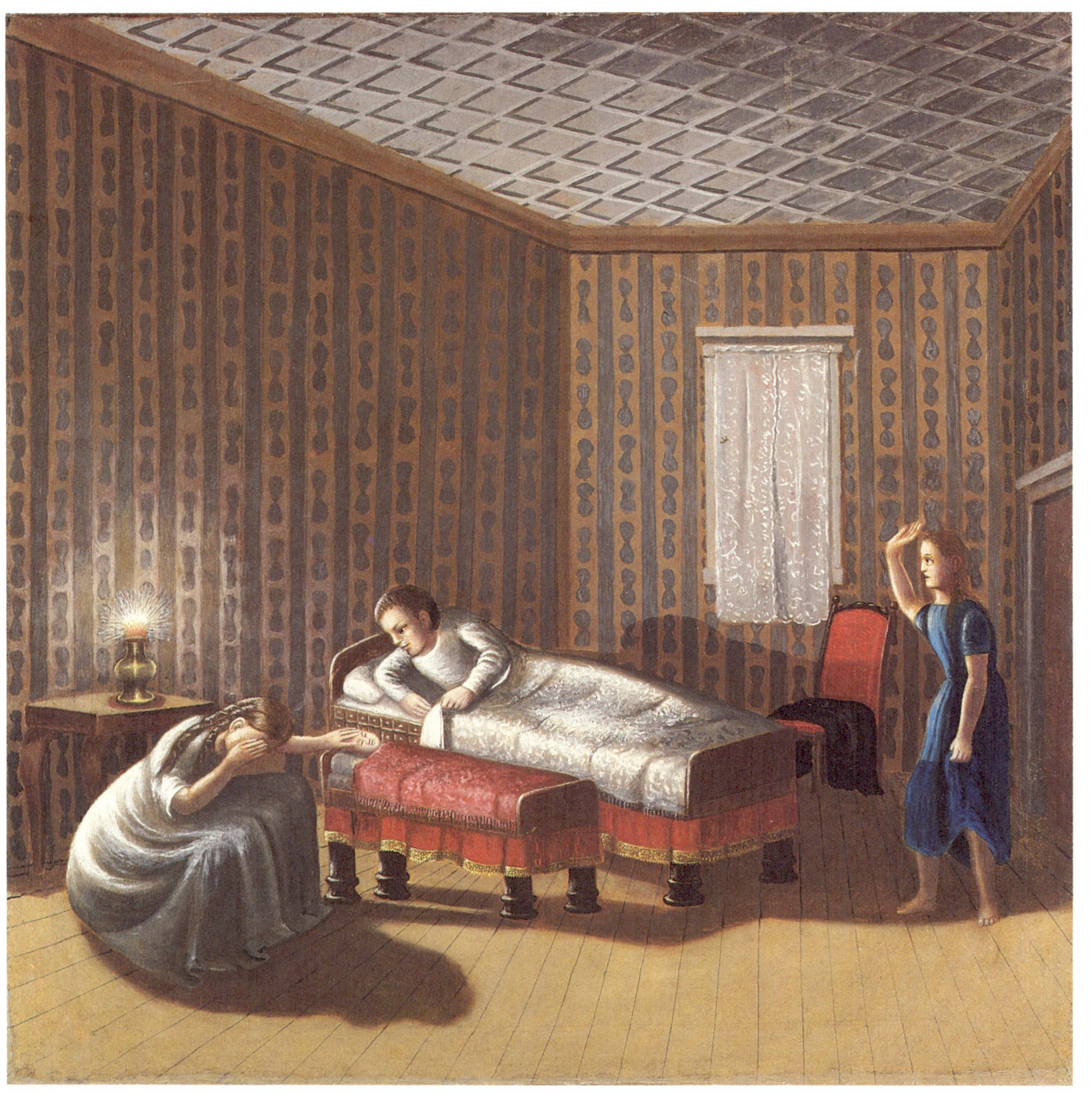

Pl. 29   *Death of the First Born*   (cat. no.89)

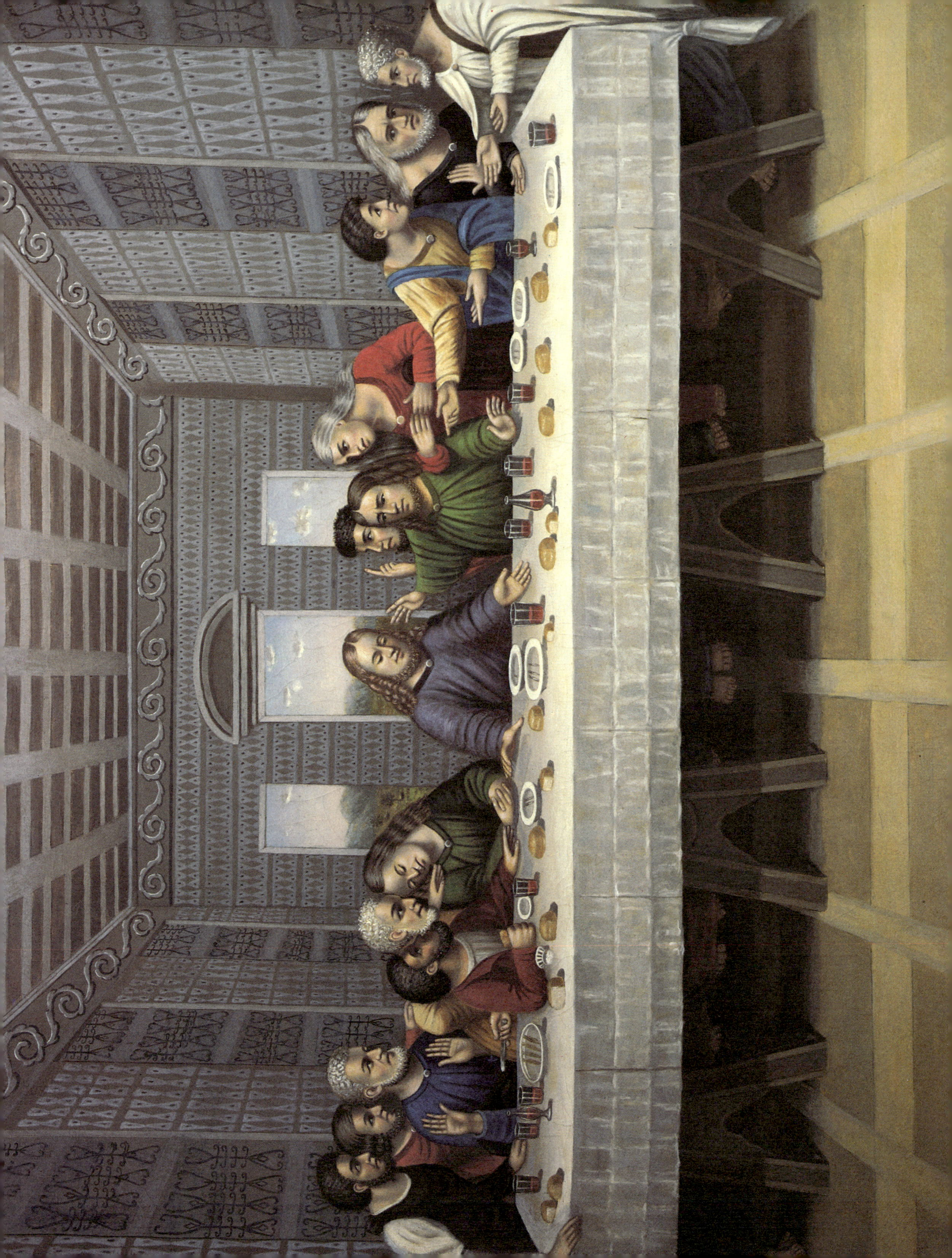

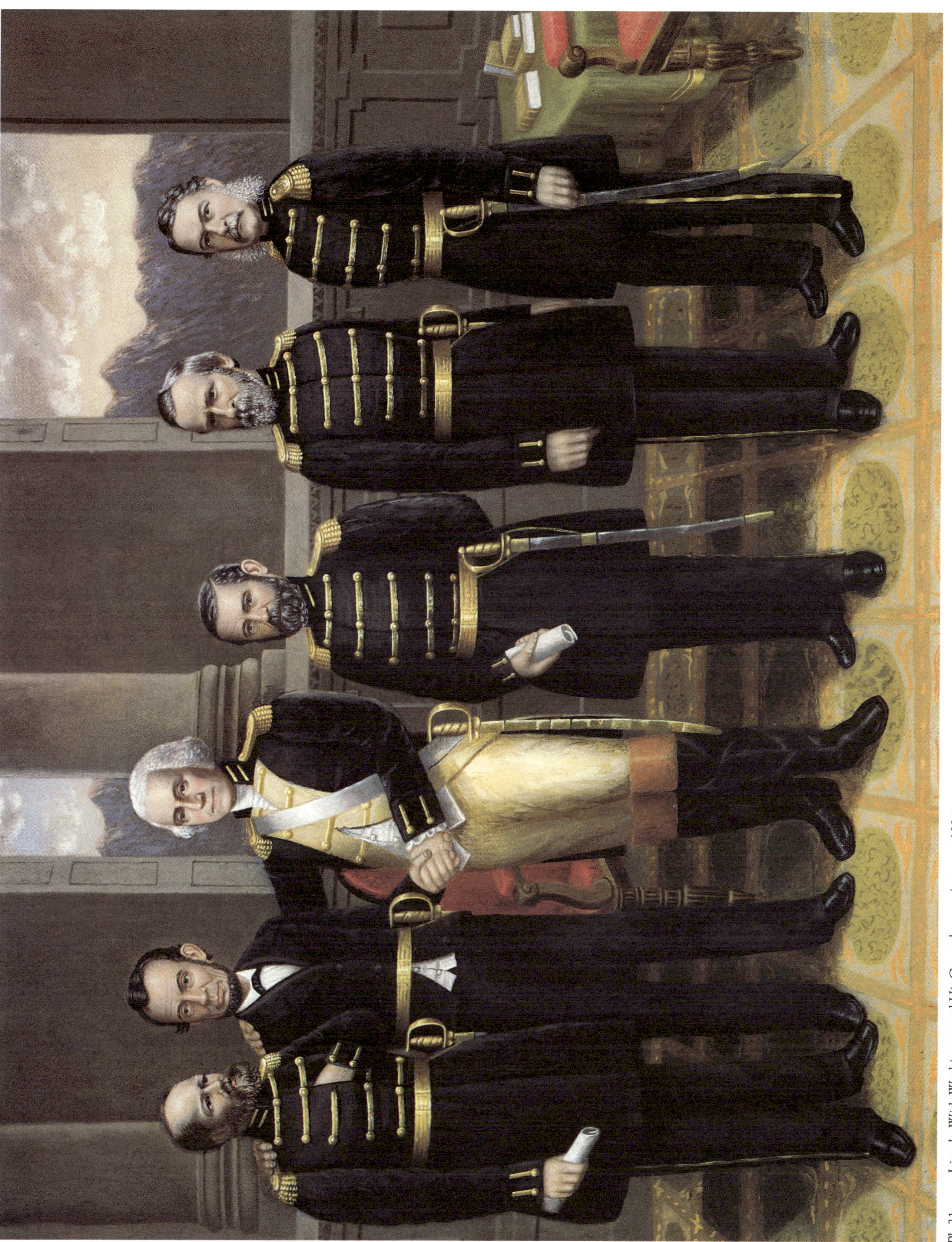

Pl. 31   *Lincoln With Washington and His Generals*   (cat. no.103)

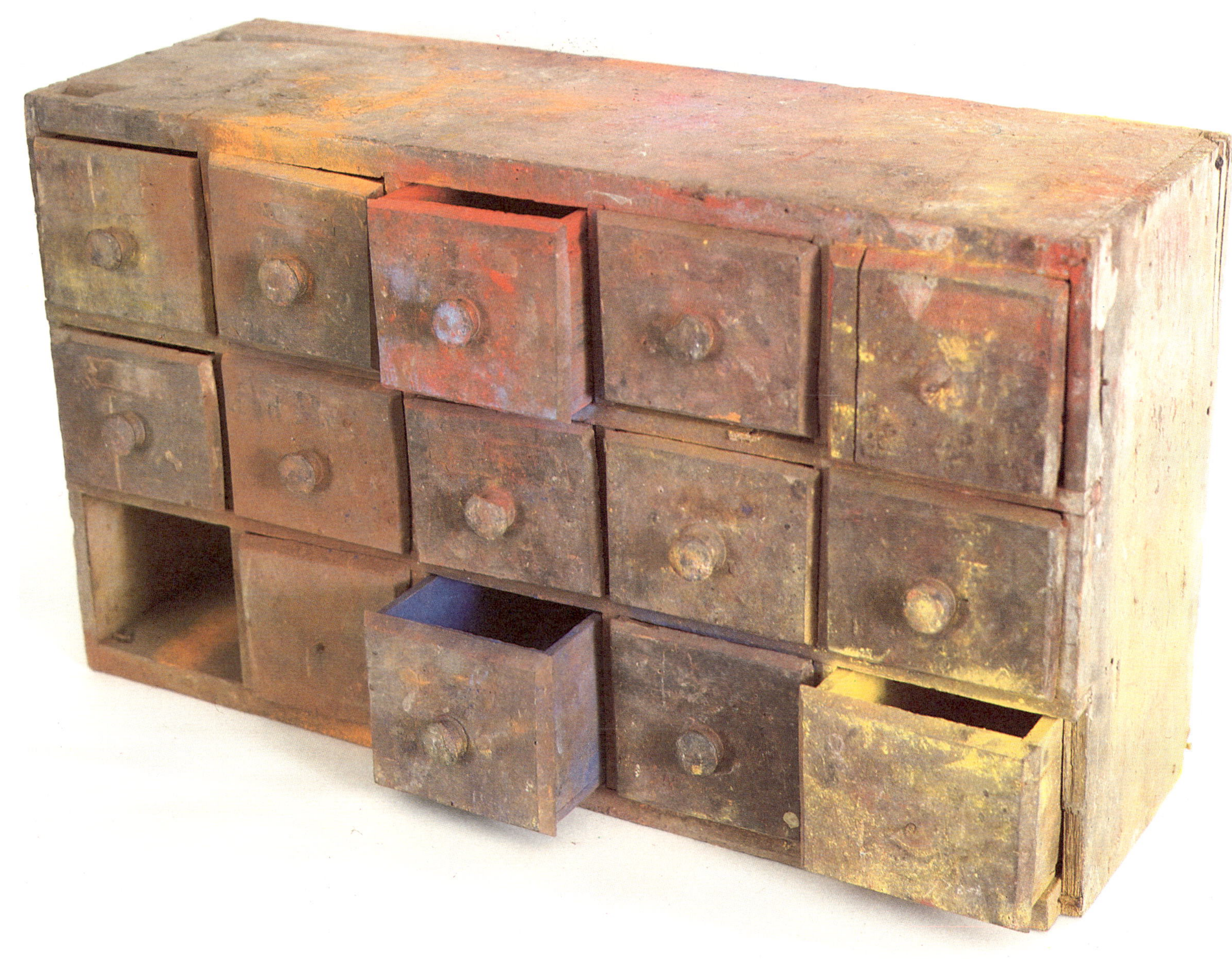

Pl. 32　　*Erastus Salisbury Field's Paint Box*　　(cat. no.108)

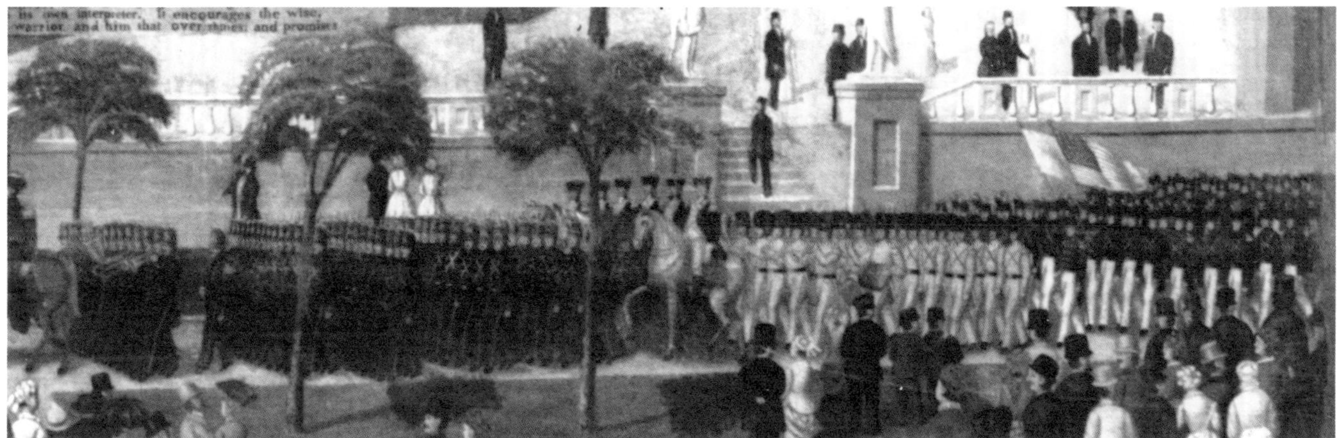

The Historical Monument of the American Republic, (detail)

Chronological Catalogue of Works

Genealogical information is from four sources: owners of paintings; George M. Smith, *History of the Town of Sunderland, Massachusetts*, Greenfield, Mass., 1899; Frederick Clifton Pierce, *Field Genealogy,* two volumes, Chicago, 1901; and the list compiled by Agnes Dods and Reginald French, "Checklist of Paintings Attributed to Erastus Salisbury Field," *Connecticut Historical Society Bulletin*, Vol. 28, No. 4 (October 1963), 105-130. CHS numbers within entries refer to the Dods-French accounting. Figure numbers refer to illustrations.

All paintings are oil on canvas unless otherwise identified; measurements are in inches and centimeters with height preceding width.

Names of additional Field sitters are capitalized within entries.

1. *Elizabeth Billings Ashley*   (color plate 1)

(1745-1826; married 1762 Stephen Ashley, son of Anna
    Dewey and the Reverend Joseph Ashley)
24½ x 22½   (61 x 57.15)   CHS 2
Museum of Fine Arts, Springfield, Massachusetts,
    The Morgan Wesson Memorial Collection 63.02

The earliest known painting by Field is this portrait of
his maternal grandmother (the daughter of Ebenezer
Billings, Jr.).

1827   *Worcester, Massachusetts*

2. *Biel Le Doyt*   (fig. 1)

(1803-?   )
30 x 23   (76.2 x 58.42)   CHS 131
Inscribed: Biel Le Doyt/Aged 24 years/Painted by
    Erastus S. Field/Worcester, Mass./1827
National Gallery of Art, Washington. Gift of Edgar William
    and Bernice Chrysler Garbisch 1971

Except for a pencil sketch of Napoleon dated 1856, this
is the only known signed portrait by Field.

c. 1828

3. *Casendiana Shumway Dowse*   (fig. 57)

(1801-1860; married SAMUEL DOWSE 1824)
38 x 32¾   (96.5 x 83.2)
Mr. and Mrs. S. Forbes Rockwell, Jr.

Formerly attributed to Field, this portrait and its
companion now appear to be by another hand. See no. 4.

4. *Samuel Dowse*   (fig. 58)

(1797-1844; married CASENDIANA SHUMWAY 1824)
38 x 33   (96.5 x 83.8)
Mr. and Mrs. S. Forbes Rockwell, Jr.

See no. 3.

1828   *Hudson, New York*

5. *Lauriette Ashley*   (fig. 2)

(1803-1870)
76½ x 53¾   (194.31 x 136.53)
The Saint Louis Art Museum, Gift of Mrs. James H.
    Spencer 345:1955

Lauriette Ashley was the artist's first cousin, daughter of
William Ashley of Hudson (oldest brother of Field's

mother, Salome Field), and Jerusha Leonard, Ashley's
second wife.

c. 1829   *Wethersfield, Connecticut*

6. *Gentleman of Squire Williams House*   (fig. 4)

32 x 24¼   (81.28 x 61.60)   CHS 202
Private Collection

See no. 7.

7. *Lady of Squire Williams House*   (fig. 3)

32 x 24¼   (81.28 x 61.60)   CHS 203
Private Collection

See no. 6.

c. 1829   *Springfield, Massachusetts*

8. *Julia Tuttle Bangs*   (fig. 59)

(1797-1884; married Joseph Bangs in 1820 as his second
    wife)
35 x 25¾   (88.9 x 65.41)   CHS 6
The Chrysler Museum, Norfolk, VA, Gift of Edgar
    William and Bernice Chrysler Garbisch

The freedom of Field's brushwork represents an advance
in painting technique over similar works of 1827.

9. *Mary Werner Bangs?*   (color plate 2)

(1816-1884)
58¾ x 30¼   (149.23 x 76.84)   CHS 7
The Metropolitan Museum of Art, Gift of
    Edgar William and Bernice Chrysler Garbisch, 1963

Although the subject was thought to be Ellen Tuttle
Bangs, she can be identified as Mary Werner Bangs
(sister of FREDERICK BANGS, no. 10), who would have
been about thirteen years old in 1829. While this and two
other Bangs family portraits by Field (nos. 8 and 10)
descended in the family of their half sister, Ellen Tuttle
Bangs, born in 1828, it is unlikely that Ellen is the subject
since the style is typical of Field's work in the late 1820's.

10. *Frederick Werner Bangs*   (fig. 60)

(1819-1890)
30¼ x 24½   (76.8 x 62.23)   CHS 8
The Chrysler Museum, Norfolk, VA, Gift of Edgar
    William and Bernice Chrysler Garbisch

The boy was the son of Joseph Bangs and the stepson
of JULIA BANGS (no. 8). He would have been ten in
1829, a date consistent with his costume.

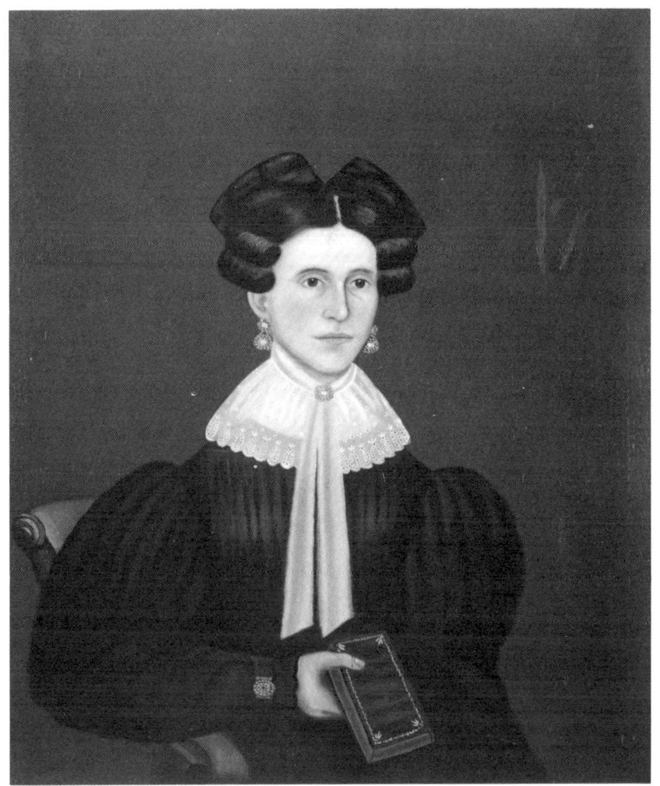

Fig. 57   *Casendiana Shumway Dowse*   (cat. no.3)

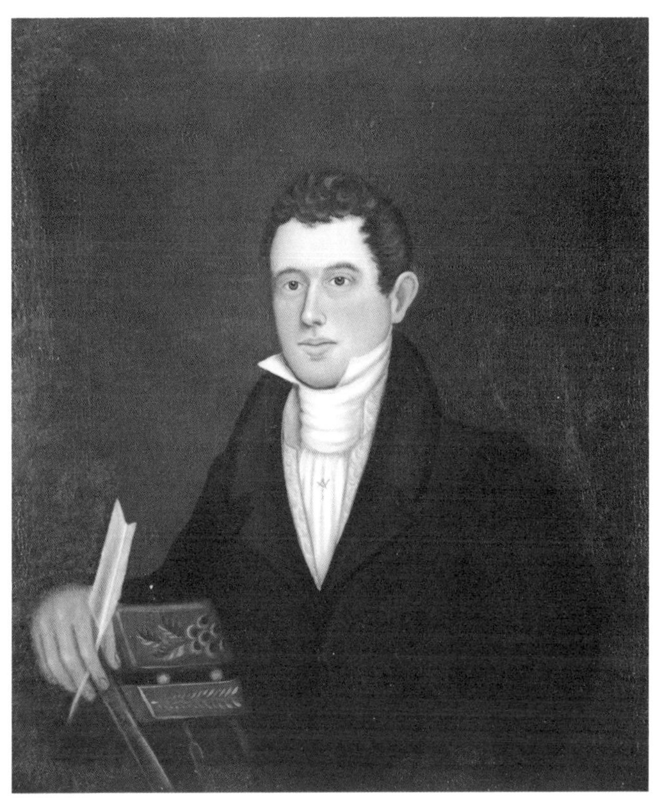

Fig. 58   *Samuel Dowse*   (cat. no.4)

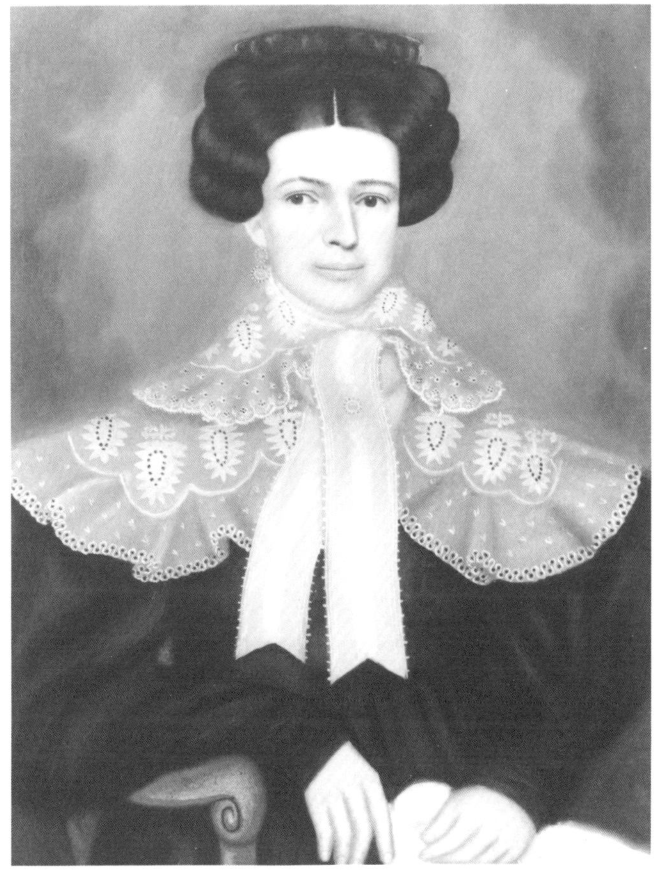

Fig. 59   *Julia Tuttle Bangs*   (cat. no.8)

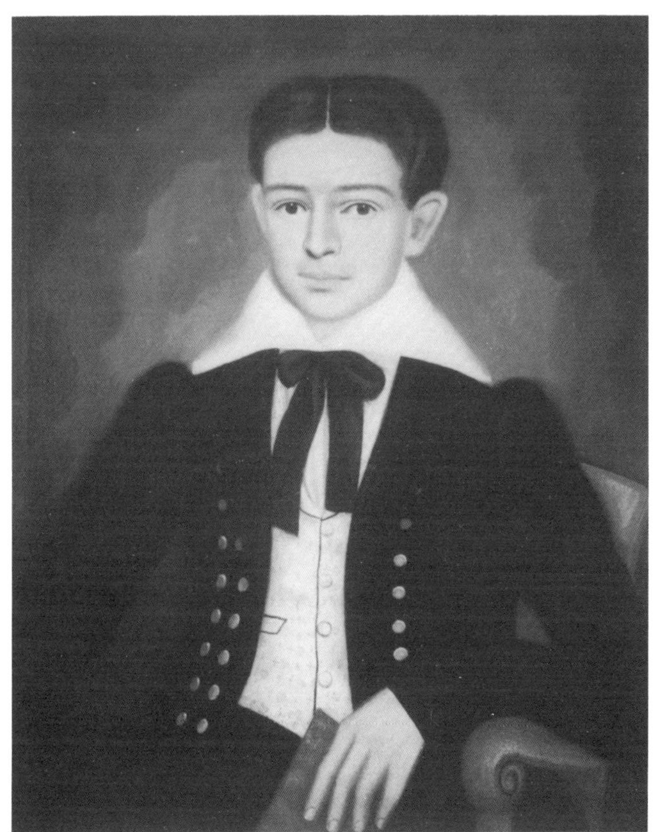

Fig. 60   *Frederick Werner Bangs*   (cat. no.10)

c. 1830   *Glastonbury, Connecticut*

11. *Member of the Hollister Family,*
    Glastonbury, Connecticut   (fig. 61)

    30¾ x 24¼ (78.10 x 61.60)
    Old Sturbridge Village

    See no. 12.

12. *Member of the Hollister Family,*
    Glastonbury, Connecticut   (fig. 62)

    30¾ x 24¼ (78.10 x 61.60)
    Old Sturbridge Village

    See no. 11

c. 1830   *Leverett, Massachusetts*

13. *Phineas Field*   (color plate 3)

    (1809-1877; married 1834 THANKFUL FIELD, daughter of
       Mary Woodbury and Silas Field)
    31½ x 26½ (80.01 x 67.31)   CHS 68
    Private Collection

    The sitter, who holds a manuscript book inscribed
    Leverett, was the painter's youngest brother.

c. 1830

14. *Dwarfed Boy in Red Dress Holding Rattle*
                              (color plate 4)

    12 x 9 (30.48 x 22.86)
    Private Collection

15. *Portrait of a Young Woman*   (color plate 5)

    35¼ x 28¾ (89.5 x 73.03)
    Portland Art Museum, Portland, Oregon; Helen
       Thurston Ayer Fund

1831   *Glastonbury, Connecticut*

16. *Three Post Children, Martha Elizabeth, William*
    Warner, Laura Elizabeth   (fig. 5)

    60 x 48 (152.4 x 121.9)
    Private Collection

This painting is Field's earliest group portrait, as well as
his earliest full-length likeness of children.

c. 1832   *Pawtucket, Rhode Island*

17. *Gentleman of Pawtucket*   (fig. 63)

    36½ x 30 (92.71 x 76.2)   CHS 214
    Museum of Fine Arts, Springfield, Massachusetts, The
       James Philip Gray Collection in Memory of Eleanor
       Williams Wesson 63.27

    This portrait and its companion (no. 18) were found in
    Pawtucket, Rhode Island, in the middle of this century. If
    Field painted them there, Pawtucket would be the most
    easterly of the locations in which he worked.

18. *Lady of Pawtucket*   (fig. 64)

    37 x 30 (93.98 x 76.2)   CHS 215
    Museum of Fine Arts, Springfield, Massachusetts, The
       James Philip Gray Collection in Memory of Eleanor
       Williams Wesson 63.28

    See no. 17.

April, 1833   *Winchester, Connecticut*

19. *Reverend Frederick Marsh*   (fig. 7)

    (1780-1873; married PARNELL MERRILL of New Haven,
       Connecticut)
    35½ x 29 (90.17 x 73.66)   CHS 135
    Winchester Historical Society

    The portraits of Frederick Marsh and his wife,
    PARNELL MARSH (no. 20), are inscribed in Field's
    hand on the back of the canvas, "April 16, 1833" and
    "April 17, 1833" respectively. The dates, a day apart,
    are a measure of Field's rapid execution of portraits.

20. *Parnell Merrill Marsh*   (fig. 6)

    (1782-1860; married the REVEREND FREDERICK MARSH)
    35½ x 29 (90.17 x 73.66)   CHS 136
    Winchester Historical Society

    See no. 19.

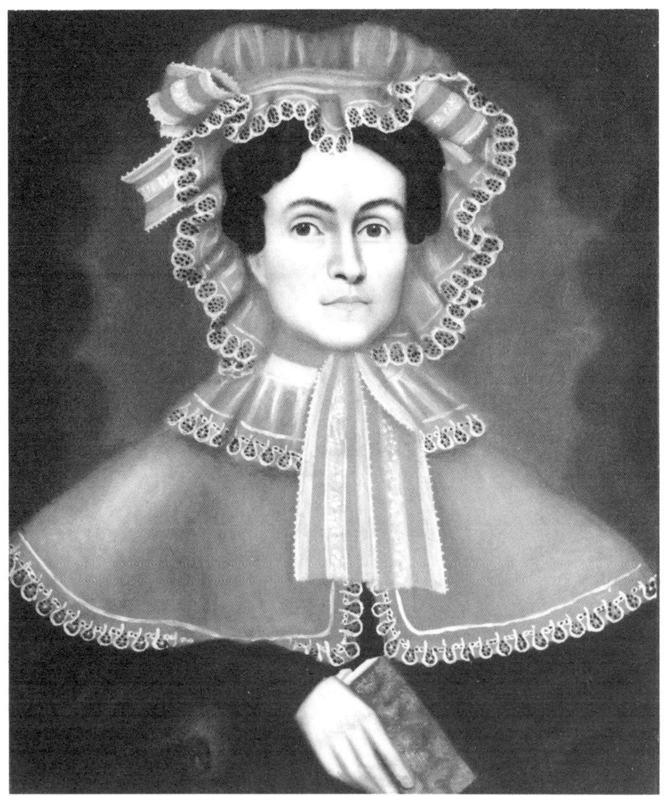

Fig. 62   *Member of the Hollister Family, Glastonbury, Connecticut*
(cat. no.*12*)

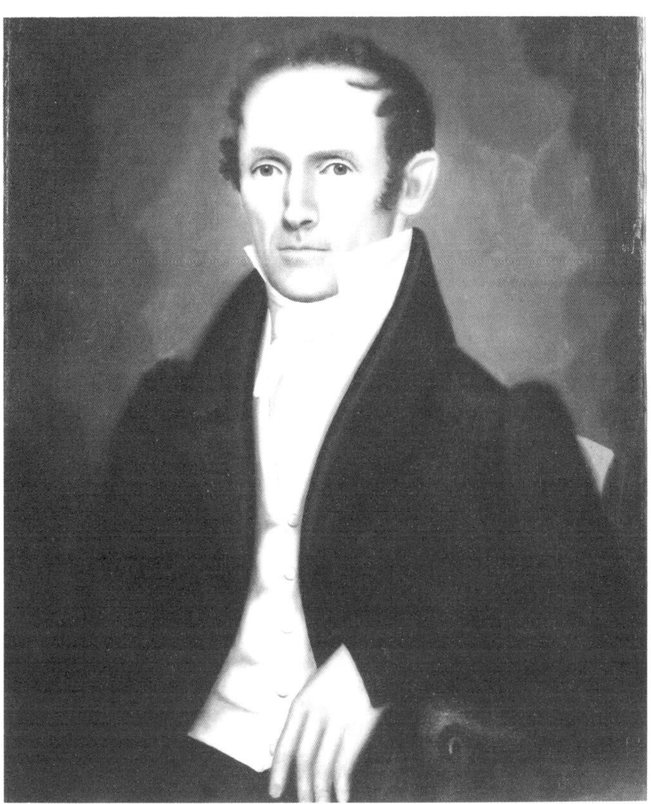

Fig. 61   *Member of the Hollister Family, Glastonbury, Connecticut*
(cat. no.*11*)

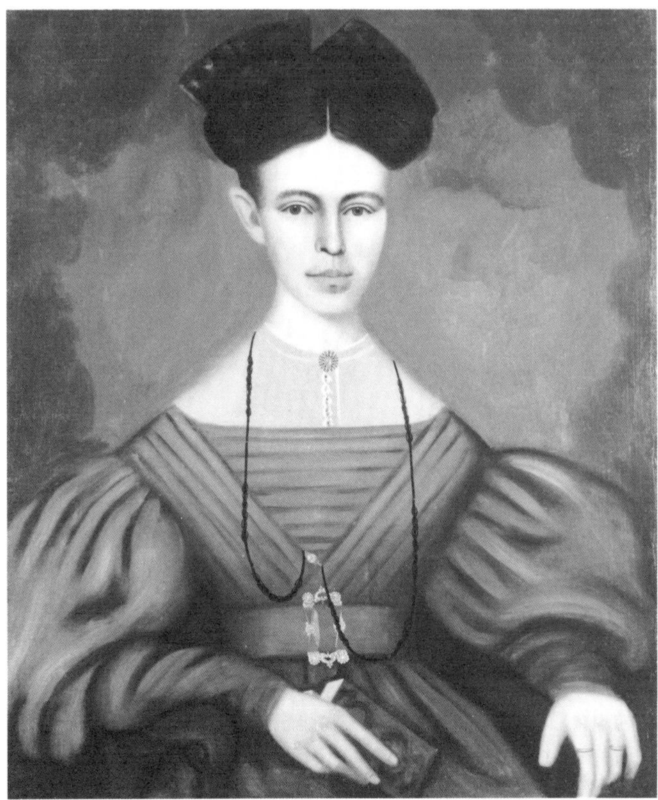

Fig. 64   *Lady of Pawtucket*   (cat. no.*18*)

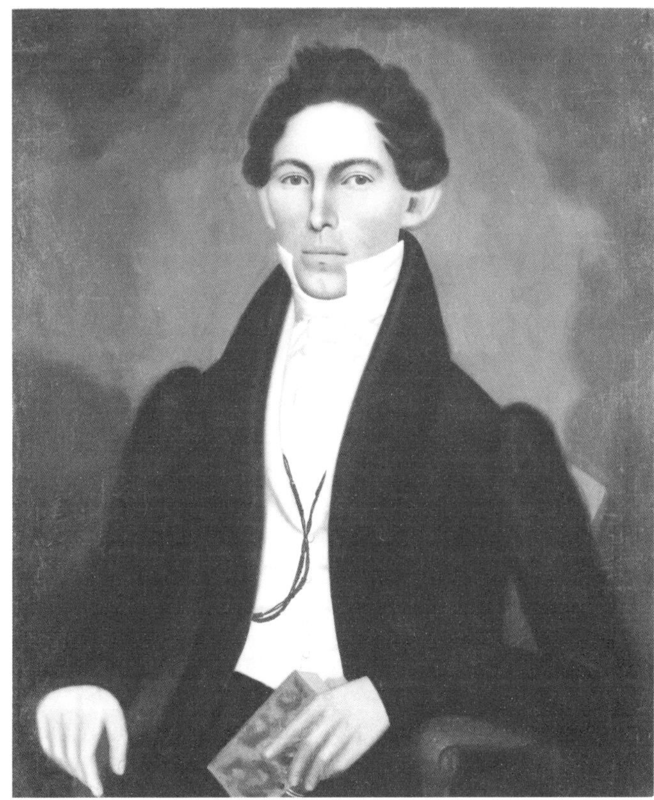

Fig. 63   *Gentleman of Pawtucket*   (cat. no.*17*)

21. *Albro Fyler*   (fig. 65)

{1808-?   ; married Jane E. Kinney, daughter of Sarah
    Wakefield and Nisus Kinney, in 1850}
35 x 29   (88.9 x 73.66)   CHS 79
Torrington Historical Society, Inc.

The subject was the son of ALMIRA WILSON and
STEPHEN FYLER, whom Field also painted in this
same period. In 1850 Albro Fyler married Ammi
Phillips' second cousin, Jane Kinney, who was
portrayed by Phillips in 1848.

22. *Colonel William Lawrence Jillson*   (fig. 13)

{1807-1861; married CHARLOTTE CURTIS 1831}
34⅞ x 28   (88.58 x 71.12)   CHS 116
The Connecticut Historical Society, Hartford, Connecticut

ASA and ANNA SABIN JILLSON, whose portraits
were also painted by Field, were Colonel William
Jillson's parents.   See no. 23.

23. *Mrs. William Lawrence (Charlotte Curtis) Jillson*   (fig. 12)

{1808-1862; married WILLIAM LAWRENCE JILLSON 1831}
34⅞ x 28   (88.58 x 71.12)   CHS 117
The Connecticut Historical Society, Hartford, Connecticut

See no. 22.

24. *Elizabeth Camilla Jillson*   (color plate 6)

{1826-1901}
48 x 29   (121.92 x 73.66)   CHS 115
The Connecticut Historical Society, Hartford, Connecticut

The subject was the daughter of ASA and ANNA
SABIN JILLSON and the sister of WILLIAM
LAWRENCE JILLSON (no. 22).

25. *Charles Backus Jones*   (fig. 11)

{ ?-1878; married SOPHIA FULLER 1828}
35¼ x 29⅜   (89.54 x 74.61)   CHS 118
Mead Art Museum, Bequest of Frank G. Nelson, class
    of 1873

See no. 26

26. *Sophia Fuller Jones*   (fig. 10)

{ ?-1894; married CHARLES BACKUS JONES 1828}
35⅜ x 29¼   (89.85 x 74.30)   CHS 119
Mead Art Museum, Bequest of Frank G. Nelson, class
    of 1873

See no. 25.

27. *Harriet Sophia Jones*   (fig. 8)

{1829-1915}
44 x 28¼   (111.76 x 71.76)   CHS 120
The Chrysler Museum, Norfolk, VA, Gift of Edgar
    William and Bernice Chrysler Garbisch

The subject was the daughter of SOPHIA FULLER
and CHARLES BACKUS JONES (see nos. 25 and 26).

28. *Thankful Field Field*   (color plate 7)

{1812-c. 1908; married PHINEAS FIELD 1834}
31¼ x 25⅝   (79.38 x 65.09)   CHS 69
Museum of Fine Arts, Springfield, Massachusetts, The
    Morgan Wesson Memorial Collection 63.05

29. *Boy on Stenciled Carpet*   (color plate 8)

43¾ x 29¼   (111.13 x 74.30)   CHS 217
The Abby Aldrich Rockefeller Folk Art Center,
    Williamsburg, Virginia

30. *Young Girl in a Pink Dress*   (color plate 9)

34 x 26   (86.36 x 66.04)   CHS 219
Collection of Peter H. Tillou

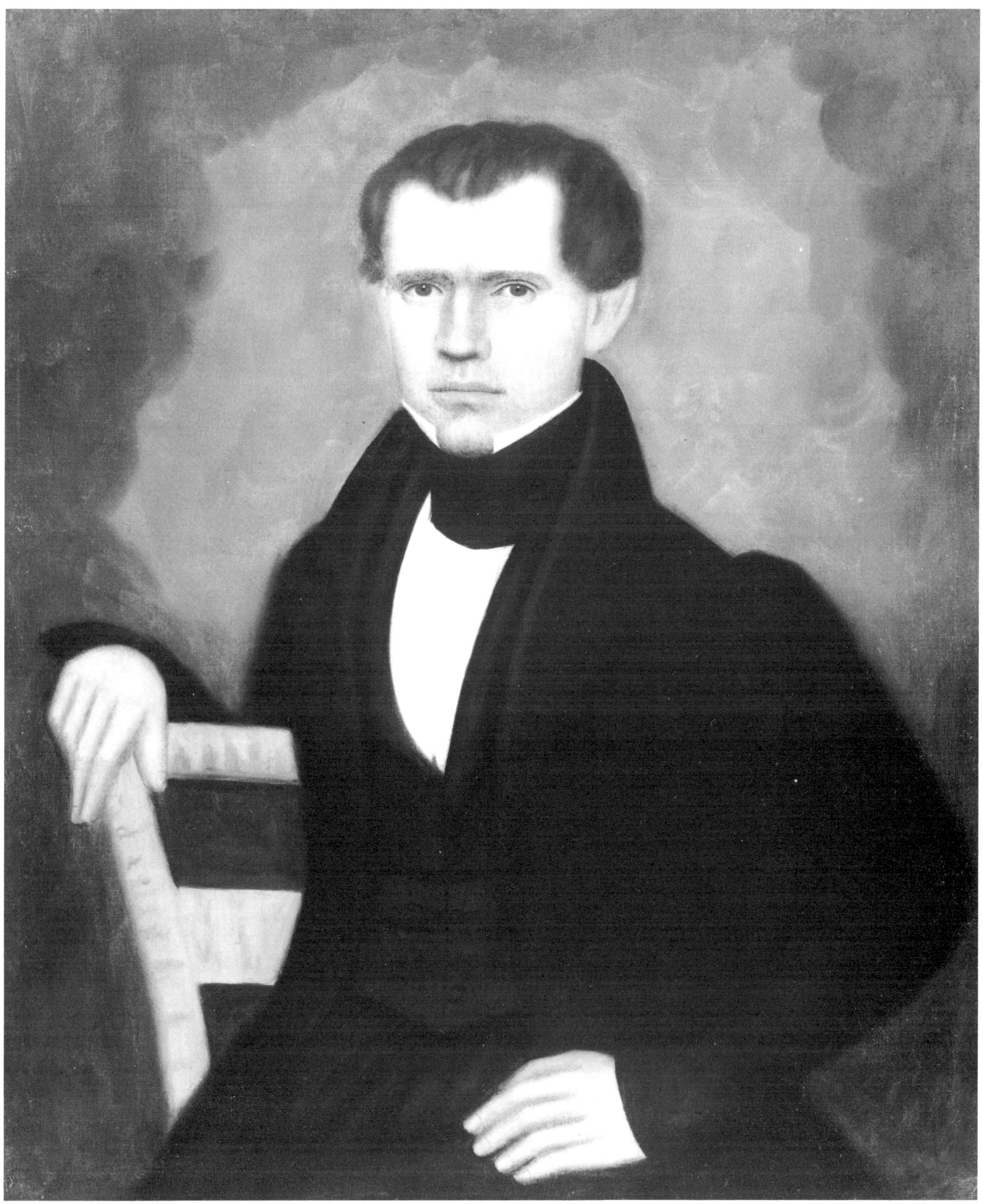

Fig. 65   *Albro Fyler*   (cat. no.*21*)

31. *Henry Allen Pease*   (fig. 9)

(1831-1870; married Emily Marion Higgins*)
35¼ x 28   (89.54 x 71.12)   CHS 165
Mrs. Joan Arden

The sitter was the son of ANNE JANE CLARK, who married a son of DEACON HARLOW PEASE. The boy's father, whose first name is unknown, was the owner of a grist mill in Alford, Massachusetts.

*Information is contained in a letter from Stewart Gregory to Mary Black, 13 March, 1964.

32. *Loring Griswold Robbins*   (fig. 66)

(1797-?   )
34¼ x 32¼   (87 x 81.92)
Mary Robbins Runyon (Mrs. Charles)

33. *Zady Tobey Robbins*   (fig. 67)

(1802-?   )
34¼ x 32¼   (87 x 81.92)
Mary Robbins Runyon (Mrs. Charles)

34. *Mary Valonia Robbins*   (fig. 68)

(1822-?   )
34¼ x 32¼   (87 x 81.92)
Mary Robbins Runyon (Mrs. Charles)

35. *Henry Thomas Robbins*   (color plate 10)

(1833-?   )
34¼ x 32¼   (87 x 81.92)
Mary Robbins Runyon (Mrs. Charles)

36. *Portrait of a Miller*   (fig. 15)

30½ x 25¼   (77.47 x 64.14)   CHS 197
Museum of American Folk Art, Gift of Cyril I. Nelson
    in Honor of Howard and Jean Lipman

37. *Anselm Bassett*   (fig. 14)

(1768-1837; married Hannah Dymoke 1793*)
34¾ x 28½   (88.27 x 72.39)   CHS 10
Collection of Mr. and Mrs. Henry Bassett Holt

Born in Sandwich, Massachusetts, Anselm Bassett was the son of Hannah Hall and Nathaniel Bassett.

*Information from Bassett Genealogy, Courtesy of Henry B. Holt.

38. *Amos Geer Hulbert*   (color plate 11)

(1799-1884; married Cynthia Bassett 1824*)
34¼ x 29   (87 x 73.66)
Collection of Mr. and Mrs. Henry Bassett Holt

Amos Geer Hulbert was a carriage maker and a prominent citizen of Lee, where he moved following his marriage in 1824 to the daughter of ANSELM BASSETT (no. 37).

*Information from Bassett Genealogy, Courtesy of Henry B. Holt.

39. *Henry Carlton Hulbert*   (color plate 12)

(1831-1912; married Susan R. Cooley, as first wife, 1854*)
29¾ x 25½   (75.57 x 64.77)   CHS 110
Collection of Mr. and Mrs. Henry Bassett Holt

Son of AMOS HULBERT (no. 38), Henry Carlton Hulbert went to New York in 1851 and worked for White and Sheffield, a paper firm in which he later became a partner. In 1858 he formed his own paper company, locating in a number of sites in downtown New York. Hulbert remained with this concern until his retirement in 1900.

*Information from Bassett Genealogy, Courtesy of Henry B. Holt.

40. *Mrs. Charles Ball Nye and Daughter Sylvina Lee*
(fig. 16)

(Eliza Cole 1813-1871; Sylvina Lee 1833-?   ; Eliza Cole married CHARLES BALL NYE 1832)
35 x 29   (88.9 x 73.66)   CHS 157
Carl V. Fasano

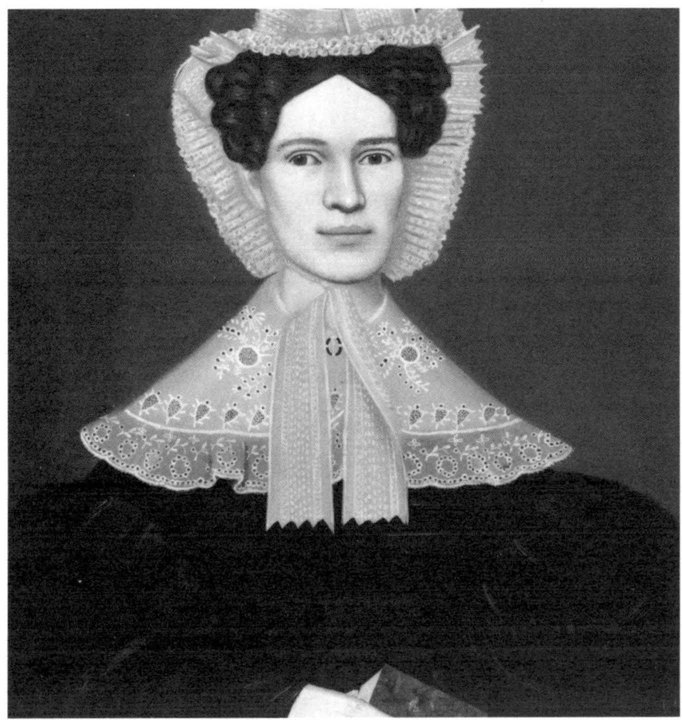 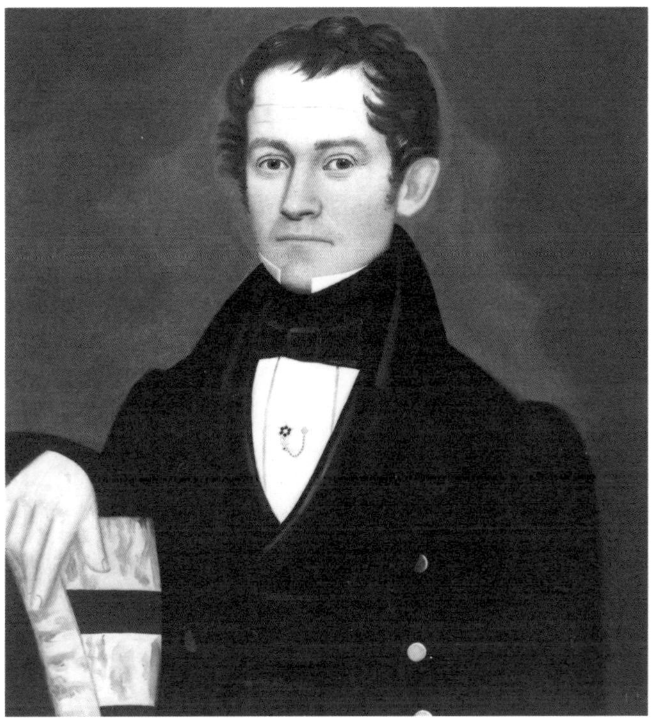

Fig. 67 *Zadey Tobey Robbins* (cat. no.33)

Fig. 66 *Loring Griswold Robbins* (cat. no.32)

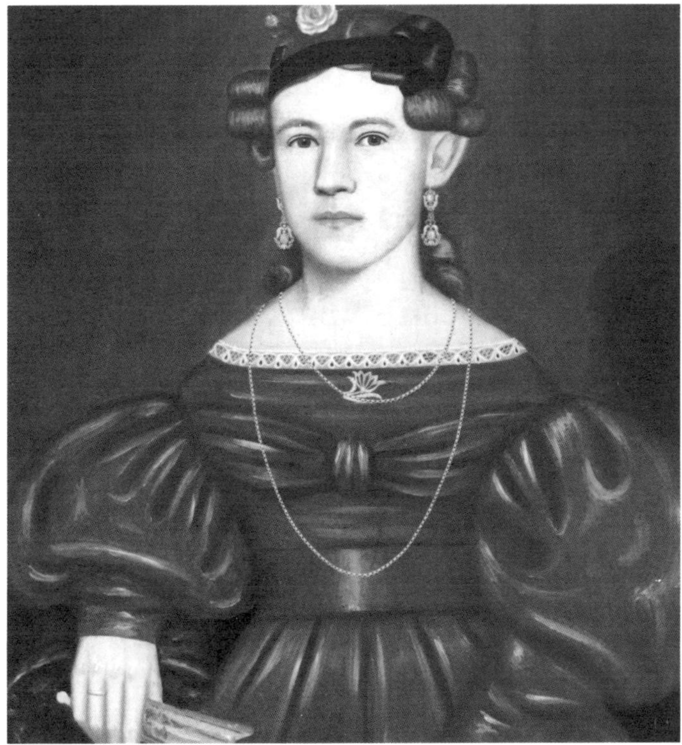

Fig. 68 *Mary Valonia Robbins* (cat. no.34)

41. Mrs. Paul Smith Palmer and Her Twins   (fig. 69)

(1804-1881; married Paul Smith Palmer 1824)
38½ x 34   (97.8 x 86.4)
National Gallery of Art, Washington. Gift of Edgar William
   and Bernice Chrysler Garbisch 1971

Hannah Ells Palmer was born in Stonington,
Connecticut. In 1824 when she married her cousin,
Paul Smith Palmer, she moved to the Berkshires, where
she lived until her death.

c. 1836   Pittsfield, Massachusetts

42. Hosea Merrill   (fig. 17)

(1761-1853; married SARAH PHILLIPS 1783)
35 x 28½   (88.9 x 72.39)   CHS 139
Museum of Fine Arts, Springfield, Massachusetts, Gift
   of Mary Black

The sitter's parents, Mary Skinner and Gad Merrill,
arrived in Pittsfield (by ox team) in December, 1755,
from Hebron, Connecticut. Hosea Merrill served in
the Revolution under Ethan Allen as a Green
Mountain Boy, later becoming a captain in the
Berkshire County militia. The remainder of his long
life was spent as a farmer, merchant, and land owner
in Pittsfield and in Onandaga, New York.* See no. 43.

*Information from Merrill Genealogy, manuscript prepared
   by John Phillips Merrill and owned by Mary Black.

43. Sarah Phillips Merrill   (fig. 18)

(1762-1850; married HOSEA MERRILL 1783)
37 x 31¾   (93.98 x 80.65)   CHS 140
Museum of Fine Arts, Springfield, Massachusetts, Gift
   of Mary Black

See no. 42.

44. Phillips Merrill   (fig. 20)

(1790-1873; married FRANCES STANTON 1815)
37 x 31¾   (93.98 x 80.65)   CHS 141
Mary Black, New York, New York

The subject, son of HOSEA and SARAH PHILLIPS
MERRILL, was a farmer in Pittsfield, Massachusetts.
See nos. 42 and 43.

45. Frances Stanton Merrill   (fig. 19)

(1794-1867; married PHILLIPS MERRILL 1815)
37¼ x 31¾   (94.62 x 80.65)   CHS 142
Mary Black, New York, New York

Frances Stanton Merrill was the daughter of Robert
Stanton of Pittsfield, Massachusetts. See no. 44.

c. 1836   Sunderland, Massachusetts

46. Austin Lysander Marsh   (fig. 24)

(1812-1840; married MARYETTE FIELD 1835)
35 x 29   (88.9 x 73.7)   CHS 132
Ruth Austin Eiseman   (great-granddaughter of subject)

Austin Marsh was the painter's brother-in-law. See
no. 47.

47. Maryette Field Marsh   (fig. 23)

(1813-1842; married AUSTIN LYSANDER MARSH 1835)
35 x 29   (88.9 x 73.66)   CHS 133
Ruth Austin Eiseman   (great-granddaughter of subject)

The sitter, sister of the painter, wears a dress identical
to the one worn by her sister-in-law and cousin,
AURILLA FIELD FIELD, in her 1836 portrait by
Field. See no. 46.

February, 1837   North Amherst,
                                          Massachusetts

48. Eleazer Cowls   (fig. 25)

(1784-1849; married Sibbel Montague 1810)
30¼ x 26⅛   (76.84 x 66.36)   CHS 40
Worcester Art Museum, Eliza S. Paine Fund

The portrait is inscribed on the reverse in Field's hand:
Eleazer Cowles (sic)/Aged 53 yrs/likeness taken/Feb.
1837. See no. 49.

49. Louisa Cowls   (fig. 26)

(1811-1868; married James Bryant Hadley 1838)
29½ x 25½   (74.93 x 64.77)   CHS 42
Worcester Art Museum, Eliza S. Paine Fund .

The portrait is inscribed on the reverse: Louisa Cowles
(sic)/Aged 25 yrs/likeness taken/Feb. 1837. Louisa
Cowls was the daughter of ELEAZER COWLS (no. 48)

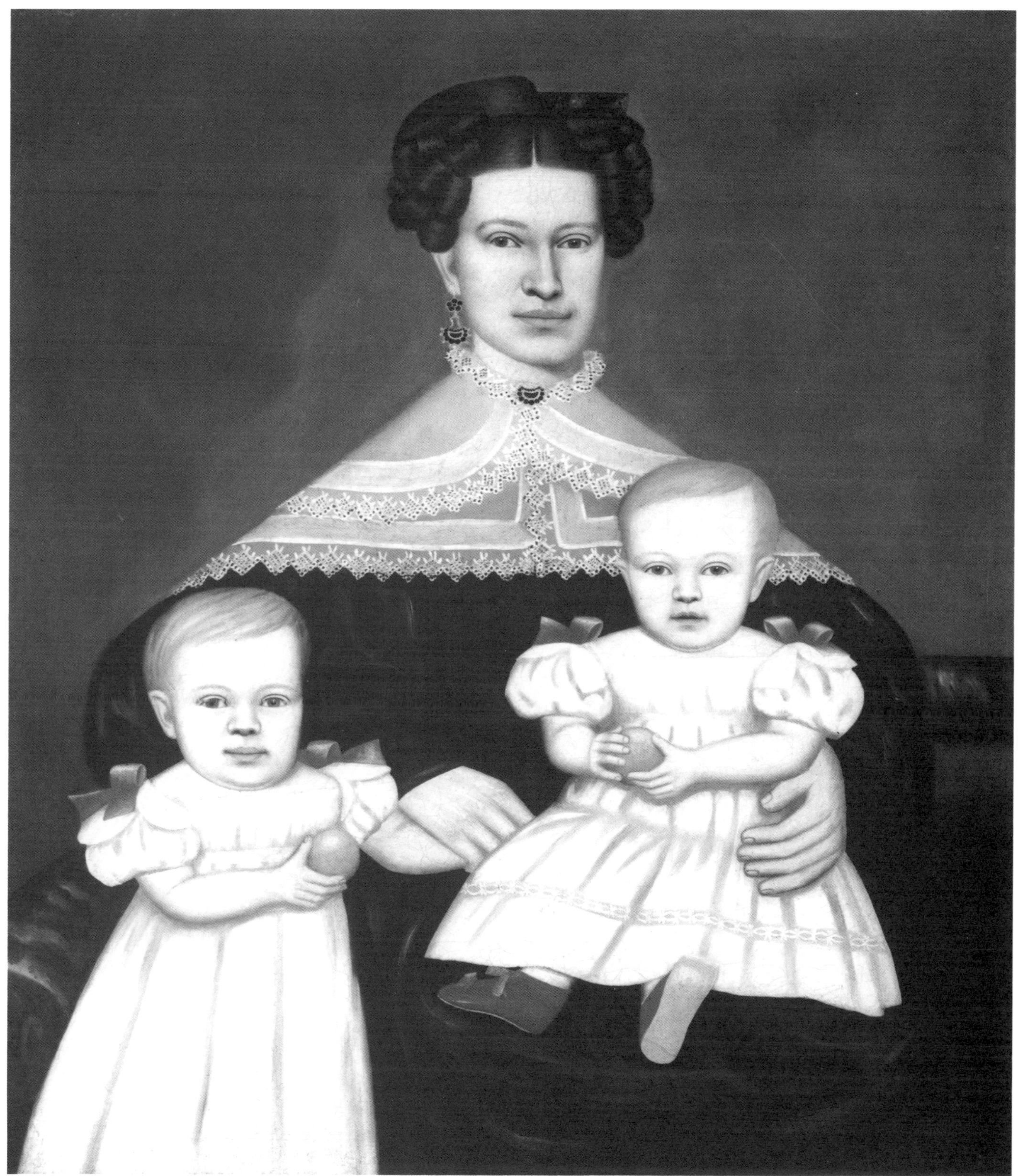

Fig. 69 *Mrs. Paul Smith Palmer and Her Twins* (cat. no.41)

1837	*Plumtrees (Sunderland), Massachusetts*

50. Dolly Floyd Wiley   (color plate 13)

(1811-1884)
35 x 29   (88.9 x 73.66)   CHS 188
Museum of Fine Arts, Springfield, Massachusetts, The
    Morgan Wesson Memorial Collection 63.08

The sitter was the daughter of CATHERINE
DUNN WILEY.

51. Climena Everentia Ball Crocker   (fig. 27)

(1812-1879; married Zacceus Crocker before 1836)
30 x 25¾   (76.2 x 65.41)   CHS 44
Museum of Fine Arts, Springfield, Massachusetts, The
    Morgan Wesson Memorial Collection 63.06

1838   *New Haven, Connecticut*

52. Reverend Dyer Ball   (color plate 15

(1796-1866; married LUCY MILLS 1827)
40¾ x 36¼   (103.51 x 92.1)   CHS 4
Museum of Fine Arts, Springfield, Massachusetts, The
    Morgan Wesson Memorial Collection 63.09

This portrait and that of Ball's wife, LUCY MILLS
BALL (no. 53), were painted by Field while the Balls
were in New Haven, delayed in their departure to
China by the Panic of 1837. The long inscription on
the letter that appears in the portrait relates to the
work of this medical missionary and is quoted in full in
the text (p.27). The Balls remained in China for the
rest of their lives; on the death of his first wife, Ball
married for the second time in Canton, where he died.

53. Lucy H. Mills Ball   (color plate 14)

(1807-1844; married the REVEREND DYER BALL, 1827)
40¾ x 36¼   (103.51 x 92.1)   CHS 5
Museum of Fine Arts, Springfield, Massachusetts, The
    Morgan Wesson Memorial Collection 63.10

First wife of the REVEREND DYER BALL, Lucy
Mills Ball died in Hong Kong in 1844 (see no. 52). The
letter in her portrait is inscribed: "New
Haven,/January 1838,/Dear Parents."

c. 1838   *South Amherst, Massachusetts*

54. Squire Bogue   (fig. 70)

35¼ x 29   (89.54 x 73.66)
The Skinner Museum of Mount Holyoke College

55. The Reverend Mason Ball   (fig. 71)

35⁵⁄₁₆ x 29³⁄₁₆   (89.70 x 74.14)
The Skinner Museum of Mount Holyoke College

56. Sarah Elizabeth Ball   (cover illustration)

35⅛ x 29¼   (89.22 x 74.30)
The Skinner Museum of Mount Holyoke College

c. 1838   *Hadley?, Massachusetts*

57. Mr. Pearce   (color plate 17)

30 x 26   (76.2 x 66)   CHS 160
The Abby Aldrich Rockefeller Folk Art Center,
    Williamsburg, Virginia

See no. 58.

58. Mrs. Pearce   (color plate 16)

30 x 26   (76.2 x 66)   CHS 161
The Abby Aldrich Rockefeller Folk Art Center,
    Williamsburg, Virginia

See no. 57.

c. 1838

59. Lavina Cook   (fig. 72)

30½ x 25¼   (77.47 x 64.14)
Douglas Williams

See no. 60.

60. Captain James Cook   (fig. 73)

30½ x 25¼   (77.47 x 64.14)
Douglas Williams

See no. 59.

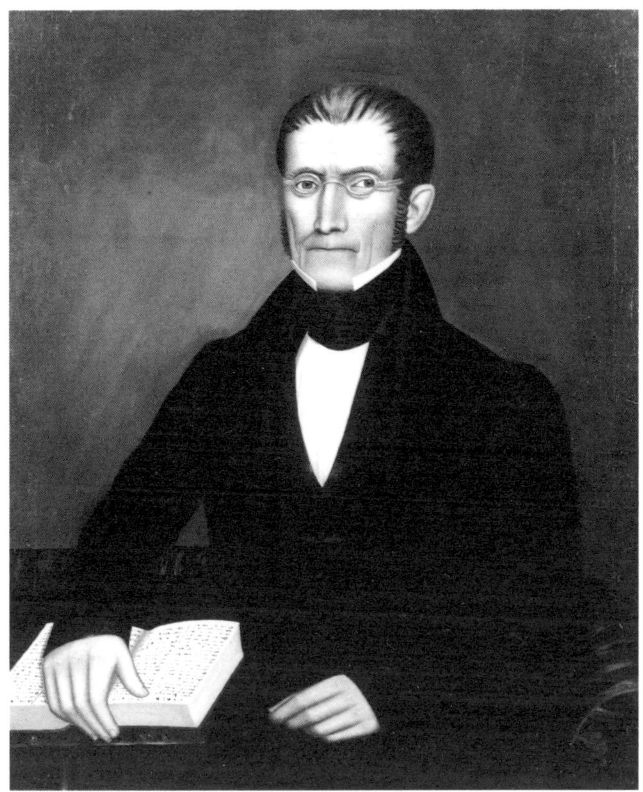

Fig. 70   *Squire Bogue*   (cat. no.54)

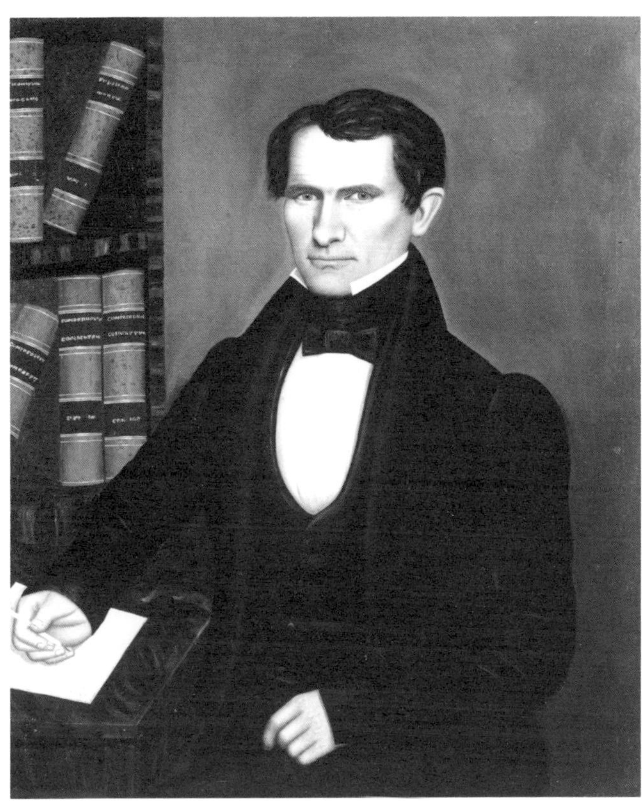

Fig. 71   *The Reverend Mason Ball*   (cat. no.55)

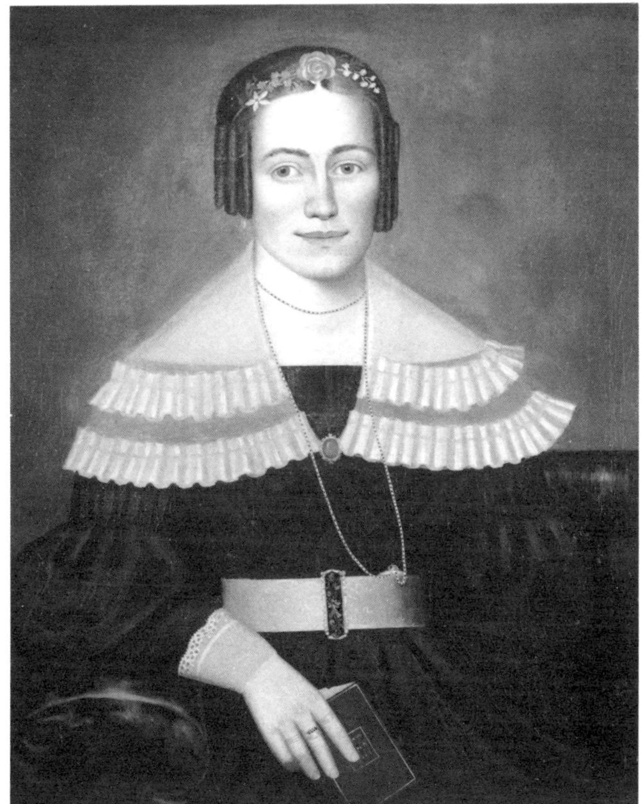

Fig. 72   *Lavina Cook*   (cat. no.59)

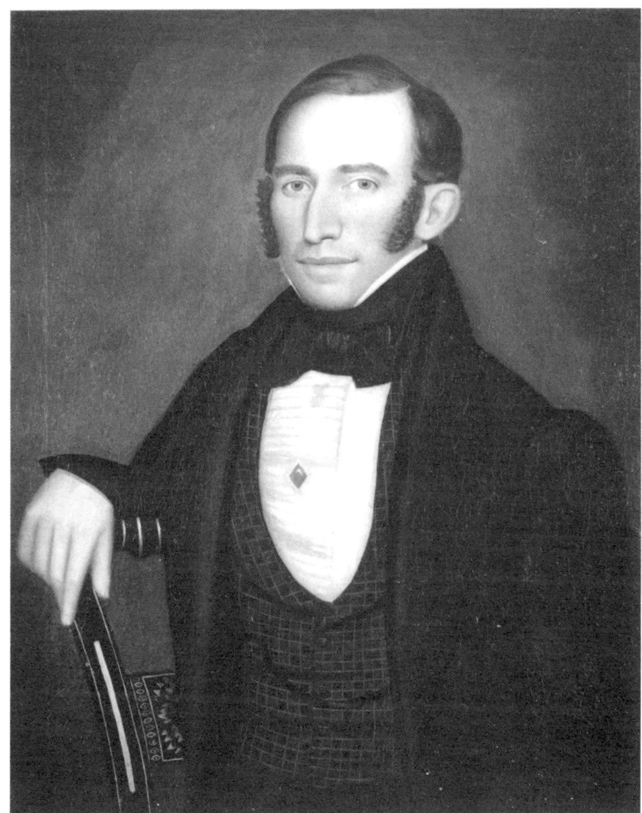

Fig. 73   *Captain James Cook*   (cat. no.60)

61. *Man with a Tune Book; Mr. Cook(?)*   (fig. 29)

{1811-1870; married 1834, as first wife, LOUISA ELLEN
     GALLOND}
35 x 29⅛   (88.9 x 73.7)   CHS 31
The National Gallery of Art, Washington. Gift of
     Edgar William and Bernice Chrysler Garbisch 1978

Identification of Nathaniel Cook as the sitter in this
portrait is based on identification of the sitter in its
companion portrait as LOUISA GALLOND COOK
(no. 62), who died in 1838.

62. *Louisa Gallond Cook?*   (fig. 28)
(also known as Woman with Green Book)

{1816-1838; married NATHANIEL COOK 1834}
35 x 29¼   (88.9 x 74.3)   CHS 32
The Art Institute of Chicago, Gift of Edgar William
     and Bernice Chrysler Garbisch, 1980.746

Although the sitter in this portrait can be identified as
Louisa Gallond Cook, she has also been identified as
CLARISSA GALLOND COOK (wife of William Cook,
NATHANIEL COOK's brother). However, the frail
appearance of the woman in this portrait supports her
identification as Louisa Gallond Cook, who died
sometime in 1838, the same year Field painted her. In
contrast, the sitter identified as CLARISSA
GALLOND COOK appears healthy and robust (no.
63). See no. 61.

63. *Louisa (Clarissa?) Gallond Cook*   (color plate 18)

{1804-1855; married 1824, William Cook, brother of
     NATHANIEL COOK}
34 x 28   (86.36 x 71.12)
Shelburne Museum, Shelburne, VT

Formerly believed to be ALMIRA GALLOND
MOORE as well as LOUISA GALLOND COOK,
the sitter is most likely Clarissa Gallond Cook.
Daughter of JEREMIAH and DORCAS BABBITT
GALLOND, Clarissa Gallond Cook was the sister of
LOUISA ELLEN GALLOND COOK and ALMIRA
GALLOND MOORE. See nos. 62 and 64.

64. *Joseph B. Moore and Family*   (color plate 19)

82¾ x 93⅜   (210.19 x 237.17)   CHS 149
Museum of Fine Arts, Boston, M. and M. Karolik
     Collection

Represented here are Joseph Moore (1804-1855) and
his wife Almira Gallond (1807-1892). From left to
right, the children are believed to be: Frederick Cook
(born 1835) and Louisa Ellen Cook (born 1837), son
and daughter of Mrs. Moore's sister, LOUISA ELLEN
GALLOND COOK (no. 62), who died in 1838;
Joseph Lauriston Moore (born 1829); and George
Francis Moore (born 1835?).

65. *Julia Ann Adams Peck*   (fig. 74)

{1817-1861}
35½ x 29   (90.17 x 73.66)   CHS 166
Collection of Peter H. Tillou

66. *Julius Norton*   (color plate 20)

{1809-1861}
35 x 29   (88.9 x 73.7)   CHS 155
The Bennington Museum, Bennington, Vermont

Julius Norton, son of LYDIA LOOMIS and JUDGE
LUMAN NORTON, operated the Bennington
Pottery and Porcelain Company in Bennington,
Vermont, from the 1830's to his death. His
grandfather, Captain John Norton, started a pottery in
Bennington as early as 1793. In 1844 Julius formed a
brief partnership with his brother-in-law Christopher
Webber Fenton.

67. *Luman Preston Norton*   (fig. 30)

{1837-?   }
43¼ x 33   (109.9 x 83.8)
Private Collection

The sitter was the son of JULIUS NORTON (no. 66),
head of the famous Bennington Pottery and Porcelain
Company. Luman became a partner in the firm
in 1859.

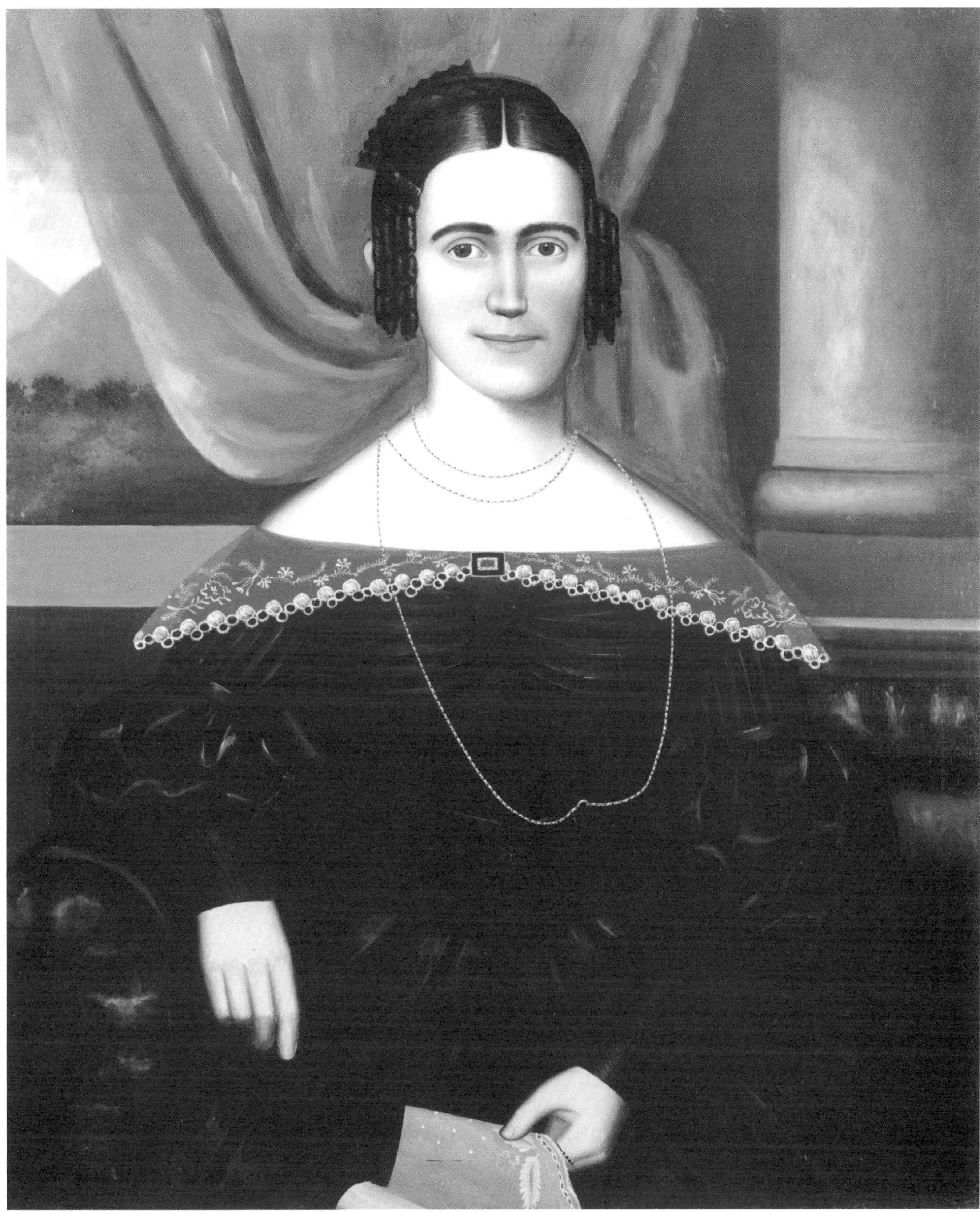

Fig. 74 *Julia Ann Adams Peck*   (cat. no.65)

c. 1844   *New York City*

68. *The Embarkation of Ulysses*   (color plate 22)

34½ x 45½   (87.63 x 115.57)   CHS 267
Museum of Fine Arts, Springfield, Massachusetts, The
  Morgan Wesson Memorial Collection 63.13

Field's wife entered "One oil painting" in the 1844
American Institute of the City of New York's annual
fair. *The Embarkation of Ulysses*, one of two versions by
Field, may have been her contribution since fair entries
often indicated owners rather than artists. The source
for both paintings was an engraving, *A City of Ancient
Greece*, published in London by J.W. Appleton in
1840. See no. 69.

69. *The Embarkation of Ulysses*   (fig. 31)

Pencil and wash drawing
9 x 13½   (22.86 x 34.29)
Museum of Fine Arts, Springfield, The Gilbert H.
  Montague Collection 66.D02

See no. 68.

1845   *New York City*

70. *Margaret Gilmore*   (color plate 21)

54 x 34   (137.16 x 86.36)   CHS 86
Museum of Fine Arts, Boston, Bequest of
  Maxim Karolik

Margaret Gilmore was Field's niece, the daughter of
David Gilmore, brother of Phebe Gilmore Field, the
artist's wife. From 1845 to 1848 David Gilmore lived in
New York City, often listed in the *New York Directory*
at the same address as the Fields. From the Field's and
Gilmore's address on Hudson Street, "M. Gillmur"
sent one "oil painting," believed to be this portrait, to
the 1845 annual fair of the American Institute of the
City of New York.

c. 1855   *Plumtrees (Sunderland),*
                                      Massachusetts

71. *Clarissa Field?*   (fig. 34)

43 x 37   (109.22 x 94.0)   CHS 59
Museum of Fine Arts, Springfield, Massachusetts, The
  Morgan Wesson Memorial Collection 63.11

Although this subject, based on a daguerreotype that
has accompanied the painting throughout its history,
has been identified as Field's sister, Clarissa, it could
not be an accurate identification. Clarissa Field died
in 1836, before the daguerreotype was brought
to America.

72. *Rattlesnake Gutter*   (color plate 23)

30½ x 27½   (71.47 x 69.85)
Private collection

c. 1855   *North Amherst, Massachusetts*

73. *William Henry Smith and Family*   (fig. 35)

36 x 47   (91.44 x 119.38)   CHS 177
The Abby Aldrich Rockefeller Folk Art Center,
  Williamsburg, Virginia

During the brief period when Field lodged with the
Smiths in North Amherst, he completed this portrait
based on a series of photographs of family members.
The sitters are, left to right: Seth (1847-1928);
Catherine (1810-1899); Mary Jane (1833-1890); Maria
Frances (1836-1917); Sarah (1844-1912); Delia
(1842-1916); William Henry (1809-1899); and Harriet
Smith (1849-1928).

c. 1858   *Palmer, Massachusetts*

74. *The Family of Deacon Wilson Brainerd*
                                      (color plate 24)

35¾ x 43¼   (90.81 x 109.86)   CHS 21
Old Sturbridge Village

Included in this group portrait are: Caroline Newton
Wilson (born 1820, married 1842 Deacon Brainerd);
John Wilson Brainerd II (born 1850); William H.
Brainerd (born 1852); Frank H. Brainerd (1847-1851);
John Wilson Brainerd (born 1843, died young);
Deacon Wilson Brainerd (1806-1881); and Charles T.
Brainerd (born 1844). Two of the children were
deceased at the time that Field included their likenesses
in the family portrait. The posthumous figures were
probably copied from photographs.

75. *Leverett Pond*   (fig. 36)

22 x 27¼   (55.88 x 69.2)   CHS 262
National Gallery of Art, Washington. Gift of Edgar
    William and Bernice Chrysler Garbisch 1978

From this period to the end of his career, Field
frequently painted *trompe l'oeil* frames directly onto
the canvas.

c. 1860   *Plumtrees (Sunderland), Massachusetts*

76. *The Garden of Eden*   (fig. 42)

36¾ x 46   (93.35 x 116.84)   CHS 243
Museum of Fine Arts, Boston, M. and M. Karolik
    Collection

One of two similar versions of this subject (see no. 77)
painted by Field, *The Garden of Eden* was inspired by a
published print, *The Temptation,* by English artist John
Martin. Details of the foliage were also influenced by a
print after a lost *Garden of Eden* by Thomas Cole.

77. *The Garden of Eden*   (color plate 25)

25 x 41½   (63.5 x 105.41)   CHS 244
Shelburne Museum, Shelburne, VT

The decorative border of this work was painted
directly onto the canvas. See no. 76.

78. *Henrietta Field*   (fig. 37)

[1832-1914]
16 x 14   (40.64 x 35.56)   CHS 64
Museum of Fine Arts, Springfield, Massachusetts, The
    Morgan Wesson Memorial Collection 63.12

This painting of the artist's daughter shown seated at a
piano was copied from a photograph.

79. *Stillman Field*   (fig. 39)

[1802-1878; married AURILLA FIELD 1832]
16 x 14   (40.64 x 35.56)   CHS 73
Private Collection

Field painted his brother and sister-in-law twice, in
1836 (private collection) and 1865. They are the only
sitters portrayed by the artist both early and late in
his career. The source of the 1865 portrait was a
photograph. See no. 80.

80. *Aurilla Field Field*   (fig. 40)

[1807-1883; married STILLMAN FIELD 1832]
16 x 14   (40.64 x 35.56)   CHS 75
Private Collection

Like the portrait of STILLMAN FIELD (no. 79), this
portrait of Aurilla Field Field, his wife, was copied from
a photograph.

81. *Lucius Field*   (fig. 41)

[1837-1863]
15⅛ x 14   (38.2 x 35.56)   CHS 66
Private Collection

1867, c. 1876, and 1888   *Plumtrees (Sunderland), Massachusetts*

82. *The Historical Monument of the American Republic*   (fig. 43 and color insert)

9'3" x 13'1"   (281.94 x 398.78)   CHS 241
Museum of Fine Arts, Springfield, Massachusetts, The
    Morgan Wesson Memorial Collection 60.16

On the ten towers of his fantasy structure, Field
narrated the history of the Republic from settlement to
post Civil War. Many of the scenes refer to Lincoln
and the war, reflecting Field's strong anti-slavery
stance. Field worked on it in several stages: most of the
work was completed by 1867; Field added references to
the Philadelphia Centennial in 1876; and he painted
the two end towers, left and right, in 1888. A
description and interpretation of each tower and bas-
relief were provided by the artist in his *Descriptive
Catalogue of the Monument of the American Republic,*
published in Amherst in 1876.

83. *The Historical Monument of the American Republic*   (fig. 44)

Photoengraving by Edward Bierstadt after the painting
    by Erastus Field
15 x 22¾   (38.1 x 57.79)   CHS 242
Museum of Fine Arts, Springfield, Massachusetts,
    Bequest of Mrs. Victor H. Wesson 63.D07

The plate size of this Albertype is 15 x 22¾ inches.

c. 1865-1880   *Plumtrees (Sunderland), Massachusetts*

84. *"He Turned Their Waters Into Blood"*
                  (color plate 26)

30⅛ x 40½   (76.52 x 102.87)   CHS 245
National Gallery of Art, Washington. Gift of Edgar
    William and Bernice Chrysler Garbisch 1964

The subject is one of the few surviving paintings in the
series called "The Plagues of Egypt," apparently
intended for the North Amherst Congregational
Church. Because of wide variations in quality among
these Biblical works, it is believed that they were
painted over an extended period of time.

85. *The Plague of Darkness*   (fig. 46)

35½ x 46¾   (90.17 x 118.75)   CHS 247
Herbert W. Hemphill, Jr.

See no. 84.

86. *Death of the First Born*   (color plate 27)

35 x 46   (88.9 x 116.84)   CHS 250
The Metropolitan Museum of Art, Gift of
    Edgar William and Bernice Chrysler Garbisch, 1966.

See no. 84.

87. *Burial of the First Born of Egypt*   (color plate 28)

33¼ x 39¼   (84.46 x 99.70)   CHS 251
Museum of Fine Arts, Springfield, Massachusetts, The
    Morgan Wesson Memorial Collection 63.18

See no. 84.

88. *Pharaoh's Army Marching*   (fig. 48)

35⅛ x 46   (89.1 x 116.84)   CHS 252
National Gallery of Art, Washington. Gift of Edgar
    William and Bernice Chrysler Garbisch 1978

See no. 84.

89. *Death of the First Born*   (color plate 29)

34⅞ x 35   (88.58 x 88.9)   CHS 258
The Abby Aldrich Rockefeller Folk Art Center,
    Williamsburg, Virginia

See no. 84.

90. *Mine Eyes Have Seen the Glory (Death of the Twins)*   (fig. 49)

34½ x 46   (87.63 x 116.84)   CHS 259
Museum of Fine Arts, Springfield, Massachusetts, The
    Morgan Wesson Memorial Collection 63.17

This subject may have had special significance for
Field, himself a twin. See no. 84.

91. *Egyptian Scene*   (fig. 45)

35 x 46 (88.9 x 116.84)   CHS 260
The Metropolitan Museum of Art, Gift of
    Edgar William and Bernice Chrysler Garbisch, 1966

See no. 84.

92. *The Israelites Crossing the Red Sea*   (fig. 47)

34¾ x 46   (88.27 x 116.84)
Private Collection

See no. 84.

93. *Ark of the Covenant*   (fig. 50)

20 x 24⅛   (50.8 x 61.28)
National Gallery of Art, Washington. Gift of Edgar
    William and Bernice Chrysler Garbisch 1956

94. *The Last Supper*   (color plate 30)

35 x 46   (88.9 x 116.84)   CHS 256
The Chrysler Museum, Norfolk, VA., Gift of Edgar
    William and Bernice Chrysler Garbisch

Field based his painting on a chromolithograph of Leonardo Da Vinci's famous work, *The Last Supper.*

c. 1880 — Plumtrees (Sunderland), Massachusetts

95. *The Visit of Ulysses Grant to India* (fig. 51)

34¼ x 45½ (87 x 115.57) CHS 236
Museum of Fine Arts, Springfield, Massachusetts, The Morgan Wesson Memorial Collection 63.19

This subject was copied from the illustration, *Entering Agra*, in James R. Young's *Around the World with General Grant*, New York, 1879. In 1880 Stephen Ashley Hubbard, Field's supporter and cousin, was in charge of arrangements for Grant's visit to Hartford, the likely impetus for a series of paintings on Indian subjects by Field.

96. *The Taj Mahal* (fig. 53)

35 x 46 (88.9 x 116.84) CHS 228
National Gallery of Art, Washington. Gift of Edgar William and Bernice Chrysler Garbisch 1978

97. *The Taj Mahal and Its Gardens* (fig. 75)

35 x 45 (88.9 x 114.3) CHS 230
Museum of Fine Arts, Springfield, Massachusetts, The Morgan Wesson Memorial Collection 63.14

Field painted the decorative frame directly onto the canvas.

98. *The Taj Mahal and Its Gardens* (fig. 76)

Pencil on Bristol board
7¾ x 10⅜ (19.69 x 26.35) CHS 231
Museum of Fine Arts, Springfield, Massachusetts, The Morgan Wesson Memorial Collection 63.D04

99. *The Taj Mahal and Its Gardens* (fig. 52)

Pencil on Bristol board
10 x 15⅛ (25.4 x 38.42) CHS 232
Museum of Fine Arts, Springfield, Massachusetts, The Morgan Wesson Memorial Collection 63.D05

Field painted the decorative frame directly onto the canvas.

100. *Palace Facade with Landscape, India* (fig. 77)

24¼ x 29½ (61.60 x 74.93) CHS 233
Museum of Fine Arts, Springfield, Massachusetts, The Morgan Wesson Memorial Collection 63.15

Field painted the decorative frame directly onto the canvas.

101. *A Temple in India* (fig. 78)

Pencil on Bristol board
12½ x 18½ (31.75 x 46.99) CHS 234
Museum of Fine Arts, Springfield, Massachusetts, The Morgan Wesson Memorial Collection 63.D06

102. *Design for a Tabernacle, India* (fig. 54)

24¾ x 29½ (62.87 x 74.93) CHS 235
Museum of Fine Arts, Springfield, Massachusetts, The Morgan Wesson Memorial Collection 63.20

1881 — Plumtrees (Sunderland), Massachusetts

103. *Lincoln with Washington and his Generals* (color plate 31)

32 x 39½ (81.28 x 100.33) CHS 237
Museum of Fine Arts, Springfield, Massachusetts, The Morgan Wesson Memorial Collection 63.16

Left to right are: Ambrose E. Burnside, Abraham Lincoln, George Washington, Ulysses S. Grant, Rutherford B. Hayes, and Chester A. Arthur.

c. 1885 — Plumtrees (Sunderland), Massachusetts

104. *An Egyptian Sarcophagus* (fig. 55)

24¾ x 29½ (62.87 x 74.93) CHS 269
Museum of Fine Arts, Springfield, Massachusetts, The Morgan Wesson Memorial Collection 63.21

105. *Relief From the Arch of Titus* (fig. 56)

20 x 24¾ (50.8 x 62.87) CHS 268
Museum of Fine Arts, Springfield, Massachusetts, The Morgan Wesson Memorial Collection 63.22

Field painted the decorative frame directly onto the canvas.

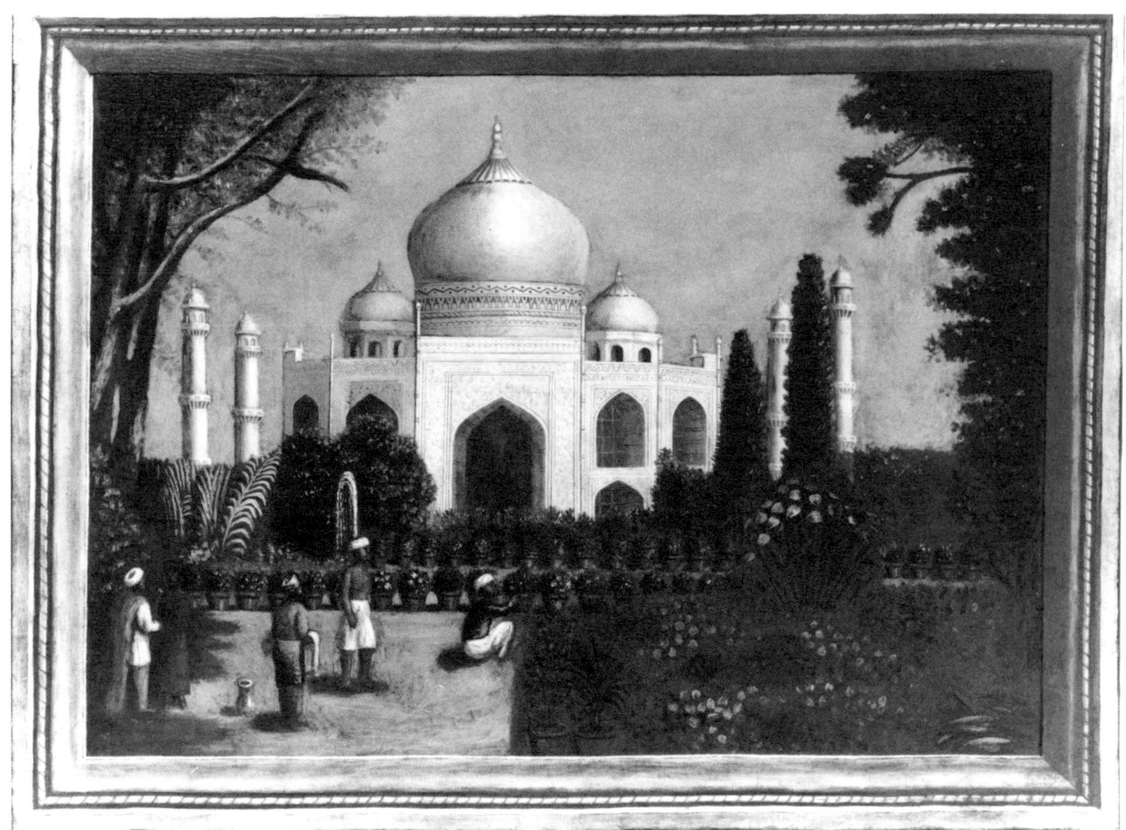

Fig. 75   *The Taj Mahal and Its Gardens*   (cat. no.97)

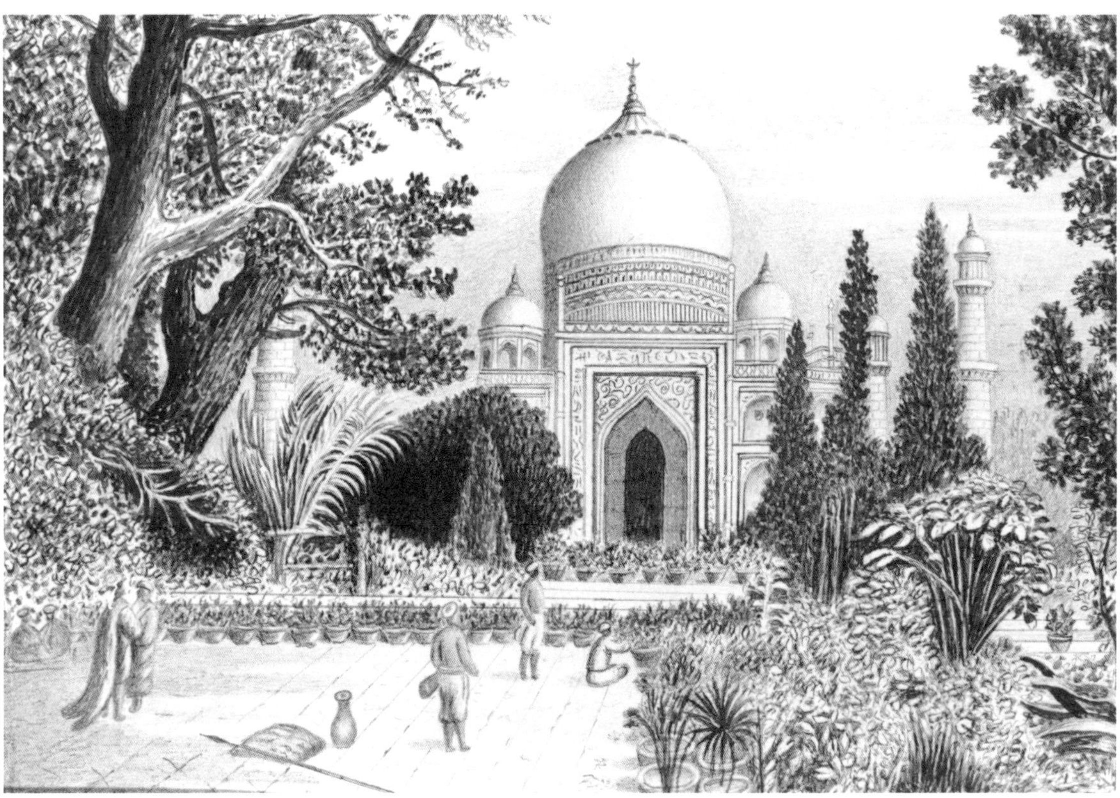

Fig. 76   *The Taj Mahal and Its Gardens*   (cat. no.98)

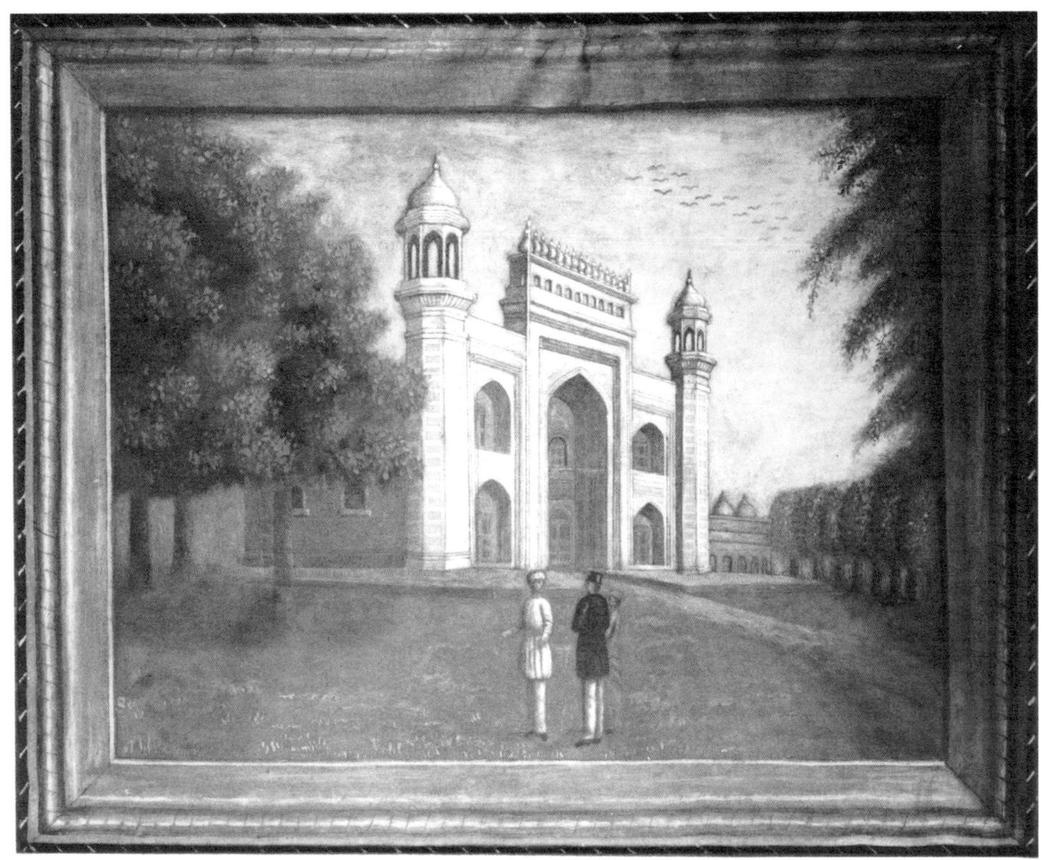

Fig. 77   *Palace Facade with Landscape, India*   (cat. no.100)

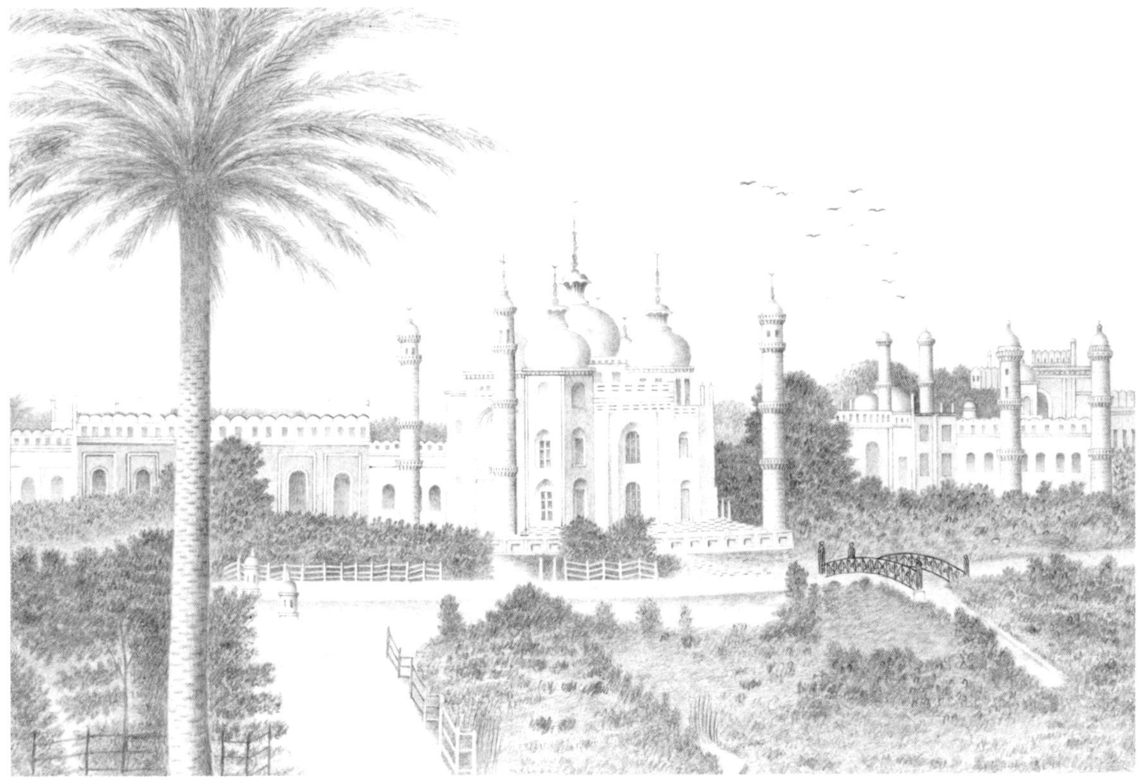

Fig. 78   *A Temple in India*   (cat. no.101)

106. *Erastus Salisbury Field*   (fig. 33)

[1805-1900]
Photograph
10¾ x 8½   (27.31 x 21.59)   CHS 62
Private Collection

The photograph, taken about 1852, is an ambrotype,
hand colored in oils presumably by the artist.

107. *Henrietta Field*   (fig. 38)

[1832-1914]
Photograph
7½ x 5¾   (19.05 x 14.61)   CHS 65
Museum of Fine Arts, Springfield, Massachusetts,
    Gift of Mr. and Mrs. Reginald French 76.Mi.02

The photograph, taken about 1860, is an ambrotype
hand colored in oils.

108. *Erastus Salisbury Field's Paint Box*
(color plate 32)

15 x 24¾ x 9   (38.19 x 62.87 x 22.82)
Museum of American Folk Art, Gift of Amicus
    Foundation, Inc.

Lenders to the Exhibition

The Abby Aldrich Rockefeller Folk Art Center,
Williamsburg, Virginia
Mrs. Joan Arden
The Art Institute of Chicago, Chicago, Illinois
The Bennington Museum, Bennington, Vermont
Mary Black
The Chrysler Museum, Norfolk, Virginia
The Connecticut Historical Society,
Hartford, Connecticut
Ruth Austin Eiseman
Carl V. Fasano
Herbert W. Hemphill, Jr.
The Historical Society of Glastonbury,
Glastonbury, Connecticut
Mr. and Mrs. Henry Bassett Holt
Mead Art Museum, Amherst College,
Amherst, Massachusetts
The Metropolitan Museum of Art, New York, New York
Museum of American Folk Art, New York, New York
Museum of Fine Arts, Boston, Massachusetts
Museum of Fine Arts, Springfield, Massachusetts
National Gallery of Art, Washington, D.C.
Old Sturbridge Village, Sturbridge, Massachusetts
Portland Art Museum, Portland, Oregon
Mr. and Mrs. S. Forbes Rockwell, Jr.
Mary Robbins Runyon (Mrs. Charles)
Shelburne Museum, Shelburne, Vermont
The Saint Louis Art Museum, Saint Louis, Missouri
The Skinner Museum of Mount Holyoke College,
South Hadley, Massachusetts
Peter H. Tillou
Torrington Historical Society, Inc.,
Torrington, Connecticut
Douglas Williams
Winchester Historical Society, Winsted, Connecticut
Worcester Art Museum, Worcester, Massachusetts
Private Collectors

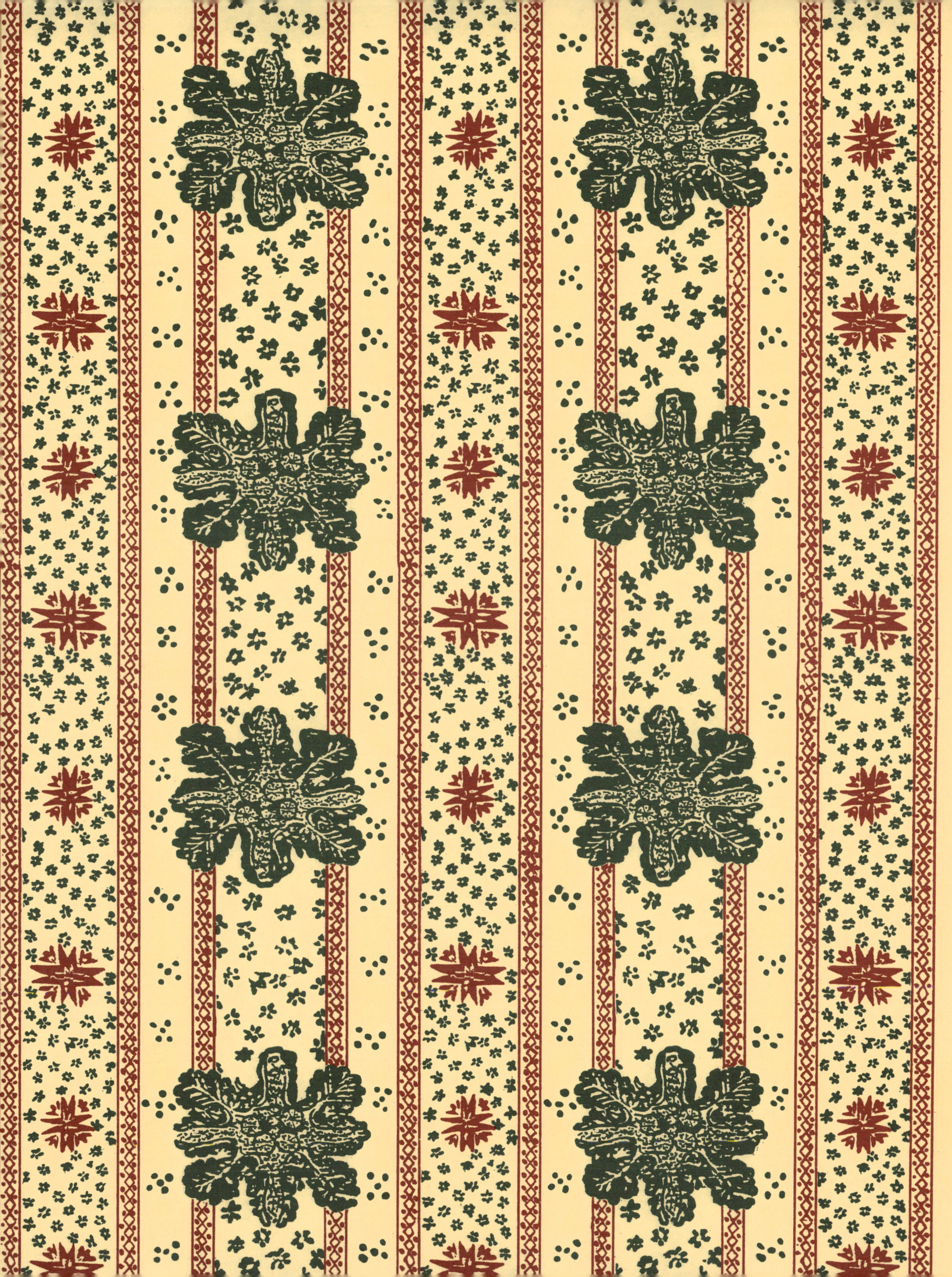

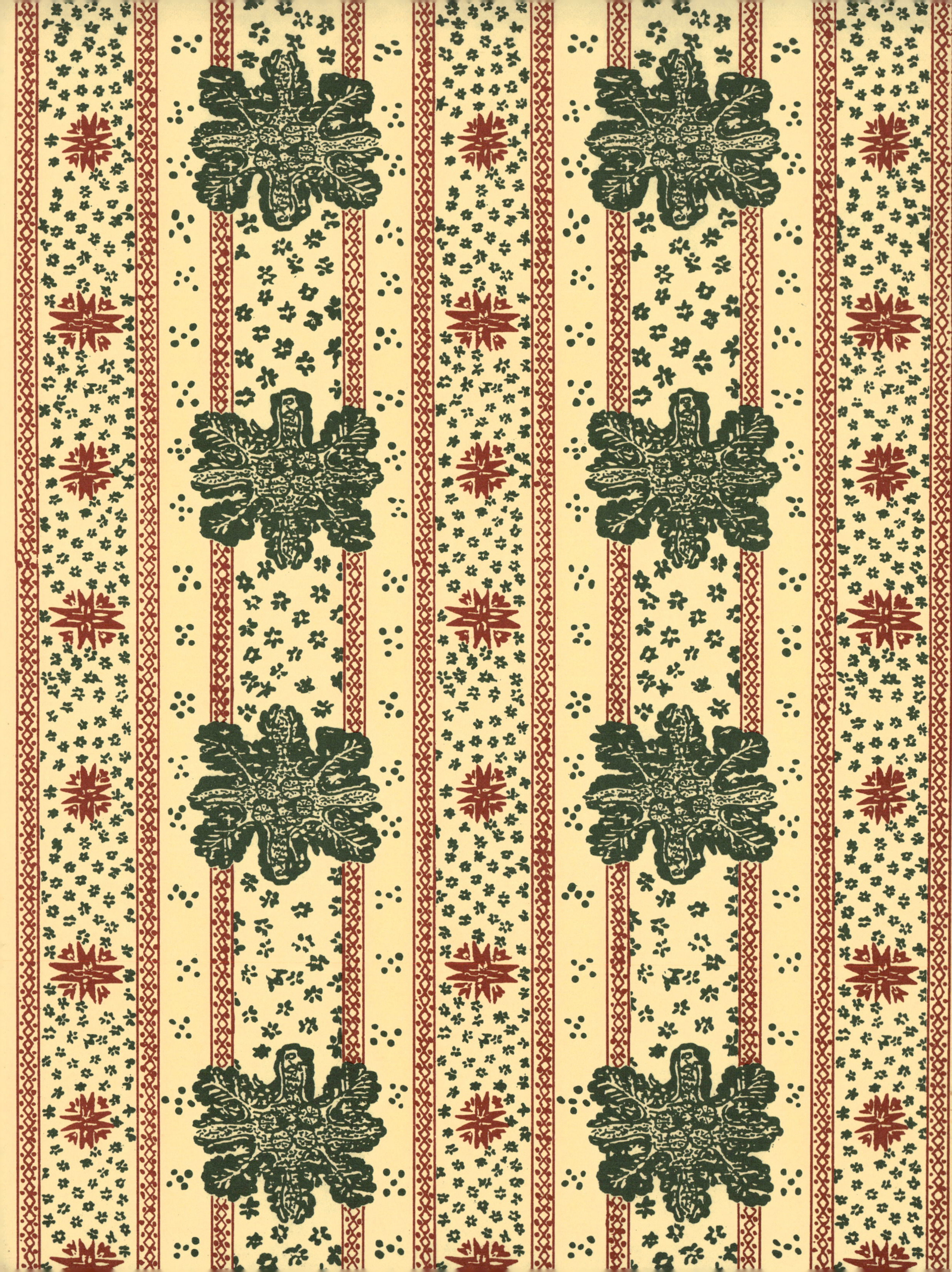